PRAISE FOR *THE NEW CHAMELEONS*

A brilliant read with the eye-opening power of *Thinking Fast and Slow* applied to marketing. Solomon challenges marketers to step away from neat and tidy methods of target segmentation in a revealing and accessible way. He provides language that reflects the reality of the post-advertising, multi-channel, hyper-fragmented, insert-buzzword-here environment that businesses need to navigate for success. Most importantly, it shows the way to think about communicating with people, not marketing to "consumers" reduced to percentages in cross-tab cages.
Sara Bamossy, Chief Strategy Officer, Pitch

When commercial borders between nations disappeared, so did many brands who could not adapt. Now that the borders between just about everything else in our culture are evaporating (home/office, work/play, consumer/producer, online/offline, us/them, male/female, humans/machines, and more), how do you make sure your brand doesn't go the way of the dinosaurs? A great starting place is Professor Solomon's *The New Chameleons*, which provides insights and opportunities that could mark the difference between success and failure for anyone involved in marketing. You know. Like you.
Martin Bihl, Executive Creative Director, LevLane, and Editor-in-Chief of the-agency-review.com

The New Chameleons brings marketers to the edge of tomorrow, revealing deep insights for building the next generation of leading brands.
Derrick Daye, The Blake Project and *Branding Strategy Insider*

Enabled by technology and accelerated by transformations of our global cultural and social ecosystems, traditional categorization of consumer behavior is out the window! Michael R. Solomon brilliantly helps us understand and navigate the continuously evolving and rapidly morphing intersections of marketers and consumers. Michael shows us how new challenges of engagement also offer new opportunities to those who are able to develop and execute strategies consistent with these dynamic consumer chameleon characteristics. Combining his unique expertise, experience, insights, and perspective with numerous relevant practical specific examples, this is a must-read not only for marketing professionals, but for all stakeholders in their brand's future, in every function and at every level (from the boardroom to the mailroom and everyone in between, and whether for-profit, nonprofit, B2C, or B2B in their focus).

John Greco, Founder and Chairman, Marketing IMPACT Council™, and former CEO of the Direct Marketing Association and former Director of AT&T Bell Laboratories' Consumer Lab

Michael R. Solomon proves yet again why he's such a trusted and insightful consumer behaviorist. In *The New Chameleons*, he explains why traditional segmentation is too blunt an instrument and outlines, in very practical terms, what marketers should do about it. This is a great read for marketing's modern age.

William F.N. Gullan, President, Finch Brands

Michael R. Solomon skillfully articulates why today's brands must understand the postmodern consumer to remain relevant. The lines between consumer categories have long been converging, and *The New Chameleons* establishes the need for a brand's horizontal appeal and offers practical examples and actionable takeaways.

Asma Ishaq, CEO, Modere

As a serial direct marketer for over 35 years, and a lifelong student of the craft, I look for books (and voices) who are taking everything we have learned up until now and turning it all on its head for deeper understanding. Michael R. Solomon is one of those voices, re-equipping us with new tools and ways of thinking to deal with

an unknown marketplace of the future... but a marketplace that is more exciting than we ever could have imagined. His latest work debunks many of marketing's sacred cows with the goal of taking us to places no one has taken us before. His experience as one of the world's experts in consumer behavior qualifies him to take us to this place, a place where he can make sure we are ready for what's coming. This is a must-read for every marketer (or anyone) who wants to be relevant, offering products and services based on what consumers demand today (and will demand even more tomorrow).
Brian Kurtz, CEO, Titans Marketing LLC, and former business builder of Boardroom Inc. and author of *The Advertising Solution*

Michael R. Solomon has scuttled the ideology of marketing experts and psychologists. No longer can consumers be neatly categorized and targeted. He gives marketers a new roadmap on how to succeed in a chameleon-led marketplace.
Andrew Mitchell, CEO, Brandmovers

When I started in design, I was always fascinated with the idea that everything around us is connected and shapes our human experiences. Design is every aspect of our human life. The floor, walls, chair, carpet, table, flatware, objects, lamp, ceiling, clothes on my body, the watch on my wrist, the building, the sidewalks, the roads, the cars, the city are one endless landscape—a horizontal connection that must be considered. To use a term of Michael's, these constellations, from interfaces to services to physical goods, make marketing today far more complex than even just 10 years ago. En masse is long over, and this rigorous dissection and complex reading made me feel like a got a master's in marketing. Kudos.
Karim Rashid, Industrial Designer

Solomon is a marketing maverick who compels you to alter the way you think about your customer, your competition, and the not so neatly defined world around you. Everything you thought you knew about marketing will make sense in a completely different context as you look through Solomon's lens.
Kimberly Richmond, Principal, richmondmarketing+communications

Michael stiches the trends of today to the future of consumerism in a way that is both provocative and inspiring. This book should be required reading for every marketer; it's a wake-up call to the undeniable truth that we need to think and attack our challenges in a profoundly new way.

Patrick Rodmell, President, Rodmell & Company Inc.

Get ready to take a sledgehammer to your old way of thinking about marketing and consumers. Michael R. Solomon's newest book turns old-school ideas on their head and helps you see marketing—and the consumers you're marketing to—in an entirely new light. This is a must-read book for anyone who wants to stay up to date on the latest developments in the business.

Jamie Turner, author, speaker, and CEO of 60secondmarketer.com

After blowing up our decades-old model for understanding consumers, the first thing Michael R. Solomon does is, thankfully, give us everything we need to rebuild a new one. Even though we marketers knew deep down that consumers didn't fit so neatly into the "cages" we put them, we didn't have a better way of thinking or understanding them. But that's what this book does: by walking us through the black-and-white thinking that got us in the mess in the first place, Solomon shows us the depth, breadth, and opportunity that lies in all the beautiful shades of gray in between.

Tamsen Webster, Message Strategist, Find the Red Thread

Solomon makes a compelling case for more enlightened marketing in a postmodern world. He shows that simply adapting to the latest consumer trends or fads is no longer enough—something more fundamental is afoot. Use these sample insights to build a better strategy for your business!

John Wittenbraker, Ph.D., Global Director, New Business Development, GfK

Michael R. Solomon introduces readers to two very different worlds. The real world, where individual consumers float seamlessly from one connection to another, defying classification. And an alternative universe, where marketers are still trapped by strictly defined consumer segments and media categories which bear no relationship to real customer behavior. It's time for marketers to make a quantum leap to the real world.

Leslie Zane, President, Triggers Brand Consultancy

The New Chameleons

*How to connect with consumers
who defy categorization*

Michael R. Solomon

KoganPage

Publisher's note
Every possible effort has been made to ensure that the information contained in this book is accurate at the time of going to press, and the publishers and authors cannot accept responsibility for any errors or omissions, however caused. No responsibility for loss or damage occasioned to any person acting, or refraining from action, as a result of the material in this publication can be accepted by the editor, the publisher or the author.

First published in Great Britain and the United States in 2021 by Kogan Page Limited

2nd Floor, 45 Gee Street	122 W 27th St, 10th Floor	4737/23 Ansari Road
London	New York, NY 10001	Daryaganj
EC1V 3RS	USA	New Delhi 110002
United Kingdom		India
www.koganpage.com		

Kogan Page books are printed on paper from sustainable forests.

ISBNs
Hardback   978 1 3986 0006 5
Paperback   978 1 3986 0004 1
Ebook   978 1 3986 0005 8

British Library Cataloguing-in-Publication Data

A CIP record for this book is available from the British Library.

Library of Congress Cataloging-in-Publication Data

Names: Solomon, Michael R., author.
Title: The new chameleons: how to connect with consumers who defy categorization / Michael R. Solomon.
Description: London, United Kingdom ; New York, NY: Kogan Page, 2021. | Includes bibliographical references and index.
Identifiers: LCCN 2020044129 (print) | LCCN 2020044130 (ebook) | ISBN 9781398600065 (hardback) | ISBN 9781398600041 (paperback) | ISBN 9781398600058 (ebook)
Subjects: LCSH: Consumer behavior. | Marketing research. | Consumers. | Group identity.
Classification: LCC HF5415.32 .S625 2021 (print) | LCC HF5415.32 (ebook) | DDC 658.8/342–dc23
LC record available at https://lccn.loc.gov/2020044129
LC ebook record available at https://lccn.loc.gov/2020044130

Typeset by Hong Kong FIVE Workshop
Print production managed by Jellyfish
Printed and bound by CPI Group (UK) Ltd, Croydon CR0 4YY

To Arya, Evey, and Rose:
My favorite chameleons

CONTENTS

LIST OF FIGURES AND TABLES

ABOUT THE AUTHOR

Michael "wrote the book" on understanding consumers. Literally. Hundreds of thousands of business students have learned about marketing from his books including *Consumer Behavior: Buying, Having, and Being*—the most widely used book on the subject in the world.

Michael's mantra: We don't buy products because of what they do. We buy them because of what they mean. He advises global clients in leading industries such as apparel and footwear (Calvin Klein, Levi Strauss, Under Armour, Timberland), financial services and e-commerce (eBay, Progressive), CPG (Procter & Gamble, Campbell's), retailing (H&M), sports (Philadelphia Eagles), manufacturing (DuPont, PP&G), and transportation (BMW, United Airlines) on marketing strategies to make them more consumer-centric. He regularly appears on television shows including the *Today Show*, *Good Morning America*, and *CNN* to comment on consumer issues, and is frequently quoted in major media outlets such as the *New York Times*, *USA Today*, *Adweek*, and *Time*. Michael is a contributor at Forbes.com, where he writes about issues related to consumer behavior, marketing, and retailing.

As a Professor of Marketing (in the Haub School of Business at Saint Joseph's University in Philadelphia) and an industry consultant, Michael combines cutting-edge academic theory with actionable real-world strategies. His articles, published in journals including *Journal of Consumer Research*, *Journal of Marketing*, *Journal of Advertising*, *Journal of Retailing*, and *Journal of Business Research*, have been cited over 30,000 times. He helps managers get inside the heads of their customers so they can anticipate and satisfy their deepest and most pressing needs—today and tomorrow. An executive at Subaru said it best: "The man is a scholar who is current and street-wise."

ACKNOWLEDGMENTS

I'd like to thank my dear friend and colleague, the late Professor Gary Bamossy, for his support and feedback. I miss you, Gary.

A special note of gratitude to my fantastic editor, Kathe Sweeney, for her encouragement and insightful feedback during the writing process.

Introduction

Meet the new chameleons

Meet Sofía:

- She's a 24-year-old of Hispanic descent with a bachelor's degree in English. She is bisexual. Her preferred pronouns are *ze* (instead of *she*) and *zir* (instead of *her*)—but on these pages I will stick with *she* and *her*, not to disrespect Sofía's use of language but so that readers not used to it are not distracted from what I am saying.

- She recently exited a three-year relationship. She has no kids, but she dotes on Kelbie, her fawn pug. She lives in a loft apartment in Manhattan.

- When she goes out for the evening, she dresses like a typical club girl. But she hates loud, smoky places.

- She's very goal-oriented, and she carefully plans out and updates her career trajectory regularly.

- She trains at a CrossFit box at least twice per week.

- She loves to cook—but only vegan recipes.

- She prides herself on having attended 50 Phish concerts in the last five years. And she's an avid poster on Shakira fan sites.

- She volunteers for Greenpeace.

- She's a strong supporter of most Democratic political positions, but because of her Catholic upbringing she's Pro-Life so she's very ambivalent about backing liberal candidates.

- During the pandemic she participated in a weekly Zoom Happy Hour with friends, where everyone sampled a different craft beer during each session.

- She makes a good salary, but she's always aware that she could lose her job and perhaps find herself homeless without much warning.

- She works for Chase Manhattan Bank. When she goes to work, she dresses very conservatively, and she always takes care to wear clothes that hide the prominent tattoos on her upper arms and chest.
- She's addicted to buying baubles on Etsy.
- She loves to hunt for food bargains at Walmart, but she does most of her casual clothes shopping online at Urban Outfitters and Topshop. She rents almost all of her work outfits from Rent the Runway.
- She's saving up for a two-week trip to the Galapagos Islands.

Just what lifestyle category does Sofía belong to? Good luck to the marketer who tries to describe her. Like Sofía, today many of us change our identities faster than a chameleon changes color.

Meet your customers—the new consumer chameleons

Whether you're based in the United States, Europe, Asia or elsewhere, you can see it all around you (maybe even in the mirror!). Today a lot of consumers defy categorization—sometimes deliberately. They (or perhaps ze, eir, thon, vae, or ne) yearn to be liberated from cubicles, labels, "market segments," especially those confining cages that restrict them from expressing the unique self they have constructed out of all the lifestyle "raw materials" that marketers of many stripes have to offer. Their lives are a work in progress and always in beta.

From monolith to multilith

We didn't appreciate it then, but in "the good old days" (say, a few decades ago), marketers had it pretty easy. Customers respected authority figures, and we had a pretty good idea of where to locate these people and how to enlist them to sell for us. There were just a handful of TV stations (ABC, NBC, CBS or BBC One and

Two, etc.), some popular radio stations, and large-circulation print magazines like *Time*, *Life*, *Vogue*, or *The Spectator* that almost everyone read to learn about the world—and about what to buy.

At that time, we thought of the world in terms of very broad categories. We had First World versus Third World, the Young and the Old, Guys and Dolls, and Our People versus the Other People. As we emerged from the throes of World War II, the marketing machine revved up to provide us with the spoils of prosperity—but without a lot of variations to choose from. There was so much pent-up demand following the deprivations of wartime that people with newly-found money to spend weren't that picky about the details—and the pressures to conform to what others chose were pretty fierce as well.

Indeed, even decades before World War II, Henry Ford famously boasted that his customers could buy one of his cars in any color they liked, so long as it was black. That one-size-fits-all approach made sense in the early days of the Industrial Revolution, when mass production was all about maximizing efficiency and output. And even though this orthodoxy started to loosen up after the Great Depression and then through the post-war years, we remained much more of a cookie-cutter society than we are now (especially since, by and large, the notion of cultural diversity was still a pipe dream).

Our shift from a monolithic structure to a multilithic one began to change in the 1950s, as consumer groups began to splinter into smaller and smaller niches. Mass-circulation periodicals like *Look* and the *Saturday Evening Post* faded into history, to be replaced by a multiplicity of specialized magazines. Editors discovered that they could better compete by helping advertisers to reach more finely defined audiences with specific needs and tastes.

Cable TV stations, internet radio and other upstart outlets also proliferated. Bruce Springsteen's famous lament about the quality of TV programming in his 1992 song "57 Channels (And Nothin' On)" seems quaint today, when even adding a zero to this number doesn't capture the full range of channels available to us (many still with nothin' on, but that's another story).

Wake up to reality

> There is a Chinese curse which says "May he live in interesting times."
> Like it or not, we live in interesting times. They are times of danger
> and uncertainty; but they are also the most creative of any time in the
> history of mankind (Robert F. Kennedy, 1966).[1]

Guess what? The party's over, folks. For years, we've been able to get away with putting our customers into neat little cages, as we grouped them according to fairly broad ranges of age or income, or we pigeonholed them by gender. New ideas, new products, and new styles came to life in mass media, so not surprisingly most people adopted them *en masse*. Year by year, we had clear winners in domains like hit songs, clothing styles, home furnishings, etc.

That monolithic strategy just doesn't wash in a world where tranquilized consumers are waking up and shaking those cages. Today many of us no longer accept the labels marketers assign to us, and with good reason. Like our friend Sofía, we just don't conform to the assumptions they make about what we do, think, and buy. There's a bit of a consumer revolution afoot.

That revolution requires marketers to revisit the cages they've erected over many years. And no one is saying that's an easy thing to do. Conventional marketing strategies are built upon predictability, stability, and the comfort that comes from knowing that we "understand" our customer yesterday, today, and tomorrow. To accomplish this, we love to put people into categories and often into super-neat dichotomies—and call it a day.

Unfortunately, that strong tendency also is a prime example of what psychologists call a nominal fallacy: the belief that because we have given a name to something, we have therefore explained it.[2] So, we blissfully describe our target markets with peppy terms like Millennials, Empty Nesters, Henrys (high earners, not rich yet), Recreational Shoppers, etc. Then we give ourselves a high-five, secure in the knowledge that we now understand what makes these folks tick. We have safely placed them into their cages and affixed cute labels on the doors. We can sleep soundly because we know we can easily find them again when we're ready to sell to them.

Those cages used to be solid, and marketers relied upon them to build a structure that formed the basis of their traditional strategic worldview. This rather simplistic approach worked really well for a lot of years, so marketers can't be blamed for continuing to rely upon it. But that's no longer the case. Now many of these comfortable cages are opening—and fast. Consumer chameleons like Sofía and millions of others are climbing out of them at warp speed, while others are sniffing the air and starting to think about doing the same.

Don't despair! Creative destruction is a good thing. We need to open these cages if we're going to thrive in today's cutthroat market. But it's really, really tough to give up the security that comes from thinking you know exactly who your customers are. So, take a deep breath, and get ready to unlock those cage doors.

Marketers sell vertically but consumers buy horizontally

Well, sorry to say things get even more turbulent! It turns out that marketers like to put *themselves* into cages as well. Again, the lure of the familiar and manageable often lulls us into these self-made containers. But there are a lot of opportunities that await us if we allow ourselves to peek out and consider other possibilities. To illustrate the advantages of this broader perspective, let's take a little quiz (indulge me):

Quick: What do white wine, Brie cheese, a squash racket, a Brooks Brothers suit, fresh pesto, a Rolex, and a BMW have in common?

The consumption constellation

Anyone who's been hanging around US popular culture for a few decades can probably come up with the answer quite quickly. These are products that defined the infamous "Yuppie" (young urban professional) consumer who dominated the marketing airwaves back in the 1980s (their counterparts the so-called Sloane Rangers were prominent in the UK). This cluster of ostensibly unrelated products is an example of a consumption constellation: a set of symbolically related brands that jointly define a social role.

But why should marketers care about an outdated media invention from the last century?

Quite simply, this "consumption constellation" reminds us that while marketers *sell* vertically, consumers *buy* horizontally. The specific items within the constellation may evolve over time (though some hang on as classics), but at any point we can identify a group of disparate products and services that stand apart in terms of function, but that nonetheless *mean together*.

Updated versions of the Yuppie stereotype roam the streets of affluent suburbs and gentrified urban areas even today. Maybe a pricey Liforme yoga mat, a Silver Cross Balmoral baby carriage (only around $4K), a smooth Cabernet with notes of cassis, cocoa and tobacco and a long finish, a Blue Apron subscription, a Daniel Wellington watch, or other indulgences have replaced some of the original Yuppie items in the current pantheon, but the idea is the same.

VERTICAL THINKING

What does this mean for the way we relate to our customers? Most CMOs (chief marketing officers) lose sleep over market share *within* a product category. They dutifully benchmark their initiatives vis-à-vis what their main competitors in that category do. That means they often confine themselves to cages where the bars are made of the industry verticals they insist on adhering to. A fixation with benchmarking strictly to the handful of other organizations that produce a very similar product or service creates a form of marketing myopia where they lose sight of why people are buying their stuff in the first place.

This is vertical thinking.

HORIZONTAL THINKING

But alas, this is not the way your customers think about what you sell. Sorry to break it to you, but they really don't care about your market share. They have other goals in mind than your annual bonus when they decide whether to buy what you sell.

Think of it this way: a marketer sells a lamp, but a consumer buys a living room. Another marketer sells a blouse, but a consumer buys an outfit. Yet another sells an entrée, but a consumer buys a dining experience. You get the idea.

So, the buyer evaluates each item not just to see how it stacks up to other direct substitutes, but also in terms of how it harmonizes with the other products and services that collectively express their taste and social identity.

This is horizontal thinking.

WE SEE WHAT ISN'T THERE

Imagine the ancient Greeks who stared for hours at the night sky (undimmed by light pollution). They saw hundreds of stars and they wondered why they were there. These people used their imagination to invent astronomical constellations. Their minds linked unrelated stars shining in the night sky together to create vivid stories. So, rather than just seeing a bunch of random points of light, they "saw" the big picture of a Big Dipper, Orion's Belt, or other images they imagined these stars spelled out. They were creative people, but their stories also came into being because that's just the way our brains work. They abhor randomness, and they ascribe meaning and patterns even where none actually exist (more on this later).

Somewhat like those stargazing Greeks, modern consumers make sense of unrelated products that blink at them in stores and media in terms of how they fit together to define a social role like a Yuppie, a Tree Hugger, Big Man on Campus, Successful Executive, Soccer Mom, and on and on. As we learn about new things, we make sense of them by trying to figure out what else they relate to that we've already encountered. That's our brains at work trying to make sense of our complicated world.

That way of looking at the world is 90° out of sync with the traditional marketer-centric perspective. If you're able to tilt your head (metaphorically, at least), you may be able to see things in a new way. You'll be able to think like your customers do. That's a huge advantage in an environment where most of us are unable or unwilling to look at things in different ways.

Tilt your head to see new opportunities

Horizontal thinking opens a cage door that may reveal strategic opportunities. These include potential partnerships, brand extensions or promotional tactics with other organizations that belong to the same constellation.

Warning: these possibilities will not seem obvious from the usual vertical view, because these other companies probably don't operate in anything like the vertical that you do. Why would a car manufacturer like BMW find common ground with Louis Vuitton, the luxury leather brand? But indeed they did. For example, Vuitton designed a travel bag set that was designed to fit into the limited space of the BMW i8 sports car.[3] To be sure, this is just a good application of cross-marketing, but it also reflects the recognition that the Beemer buyer and the Vuitton buyer are probably one and the same.

Research supports the notion that we think in terms of these product sets. When consumers encounter a brand that is part of a consumption constellation, they expect to find other (functionally unrelated) brands that belong to it as well. In laboratory studies where we prompt respondents with a constellation brand, we find that their reaction times when they are exposed to other constellation members are faster than for unrelated brands.[4] That means that these cross-category associations have become part of a memory network, so they are more accessible when our brains look for linkages. And these inter-brand associations start early; other work shows similar effects even for children.[5]

In plain English, once we start to think about a specific constellation because we see a product that we associate with it, our brains are quicker to recognize other products from other verticals that we also link to this social structure.

These constellations are all around us, once we start to look for them. For example, they often (albeit subtly) help us to make sense of the stories we encounter in books, plays, movies, TV shows, and of course, advertisements. Indeed, the job of a set designer or prop master is to populate the backdrop of the action so that we instantly recognize the types of characters we're dealing with. In fact, it's common practice for these experts to scour garage sales or stores near where a show is being filmed to procure "realistic" furnishings that will clinch the deal.

Take a close look at sets of TV shows, ads, etc. and you'll quickly see that you can often tell a story about the people who supposedly live in these fictional worlds without even seeing the characters. In a study I did some years ago with MTV Europe, we showed kids a set of diverse music videos they had not seen before (back in the days when MTV primarily played music videos!) with the sound off. We then asked them to guess the music genres that were probably playing in the background. As you might not be surprised to learn, virtually all of the respondents gave the correct answers simply by scrutinizing where the videos were shot and what the musicians and their fans were wearing.[6] They didn't need to hear the notes to know the genre.

What does a shift from a vertical to a horizontal perspective mean for strategic thinking? After all, lifestyle marketing is already a well-oiled weapon in the marketer's arsenal. When Courvoisier partners with Def Jam Recordings because cognac is part of the hip-hop subculture, or Pringles creates a "Hunger Hammer" device that feeds chips into a gamer's mouth while they shoot at trolls, that's a healthy start toward linking a brand with the consumer's broader experience.

Lifestyle marketing is a valuable first step, but marketers can do a deeper dive as well if they really want to understand how their brand relates to other products and services that jointly help to create the consumer experience. Locate consumers who use your brand, and probe further to figure out how they use it and—importantly—what other brands they use concurrently as they perform various social roles.

For example, let's say you manage a perfume brand: Guerlain Mitsouko by Guerlain. As you talk to women who wear this fragrance, you may discover that many of them apply the scent specifically when they go clubbing. Perhaps when you ask them to elaborate on how they prepare for this activity, you discover that many of them say they're likely to wear a slim-fitting bodysuit with palazzo trousers or a jumpsuit with high heels. Perhaps specific brands like Shein or BCBGMAXAZRIA tend to pop up. Maybe a choker necklace by Kendra Scott or Steve Madden makes the list as well, or heels by Shelly London or Kate Spade. Before you know it, you've built a "Club Girl" constellation that may provide some insights to help you position your brand. Who knows, you may also identify potential partners for cross-brand promotions that span a range of verticals. And of course if your brand doesn't play well with other brands, this may be a sign that it just isn't resonating as well as it should with your customers.

Big Data applications offer us more opportunities than ever to predict usage in one category from purchases in others. Even a fairly straightforward web-scraping exercise can do the trick. You simply extract large amounts of online data and analyze it for thematic patterns that can help to identify other (noncompeting) brands that consumers post about when they also mention your brand.

CONSTELLATIONS VS. PSYCHOGRAPHICS

If you do this, remember to be consumer-centric: in addition to checking out datasets, if possible, let your customers tell you what other products and services *they* associate with people who use your brand. And don't forget about the other potential windows you can open. Ads that accurately position a brand within a constellation context by depicting the protagonists as members of a social role category may more readily resonate with target customers, and new products may be more easily accepted if creatives pair them with existing constellation members.

Marketers who do psychographic work typically collect data on a wide range of identifying markers, such as political beliefs, participation in community groups, and of course where possible the brands their respondents use frequently. These indices go by the label AIOs (activities, interests and opinions).

However, these studies often operate much like a fishing expedition, where the idea is to collect a huge amount of data and slice and dice it to see which measures correlate with others in the dataset. We may wind up with intriguing combinations; for example a 2016 analysis reported that Americans who liked to watch the *Duck Dynasty* reality show about a clan of self-professed rednecks were also likely to vote for Donald Trump.[7] But this kind of insight is post hoc only; these relationships emerge organically rather than being validated by some a priori plan or relationship—like a social role that members agree is likely to use these products.

In contrast, a product complementarity approach works *backward* from a social role to identify a relevant constellation of products and services. This approach is more in sync with the fast-growing practice of creating a brand persona that describes your heavy user in detail, and then building a marketing campaign around that mythical person.[8] Add in a proactive strategy to actually *engage* with the other brands that pop up in that profile, and you've got a constellation initiative.

Don't just think vertically when your customers think horizontally.

It's time to unlock some cages

As we've seen, our minds love to classify what we know about the world. Like those ancient Greeks, they often create meanings where none actually exist. And it can be really, really difficult to unlearn these associations once we've forged them.

That's often a big help as we each try to assimilate the millions of discrete pieces of information we have to absorb during our lives. But this need for categorization also creates roadblocks when we allow the labels we assign to people, places, and things to guide our marketing strategies, even when these designations have outlived their usefulness.

This problem is easy to understand when you compare it to the similar practice of stereotyping. A stereotype is basically a set of assumptions about a particular person or group that is not modified or eliminated in the face of conflicting information: "Don't confuse me with the facts!"

We observe this unfortunate tendency, for example, when a person who belongs to a different social group (racial or otherwise) behaves in a way that's inconsistent with what we believe people in that group will do. In these situations, we may engage in mental gymnastics to justify this contradiction by deciding that this person is somehow not a "real" member of that group, he had other reasons to behave the way he did, etc. Our overworked brains loathe inconsistencies, and they will bend over backward to resolve them rather than admit that a well-worn preconception actually is not true after all.

As part of this desire to simplify a confusing buzz of information, we marketers have a pervasive tendency to prefer simple dichotomies that may obscure important nuances. We like to think in terms of black vs. white, even when we know deep down that there are many shades of gray mixed in there (even more than the infamous book *Fifty Shades of Gray* talks about!). And once we create such a dichotomy, we create "cages" as we assign our customers to one group or the other.

In this book, we'll visit seven of these basic dichotomies (and mention lots of others, too). Then we'll show why they no longer exist. The opening of these cages (whether partially or fully) signals earthshaking changes for marketing and consumer behavior going forward. Like it or not, our customers are becoming *consumer chameleons* who will work hard to leave these cages as soon as the doors start to creak open. They're defying these labels and escaping as fast as they can run. These shifts in the basic bedrock of the marketing landscape in turn require us to rethink what we think we know about consumers—and the way *they* think about marketers.

To set the stage, here are the seven fundamental oppositions that we'll examine in subsequent chapters (we'll throw in a bunch of others as well). In each case, we'll see that these contrasts no longer work nearly as well as we think they do. This is because our customers stubbornly persist in defying them. That may be unsettling to the traditionalist. But as you contemplate how you'll market in this strange new world, I encourage you to bear in mind the words of Winston Churchill: "A pessimist sees difficulty in every opportunity; an optimist sees opportunity in every difficulty."[9]

The seven (obsolete) dichotomies

1 Us vs. Them: Some widely used demographic dichotomies such as Rich vs. Poor and Young vs. Old.

2 Me vs. We: The sole decision maker versus his/her peers.

3 Offline vs. Online: Consumer behavior in the physical world versus the digital world.

4 Producer vs. Consumer: People who make things versus people who buy things.

5 Male vs. Female: The end of gender binarism.

6 Body vs. Possessions: Our biological bodies versus the things we put on or in them.

7 Editorial vs. Commercial: Communications that intend to inform us versus those that intend to sell to us.

I hope you enjoy reading about these cages as much as I enjoyed unlocking them.

Endnotes

1 Robert F. Kennedy, 1966, http://www.jfklibrary.org/learn/about-jfk/the-kennedy-family/robert-f-kennedy/robert-f-kennedy-speeches/day-of-affirmation-address-university-of-capetown-capetown-south-africa-june-6-1966 (archived at https://perma.cc/8N8A-HW9H).

2 Kenneth S. Pope and Melba J.T. Vasquez, "Common Logical Fallacies in Psychology: 26 Types and Examples," *Fallacies and Pitfalls in Psychology*, https://kspope.com/fallacies/fallacies.php (archived at https://perma.cc/6HXZ-6TY7).

3 "How to Open Up New Growth Opportunities with Cross Marketing," *Lead Innovation Blog*, April 27, 2018,

https://www.lead-innovation.com/english-blog/cross-marketing (archived at https://perma.cc/RU78-EYQG).

4   Tina M. Lowrey et al., "Response Latency Verification of Consumption Constellations: Implications for Advertising Strategy," *Journal of Advertising* 30, no. 1 (Spring 2001): 29–39.

5   Lan Nguyen Chaplin and Tina M. Lowrey, "The Development of Consumer-Based Consumption Constellations in Children," *Journal of Consumer Research* 36, no. 5, (February 2010): 757–77, doi.org/ 10.1086/605365 (archived at https://perma.cc/D2AB-LXWP).

6   Michael R. Solomon and Lawrence Greenberg, "Setting the Stage: Collective Selection in the Stylistic Content of Commercials," *Journal of Advertising* 22 (March 1993): 11–24; Basil G. Englis, Michael R. Solomon, and Anna Olofsson, "Consumption Imagery in Music Television: A Bi Cultural Perspective," *Journal of Advertising* 22 (December 1993): 21–34.

7   Josh Katz, "'Duck Dynasty' vs. 'Modern Family': 50 Maps of the U.S. Cultural Divide," *The New York Times,* December 27, 2016, https://www.nytimes.com/interactive/2016/12/26/upshot/duck-dynasty-vs-modern-family-television-maps.html?_r=0 (archived at https://perma.cc/Q8AQ-CMSU).

8   "How to Craft the Ideal User Persona for Your Brand," *Forbes,* March 14, 2018,

9   https://www.forbes.com/sites/forbesagencycouncil/2018/03/14/ how-to-craft-the-ideal-user-persona-for-your-brand/#4c4013ec6ead (archived at https://perma.cc/TH4Q-TXUF).

01

The evolution of marketing categories

There are two kinds of people… people who think there are two ~~hc~~
kinds of people, and people who don't.

Why is our urge to categorize consumers so pervasive? One simple answer: this is the way our brains work. Psychologists know that when we encounter a new object (or person), within milliseconds our immediate response is to put it into a familiar category. Good or bad? Weak or strong? Binary code: 0 or 1? Regular or decaf? Ready-to-wear or haute couture? Swipe left or swipe right?

Build cages and put people into them, depending upon the categories we assign to them in those first fleeting moments. Perhaps this mindset is a holdover from the caveman days, when the choice about how to label a person literally was life or death.

Imagine a prehistoric man wandering across the savannah. Suddenly he spies a stranger heading his way. It's time for a really quick judgment call: friend or foe? The wrong answer can turn out quite badly for him, to say the least. Today we short-circuit this dilemma with a handshake, a gesture that evolved to assure others that you are not holding a weapon. And this stand-in looks like it will evolve to an elbow bump post-pandemic. Even with this more civilized solution, our "good or bad" decision process isn't that much different from that of our ancient ancestors.

Marketing categories are cultural categories

If you stop to think about it, just about everything you know belongs to a category. In some cases, your brain has done the heavy lifting of assigning an object a label, but often each of us simply obeys preexisting structures our culture has taught us. Meanings that we impart to products reflect underlying cultural categories, which correspond to the basic ways in which we characterize the world.[1] Our culture makes distinctions between different times of the day, such as between leisure and work hours, as well as many other differences, such as between genders, occasions, groups of people, and so on.

And the marketing system conveniently provides us with products that signify these categories. For example, the clothing industry gives us labels to denote certain times and wearing occasions such as formal, business professional, business casual, resort wear and even (shudder) Casual Fridays. It differentiates between leisure clothes and work clothes, and it promotes masculine, feminine or unisex styles. It labels itself in other ways to denote price points and suitable age groups, such as Haute Couture, Designer, Ready to Wear, Bridge, or Contemporary.

We find similar gradations no matter where we look across the cultural spectrum. Think about the following categories we use every day: Appetizer, Entrée, or Dessert? Conservative and Unionist Party, Liberal Democrats, Labour Party, or Scottish National Party? Danish Modern, Rustic, Shabby Chic, or Industrial? FA Premier League, League 1, Bundesliga, or Serie A? Novice, Intermediate, or Expert? Sedan, Coupe, Convertible, or SUV? Fiction or nonfiction? Slapper, Prim, or Chav?

We internalize these underlying configurations almost from birth, even though we may not be aware just how well-worn our judgments may be. Consider for example the categories that underlie the TV shows, movies, and popular novels we avidly consume. In an extreme case like a romance novel, you can actually work with a template to "write" your own tearjerker by systematically varying certain set elements of the story! Essentially, all you need to do is fill in the blanks as you decide whether the beleaguered heroine will be an innocent teenager, a jaded socialite, an ambitious career woman, and so on.[2] Add a few familiar clichés like a "heaving bosom" and the "brutish hero who's really a scared little kitten" and perhaps you've got a hit on your hands.

Other familiar art forms such as TV follow the same pattern. Consider well-known genres like these types of shows, and some of the cultural formulae they almost always follow:[3]

TABLE 1.1   Cultural formulae in media genres

Genre	Classic western	Science fiction	Hard-boiled detective	Family sitcom
Time	1800s	Future	Present	Any time
Location	Edge of civilization	Space	City	Suburbs
Protagonist	Cowboy (lone individual)	Astronaut	Detective	Father (figure)
Heroine	Schoolmistress	Space girl	Damsel in distress	Mother (figure)
Locomotion	Horse	Spaceship	Beat-up car	Station wagon/SUV
Weaponry	Six-gun, rifle	Ray guns	Pistol, fists	Insults

Who builds the cages?

Where do the cages we've been discussing come from? Did Moses come down from the mountain and declare that the fashion industry will follow four seasons: Spring/Summer, Fall/Winter, Resort, and Pre-Fall? Did he give us other schemes, like Fiction/Nonfiction, etc. or Danish Modern/Shabby Chic, etc.? Obviously not, but most businesses are very reluctant to challenge the established order— even if their customers do.

Traditional knowledge structures use preestablished systems to sort content. Taxonomies are classifications that experts create; for example, you may have learned (and perhaps forgotten) the classic system that biologists use to categorize organisms (the Linnaean taxonomy) that places any living thing in terms of Kingdom, Phylum, Class, Order, Family, Genus, and Specie.[4]

These taxonomic structures are often logical, comprehensive, and quite useful. The problem is, they don't necessarily mirror how people actually think. Unless we've been trained (or indoctrinated) to follow a certain preordained system, we're likely to come up with other ways to sort out what we know. We may develop folksonomies instead. These are sets of labels, or tags, individuals choose in a way that makes sense to them, as opposed to using predefined keywords. You may sort your own clothing inventory in your own way, perhaps with labels such as Good for Clubbing, Out of Style, or No Longer Fits.

The divergence between taxonomies and folksonomies can create two problems for a business or other organization:

- Customers may need help to translate the language an industry uses into parameters they understand.
- As customers create their own knowledge structures, they may be comparing purchase alternatives that don't track the way the vertical professionals view their competitors.

Thus, a perfumer distinguishes among fragrances in terms of their top notes, heart notes, and base notes. A customer is more likely to label competing brands as citrusy, bold, pricey, feminine, or the one that Kim Kardashian recently blogged about.

We can readily observe this disconnect when we compare the way that Amazon organizes its e-commerce platform with the way that customers talk about what the company sells. Amazon uses a logical taxonomy as it subdivides the site into sections such as (1) books; (2) movies, music, and games; and (3) computer and office products. Then, within the books section, the customer can explore genres such as sci-fi and fantasy.

The scientific method needs categories

Rigorous research in the hard sciences and a substantial bit of the social sciences rests on the scientific method, which emphasizes the importance of an objective approach to understanding natural phenomena. As an outgrowth of modernism, this paradigm tried to correct for what its founders believed was an understanding of the world based upon superstition and "nonrational" explanations for everything from the movement of the stars to social deviance.

In tandem with the Industrial Revolution that began in the late nineteenth century, technology rather than religion reigned supreme. Engineers, inventors, and scientists became the "new priests" who celebrated a dawning age of rationality.

Streamlined, symmetrical skyscrapers took the place of ornately decorated cathedrals. People began to "worship" science as a panacea. The 1964 World's Fair in New York was the apogee of this belief in technology to solve the world's problems. It unveiled wonders like the Picturephone (long before Zoom Happy Hours), jet packs, and a General Motors exhibit that promised us moon colonies, commuter spaceships, moving walkways, and underwater hotels in the near future.[5]

The modernist, or positivist, searches for objective facts. Through a process of systematic discovery, he or she believes it is possible to identify basic laws that govern the way things work in this world. The truth is out there. We just have to find it.

Laboratories vs. the real world

A basic dichotomy scientists revere is In Here vs. Out There. To study a phenomenon, we need to isolate it from its naturally occurring context. This enables us to eliminate "confounds" that may obscure the true cause of what we observe. We dutifully take a sample, bring it into a sterile laboratory, and manipulate it while we hold everything else constant (to the extent possible). If we observe any changes after we're done, we have much greater confidence that they relate to what *we* did, rather than to some other unruly stuff going on in the real world.

For years, we've put customers into neat little cages, such as age groups, income groups, or gender groups. We might collect (or more likely, purchase) data on buyers who have been classified in certain ways such as male or female, married or single, low-income or affluent. Then we'll create cross-tabulations within the dataset so that we can compare people whom we've identified as, say, married males who don't make a lot of money vs. single females who do quite well. We happily slice-and-dice the data in many ways to compare purchase rates, attitudes toward our brand, or whatever we need to explore.

A little secret that statisticians know: if you relentlessly try different analyses as you go on what they like to call a fishing expedition, you may well come up with "results" just by chance. But it's hard to argue with positive results. If we discover a difference in these cross-tabs, we're happy because now we "know" people who fall into one cell differ from those in another.

CAUSATION VS. CORRELATION

When we find these disparities, it's tempting to conclude that our descriptive variables "cause" the differences. But that's a tough sell to a statistician—even when the relationships seem "obvious." For example, descriptive studies show that people who buy more diapers are also likely to buy more beer. Is the act of buying diapers so stressful that it motivates us to double down on our brew purchases? Do people who put on a beer buzz wind up going on a diaper buying spree? You can guess that instead, both types of purchases most likely are driven by something else going on in these people's lives.

The familiar caveat, "correlation does not imply causation" can be a hard pill to swallow. That's the case especially when an industry's hired guns use it to rebut compelling findings, such as the oft-reported relationship between heavy cigarette smoking and high mortality rates. As much as we "know" this makes sense, the tobacco industry has pushed back for decades by reminding us that heavy smokers may also exhibit other lifestyle factors that could (at least in theory) account for their tendency to keel over at higher rates than nonsmokers.

In fairness, let's not throw the baby out with the bathwater. The tried-and-true scientific method still offers many powerful applications, even in the soft sciences. This controlled approach is especially valuable to understand more micro-level marketing questions that don't rely so heavily upon the respondent's external environment, such as those that involve physiological changes or basic perceptual processes.

For example, if we want to understand how shoppers respond to minute changes in package designs, or perhaps whether the way we frame a statement about a product specification influences the likelihood shoppers will remember it accurately, this is still the way to go. If we want to see whether a teenager is less likely to vape when he knows his friends disapprove, or if a young woman will order the cheap burger or the pricey steak on a first date, perhaps not so much.

THE REAL WORLD IS YOUR MARKETING LABORATORY

If we want to understand a lot of social phenomena where a customer's thoughts, feelings, and behaviors probably depend upon social cues such as how others in the same situation respond, *context is king*. The other squishy things going on in the real-world environment are precisely the things that influence our interpretations of the social setting and that give us clues about how we should be thinking and acting.

So, ironically, the better we are at purifying the research setting, the less likely that setting will mimic what really goes on when the subject leaves the laboratory. That's one reason why it's valuable to use multiple research methods where possible in order to triangulate on an issue. This might involve a combination of controlled/sterile experiments with uncontrolled/realistic observations of consumers in their natural habitats so that hopefully the results will converge across methods.

For example, Campbell executed a variety of approaches to help the venerable company grapple with a big problem: young people just don't eat as much soup as they used to. A research team immersed itself in Millennial culture. They conducted face-to-face interviews and focus groups, but they also ate meals with young people in their homes, checked out their pantries, and tagged along with them on shopping trips to the grocery store.

It was only after this immersion process that the team was able to identify the "pain points" that younger consumers seem to associate with canned soups. For example, their Millennial respondents told them that the soups are too "processed" and they taste bland, homogeneous, and unexciting. Another common complaint was the lack of healthy ingredients these young consumers look for, such as quinoa and on-trend veggies like kale. This group includes "flexitarians," that is, they eat vegetarian for a few days and then eat meat on the weekends, special occasions, to satisfy a craving, etc. They tend to care about sustainability, local sourcing, and company practices.

These insights led the company to tweak its approach; one obvious response was to change the packaging from a can to a pouch, because respondents said that a pouch communicates a "fresher ingredients" message.[6] In some additional work I did with the company, we recruited Millennials to work together in a virtual environment as teams competed with other teams to come up with novel soup flavors that would appeal to people like them. These are the kinds of insights that just won't turn up in a large-scale, statistically reliable but rather sterile attitude survey.

FIGURE 1.1   A "virtual world" we created to help Campbell engage Millennials

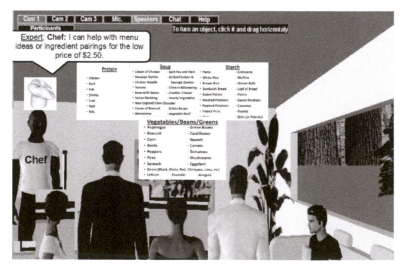

How our schemas shape our decisions

If we want to evaluate an object in isolation rather than judging it relative to other somewhat similar things we've already encountered in the world, we're probably fighting a losing battle. Our brains are literally wired to process new information by comparing it to what we already know and then assigning it to a tidy category: a place for everything, and everything in its place. The meaning we assign to a stimulus depends on the schema, or set of beliefs, to which we assign it. This in turn leads us to compare the stimulus to other similar ones we encountered in the past. And these judgments have a nasty tendency to persist even when they're downright wrong.

Identifying and evoking the correct schema is crucial to many marketing decisions. This labeling process determines what criteria consumers will use to evaluate the product, package, or message. Thus, if we determine that a new product is a dark, carbonated beverage we'll probably compare it to colas we've tasted in the past. Our poor, overworked brains would probably start to emit a cloud of steam if that liquid is poured out of a can that features colors like green rather than red or blue. We've learned to assume that citrusy soft drinks always reside in green containers, while colas reliably live in red or blue ones.

These learned assumptions can make or break a new product that doesn't conform to what we expect to find. Extra Strength Maalox Whip Antacid flopped, even though a spray can is a pretty effective way to deliver the product. To consumers, aerosol whips mean dessert toppings, not medication. A new brand of frozen dog food met a similar fate; we just don't expect to find Fido's meals in the frozen foods section of our grocery store.[7]

In one study that looked at how labels impact our preferences, a college cafeteria gave menu items descriptive labels (e.g., Red Beans with Rice versus Traditional Cajun Red Beans with Rice, Chocolate Pudding versus Satin Chocolate Pudding) so that diners could more easily categorize it. Sales increased by more than 25 percent with the enhanced labels.[8]

Again, the way we make sense of the world—and readily assign objects as well as people to categories—depends on the fundamental assumptions we form about the way that world works. For example, something as simple as the location of a product's image on a package influences the way our brains make sense of it. Due to what we have learned about the law of gravity (heavy objects sink and light objects float), we assume that if a product's image appears lower down on the front of the container, it must weigh more than products that appear higher up in the photo.

In addition, objects on the right of a frame appear heavier than products that appear on the left of a frame. This interpretation results from our intuition about levers: we know that the farther away an object is from a lever's fulcrum, the more difficult it is to raise the item. Because we read from left to right, the left naturally becomes the visual fulcrum, and thus we perceive objects on the right as heavier. Manufacturers should bear these package schematics in mind because they may influence our feelings about the contents in a package, for better or worse. Think, for example, about a diet food marketer who wants shoppers to think about its products as "lighter" than other options.[9]

How our brains create schemas

Our brains don't just assign a new piece of information to one category. The schemas we form look more like spider webs than they do cages with only one door (no, not literally: don't panic; we don't have actual webs lurking inside our heads, even though a hangover may feel like you do).

We develop knowledge structures that link individual pieces of data to one another in terms of some relation we think they have. This connection is a node. Actually, these structures also resemble the social networks we belong to that allow messages to pass among individuals who are linked to one another in some way. This sort of structure probably is more familiar to you after the pandemic, because it turns out even a virus travels this way. That's why we heard so much talk about "connectors" and "vectors" of infection as people passed the virus to those they encountered in their various networks.

If a marketer shows us a picture of a package, this stimulus may directly activate a memory of that brand. But this may also work indirectly, if that memory connects to others you've acquired. It's much like tapping a spider web; other parts of it reverberate as well. For example, say a person catches a snippet of the song "Conversations in the Dark" by John Legend. She may start to hum the rest of it—or perhaps an image of herself in her bridal gown suddenly pops into her mind because (as it turns out) this was her wedding song. And then she finds herself dwelling upon related memories such as the taste of the wedding cake or even how her rich uncle had the nerve to give such a paltry gift.

We store our memories for brands in different ways. For example, a male teen rolling his trolley through the personal care aisle may see a bottle of Axe deodorant; this could trigger a memory of a commercial he saw for the product, or perhaps the last time he applied the product to get ready for a hot date. Here are some ways that our memories can represent brand information:

- **Brand-specific**—Memory is stored in terms of claims the brand makes ("it's macho").
- **Ad-specific**—Memory is stored in terms of the medium or content of the ad itself (a macho-looking guy uses the product).
- **Brand identification**—Memory is stored in terms of the brand name (e.g., "Axe").
- **Product category**—Memory is stored in terms of how the product works or where it should be used (a bottle of Axe sits in a guy's medicine cabinet).
- **Evaluative reactions**—Memory is stored as positive or negative emotions ("that looks cool").[10]

How does this elaborate storage process benefit us? One reason that our brains love to assign things to categories is simple efficiency. It's quite difficult to decide if something is good or bad unless we answer the question, "Compared to what?" Every industry creates nomenclature and categories so that both buyers and sellers can quickly identify a relevant set of competitors. This labeling process also facilitates judgments about which of the entrants in a category are "better" than the others.

That assignment is absolutely crucial to your brand's fortunes. The reason is that the way people evaluate it depends a lot upon the other members of the category to which it's been assigned. The most successful welterweight boxer might not so fare so well if he fights men in heftier categories such as super middleweight, light heavyweight, or cruiserweight.

In the same way, brands in the apparel space such as Maje, Jaeger, and Ted Baker are classified as bridge lines. A manager for Ted Baker might be quite happy to compete against other similar lines—but not too thrilled to be lumped into the luxury brand category and be compared against the likes of Hermès, Chanel, and Prada. Suddenly he's "punching above his weight."

The question of which category you get assigned to holds enormous strategic ramifications. Ideally, you want to choose a category you can dominate. You won't have that option if, for example, you launch a new basketball shoe that immediately gets compared to heavyweights like Nike.

This is yet another reason why inventing a new, or hybrid, category can be a great solution; you get to write the rules. Determinant attributes are the criteria that buyers use to choose one brand over others in a category. To the extent possible, don't allow your brand to be judged on the attributes at which your competitors excel if you can introduce your own where you do instead. One of my favorite examples is a move PepsiCo made in the 1990s when the company suddenly introduced "freshness dating" on its soda cans. At least for a time, it turned a nonissue into a determinant attribute—even though buyers consume the very large majority of cans before they ever approach the point of becoming stale![11]

Me vs. other

The most basic and powerful distinction we humans make is Me (or Us) vs. Other. Our history is essentially the story of ingroups vs.

outgroups. We seem to be "wired" to favor others whom we feel share the same identity, even when that identity is superficial and virtually meaningless.

This urge to distinguish ourselves from others is so pervasive that we will seize upon virtually any reason to do so. The fact that one person is placed in a group with some other people and not with others, even when there is absolutely no reason to differentiate, is enough to create a powerful group identity.

Social psychologists have demonstrated this tendency in numerous studies that use a methodology they call the minimal group paradigm. They will take a set of people, previously unknown to one another, who show up for a laboratory experiment and arbitrarily form them into groups. Perhaps they will ask one group to wear a name tag that says "A" and another to wear a "B." Even though there is no discernible reason to do so, inevitably researchers find that if you're an "A" you favor other "A's" and you believe your group is "better" than others.[12] And we wonder why we have so many wars.

The imperative to make these distinctions becomes even more salient during uncertain times such as the recent pandemic. Fear of the Other was drastically magnified. Suddenly the need to practice extreme "social distancing" elevated everyone's awareness of Self vs. Other to almost hysterical proportions. Not surprising, since virtually any person who is not Me (even a loved one) has the potential to make Me sick.

The quest to identify "friend vs. foe" will always be there for us. But our definition of what makes others into the good guys vs. the bad guys does change. Sometimes brands and the people who work for them are the Other. For example, in recent years we've seen that consumers increasingly mistrust marketers (in addition to politicians and others who control mass media and economic resources). A 2019 survey of 25,000 respondents in eight global markets was concerning: only a third of respondents said they trust most of the brands they buy and use, and even that abysmal figure dropped to less than a quarter in some markets including France and Germany.[13]

But in the silver linings department, a curious thing happened during the pandemic: consumers increasingly looked to brands to play a major role in recovery. In fact, in another global survey in March 2020 by the same organization, more than half of respondents agreed that marketers are responding more quickly and more effectively to the pandemic than have their governments![14]

As Rahm Emanuel, the former mayor of Chicago, observed, "Never let a serious crisis go to waste. And what I mean by that it's an opportunity to do things you think you could not do before."[15] Friends change, enemies change. So do labels.

Gain insights by studying consumer chameleons in their real-world habitats

To truly understand today's customer, it's often smart to use naturalistic techniques that require researchers to "live with the natives." Breach the cage that separates you from your customers. Get out of your office and meet the people who love your brand. Be sure to talk to some who don't as well. What do they love about your brand? What do they hate? What would they improve?

True, many marketing researchers still pursue "the truth" via basic survey research, but this gets more difficult in our frenzied world. When was the last time you happily interrupted your dinner to respond to a phone survey?

The secret to predicting consumer behavior

Well, it's actually not such a secret after all. But it's worth keeping in mind: the best predictor of future behavior is past behavior.

To the extent that we're able to know what our customers have done before (and hopefully why), we're better able to make an educated guess about what they will do the next time a similar situation arises. Obviously. Indeed, this simple (yet profound?) statement is what's behind the entire science of tracking what people buy and where they buy it, whether in stores or online. It's particularly crucial in the e-commerce space, where algorithms serve up new ads based upon the places we've already browsed.

But note that even this knowledge is not a panacea, and our informed predictions will never come close to being 100 percent accurate. People have a nasty tendency to crave novelty if they can get it without sacrificing too much. It may not be rational to try a new brand when you're perfectly happy with your current one—but we do it all the time.

Even so, there's no better way to come close to hitting the mark when it comes to estimating what consumers will do in the future. The quest for variety-seeking is likely to be stronger among people who like to flirt with a variety of brands—so it's the ones who are in a strong relationship we want to identify. That's why it almost always makes sense to identify a brand's heavy users, even though numerically they are unlikely to be in the majority of all buyers.

Remember the famous 80/20 rule. This is the marketing version of a broader principle known as the Pareto's Law, named after the economist who proposed that in many scenarios the majority of the effects come from a small number of causes.

So, in our world, this means that 80 percent of your revenues will come from 20 percent of your customers. Although this ratio is not set in stone, it's surprising how often it comes close. That's a potent reminder of the importance of your heavy users—and they're also crucial because they can be your most powerful salesforce. But more on that later.

THE POWER OF THE BUYER PERSONA

How do we understand that heavy user? It's common today for a brand to create a fictional profile of a "core customer" who inspires product design and communications decisions. Marketers refer to these profiles as buyer personas (or sometimes brand avatars). Essentially you write a "story" about your ideal customer based on market research and real data about your existing customers.[16] The character helps you to connect with the type of person you hope to reach, and he or she gives you a more concrete way to think about your customers.

FIGURE 1.2   A hypothetical persona of a marketing manager

Byron

Age
25 to 34 years

Highest Level of Education
Bachelor's degree (e.g. BA, BS)

Social Networks

Industry
Technology

Organization Size
501–1000 employees

Preferred Method of Communication

• Social Media

Tools He Needs to Do His Job

• Content Management Systems
• Business Intelligence Dashboards
• Email
• Project Manager

Job Responsibilities

Content creation, build inbound traffic

His Job Is Measured By

Team productivity, sales revenue

Reports to

CMO

Goals or Objectives

Maximize revenue
Demonstrate his value to superiors whenever possible

SOURCE Kindly reproduced with permission of Hubspot.com

For example, Chip Wilson, who founded the popular clothing company Lululemon, relied upon a "muse" he made up: a 32-year-old professional single woman named Ocean who makes $100,000 a year. He described Ocean as "engaged, has her own condo, is traveling, fashionable, has an hour and a half to work out a day." This ideal user, according to Wilson, appeals to all women: "If you're 20 years old or you're graduating from university, you can't wait to be that woman. If you're 42 years old with a couple of children, you wish you had that time back."

Lululemon added a male "muse" when the company moved into menswear: Duke is 35 and an "athletic opportunist" who surfs in the summer and snowboards in the winter. When Wilson got involved in a new company, Kit and Ace, sure enough he helped to come up with two new muses: One was a woman he called Kit, a 29-year-old single woman who works in graphic design or fashion and loves to bike on weekends. The other was Ace, a 32-year-old male who likes to drink strong coffee, hang out with friends in breweries, and who dabbles in CrossFit."[17] Sound like anyone you know (hint: definitely not your humble author!)?

A cautionary note: it's often very useful to create personas for your brand but be very careful about the assumptions you make. Brand managers have a tendency to envision the customer they want to have, not necessarily the one they actually serve. Research (including my own) shows that marketing professionals are notoriously inaccurate when it comes to predicting the consumption behaviors of the public.[18]

And another: don't get trapped in the cage you build for your persona! As we've already seen, consumer chameleons take on multiple identities—sometimes in the course of a day. That's why at the least it's important to recognize that your persona more likely is really *several* personas. Different versions may emerge on different occasions. The persona you painstakingly create to understand the primary buyer of, say, industrial equipment is probably not the same one who heads to a club after she clocks out of the office.

Naturalistic research methods add flavor to the mix

We're witnessing a rebirth of qualitative methods like ethnography that encourage analysts to observe their customers in their natural settings. In other words, watch how consumers actually use products in their everyday habitats. A brand that wants to get the real lowdown on what drives the choices of teenage girls is probably better off sending a young female employee to crash a real-life slumber party than bringing these girls into a laboratory and asking them to gossip about their fantasies, frustrations, and favorite exfoliators.

Fish where the fish are.

Although we may pick up a lot of static in natural environments, we also get a level of richness that is very hard to come by in more well-ordered research settings. As we've already seen, the goal of a controlled experiment is to do just what the term implies—control as much of the environment as possible so that only the specific factors (we call them independent variables) of interest get manipulated.

THE CUSTOMER JOURNEY MAP

This ever-changing customer is one reason that many organizations buy into the idea of creating customer journey maps. A mapping project involves a very precise tracking of the experiences your customers actually have when they interact with your product, store, or service. One important goal is to identify the "pain points" they encounter along the way to reduce the amount of friction people experience. This process involves several basic steps:

1 Identify your buyer persona

2 Identify goals

3 Map out buyer touchpoints

4 Identify pain points

5 Prioritize and fix roadblocks

6 Take the customer journey yourself!

7 Update and improve

There are many ways to measure these experiences, such as identifying KPIs (key performance indicators), devising customer satisfaction measures, or simply adopting the widely used NPS (net promoter score). The important thing is to measure, and measure often.

But perhaps the most important step is #6: take the customer journey yourself! Too many times managers sit in their plush offices and imagine what their customers experience rather than doing what the Japanese call going to the *gemba* (roughly, the exact place at which the event occurs).

It's only by living through the experience in their shoes that you can truly appreciate the problem. For example, in one project a company that operates food concessions in big airports dispatched its executives to buy meals at these sites. It was only when they lived this process for themselves that they stumbled upon a problem with which many of us can identify: when you're traveling by yourself with luggage, it's very stressful to have to leave your bags in order to procure your meal—especially when you can't see these belongings across the room. The company was able to reconfigure the setting so that there was a clear line of sight between the cash register and all the tables. Now if they could do something about the food...

Understanding and marketing to the new consumer

The fluidity of consumer identity actually is not a new story. A chapter in Douglas Coupland's influential 1991 book *Generation X* (that's where the term came from) declared, "I am not a market segment."[19] People have been trying on different personalities for years as they strive to break out of their own little cages. We've come a long way from the drab, conforming "Organization Man" of the 1950s.

Welcome to the wild, wacky world of the postmodern consumer. Today, a consumer's consumption choices are a lot more varied and complicated than they used to be, as seemingly endless options to spend our time and money entice us. It's a fertile environment for consumer chameleons.

In fact, it's fair to propose that one of the biggest challenges of modern life today isn't that there isn't enough choice. *Au contraire.* It's that there's too much. Consumer researchers refer to this problem as hyperchoice.[20] Want to buy a new shade of lipstick? Here's a few hundred for you to ponder. A new tie? Ditto. During the 1990s, the average grocery store sold 7,000 products. Today that number exceeds 40,000 items.[21]

Our job isn't getting any easier, as companies overwhelm us with more and more features. We deal with 50-button remote controls, digital cameras with hundreds of mysterious features and book-length manuals, and cars with dashboard systems worthy of the space shuttle. Experts call this spiral of complexity feature creep. As evidence that the proliferation of gizmos is counterproductive, Philips Electronics found that at least half of the products buyers return have nothing wrong with them; consumers simply couldn't understand how to use them! What's worse, on average the buyer spent only 20 minutes trying to figure out how to use the product and then gave up.

Choice abounds, but so does an important paradox: as consumers get more options to choose from, they actually make poorer choices!

And to rub salt into the wound, research evidence suggests shoppers are less likely to buy anything at all as the number of options increases. Essentially, they get so overwhelmed that they throw up their hands and make a quick exit to avoid having to wade through all of their options. That's why—as we'll see later—it's so crucial for marketers to understand that they play a hugely important role as editors or curators who intervene to whittle down options to a manageable number.

The new consumers belong to microsegments

Although we're faced with a profusion of brands, until fairly recently we didn't see huge differences in consumption across groups of people, especially when we control for income. As "tribes" waxed and waned, they were likely to include large swaths of the population. For example, Flower Children in the 1960s did their own thing, but because most were tuned in to the big record labels and magazines of the time everyone's sartorial rebellion looked pretty much the same. Are those your tie-dyed jeans or mine?

Fast forward to today, when we truly live in an era of market fragmentation. Just as our TV viewing options have expanded to thousands of channels today, the monolithic market segments of that time have decomposed into innumerable micro-segments. In the period from 2009 to 2015 for example, the total number of

TV channels the European Union established grew by 49 percent from 3,615 TV channels to 5,370.[22]

The postmodern consumer blithely travels from one micro-segment to another. The only constant we can count on from our new consumer chameleons is that they will adopt the coloration of many segments in the course of a decade, a year, or perhaps even a day.

To see this splintering in action, just visit any decent-sized magazine stand. Count the staggering number of publications that give us a glimpse into obscure lifestyles ranging from yachting to coding to pumping iron. Stroll through the food court in a typical shopping mall. You can choose from a dizzying range of ethnic foods—Chinese, Italian, American, sushi, Thai, and Mexican—or perhaps combine them all on the same plate.

Clearly, the long-standing "one size fits all" (or at least "three networks fit all") model has to go. At least a handful of consumer behavior researchers have advocated a more fluid approach to understanding our brand choices for quite a while. These "interpretivists" like to muddy the waters rather than clearing them up. They stress the importance of symbolic, subjective experience and the idea that meaning is in the mind of the person.

In this view, we each construct our own beliefs based upon our unique and shared cultural experiences, so there are no objectively right or wrong answers. No black and white, just shades of gray. "Beauty is in the eye of the beholder." "One man's meat is another man's poison." "That's why they make chocolate and vanilla." You get the idea…

This subjective thinking is one of the hallmarks of postmodernism.

To Amazon's credit, its system does allow customers to create their own folksonomies by tagging items with labels that make sense to them. Amazon empowers its users to organize and classify its offerings using their own tags. These tags are entirely user-generated, so users can search their own tags and the tags of others. Thus, we can find George R. R. Martin's *Game of Thrones* under Sci-fi & Fantasy, but we can also search using words and phrases

FIGURE 1.3   An example of a tag cloud

according amount avidly billion boards categorize content count customers data

designate   easier   enterprising   example   folksonomy   harvested   identify

images

important   knowing   knowledge   logic

marketer

media million multiple people pin pinterest

platforms post sitting social structures tags understand # users various

vast waiting

SOURCE Created at www.tagcrowd.com

that past readers have included in their reviews, such as "highly recommend," "HBO series," and "ice and fire."

Why wouldn't a marketer want to use the same knowledge structures as his or her customers? It's easier than ever to identify these, because so many social media platforms allow users to designate multiple tags that categorize the content they see or post according to their own folksonomy. For example, more than 320 million Pinterest users avidly pin images to various boards (more than 200 billion at last count).[23]

This vast amount of data is just sitting there, waiting to be harvested by enterprising marketers who understand that knowing what people do with their images is even more important than whether they "like" them or not. For example, a quick search using the keyword "sophisticated" brings up a slew of brands and celebrities including Victoria Beckham, Bulgari, Jones New York, Emma Watson—but also descriptors such as street style, classy, and even bathroom design. Folksonomies rule.

At a more modest level, you can mine virtually any text that people post to give you a handle on how they're describing a brand or other concept. A tag cloud is a visual display of the frequency with which words are used. It's easy and useful to parse content, whether textual or visual, just by identifying the elements people use and how much overlap there is among customers. Figure 1.3

shows a simple example of a tag cloud that diagrams the content of the paragraphs just above this one.

The new consumer buys horizontally, not vertically

In this postmodern view, our world is a *pastiche*, or mixture of images and ideas.[24] Our consumption choices are most valuable when they question boundaries and force us to venture outside of our little cages. Perhaps it helps to think of this process like a music playlist: a record company thinks in terms of specific musical genres like Hip-Hop, Country, and Classical. It has to, because that's the way industry groups and publications count purchases and downloads.

But listeners don't always think in these terms at all. They build different playlists for different occasions in their lives. Their MP3 files may carry labels like Working Out at Home During the Coronavirus, Our Courtship Days in College, or Doing Housework. And each of these lists may include entries from multiple industry classifications as they weave from Rihanna to the Beatles to Taylor Swift.

We see the impact of postmodernism quite vividly when we look at how consumers around the world integrate foreign products with indigenous practices in a process of creolization:

- The Indian music hybrid called *Indipop* mixes traditional styles with rock, rap, and reggae.[25]
- Natives in Papua, New Guinea, pound on drums adorned with Chivas Regal wrappers and substitute Pentel pens for their traditional nose bones.[26]
- Young Hispanic Americans bounce between hip-hop and *Rock en Español*, blend Mexican rice with spaghetti sauce, and spread peanut butter and jelly on tortillas.[27]
- In Turkey some urban women use their ovens to dry clothes and rinse muddy spinach in their dishwashers.
- When an Ethiopian princess marries a Zulu king, tribesmen watch *Pluto Tries to Become a Circus Dog* on a Viewmaster while a band plays *The Sound of Music*.[28]

In today's "interesting times," technological and societal changes free up more of us to be cultural chameleons. The fragmentation of society, and of media, exposes the consumer to many more possible selves, or visions of possible identities that weren't accessible just a few decades ago.[29] A postmodern society that refutes the tenets of modernism by blending categories together allows us to experiment with new options. It demolishes the cages we keep trying to use to squeeze postmodern customers into modernist containers.

Create new products that defy conventional categories

What business are you in—really? Answer this seemingly obvious question not in terms of what you produce, but what people consume. If you run a dance company, your competitors include other dance companies—but also perhaps museums, cooking classes, or even bars. Remember, a company makes pillows, but buyers consume sleep.

Consider a pathway to success that's a bit unorthodox—but often quite effective. See if you can create a roadmap of the established categories in your vertical. Then, disrupt them. This strategy worked for Uber and the taxi industry, Netflix and the video rental industry, and Amazon for the publishing industry.

Of course, sometimes a failure to play by the rules can come back to bite you if your product is so different from the norm that customers don't understand it. For example, a men's hair-removal product met a quick demise. Even though the solution is more efficient than a daily shaving routine, the potential buyers couldn't buy into an alternative method that they associated with women's products.

Still, there are lots of great opportunities if you can create a new category or "color between the lines" of two existing ones. Chrysler did that when its designers combined the features of a station wagon and a sedan, and then again when the company created the new SUV category in the 1990s. Swarovski did it too, by creating a stylish piece of jewelry that is also a wearable computer to monitor the wearer's heart rate. And there's the exploding athleisure category in apparel, a hybrid of the athleticwear and leisurewear spaces that is so successful the *Merriam-Webster Dictionary* now lists it.

Or, maybe you can fuse a fashion product with a functional one. We saw this during the pandemic when designers like Gucci and Fendi started to produce high-end facemasks for trendy social distancers.[30]

When I worked as a consultant for a very large textile company, I came to appreciate what opening cages can mean. As I worked with engineers who were developing "smart garments," I found that they saw something other than silky legs when they thought about pantyhose. Instead they viewed the product as a "delivery system" they could use to apply a variety of substances directly to the body, such as vitamins, medications, and even caffeine (which reduces the appearance of cellulite) to the body. By adding microencapsulation that releases small amounts of these things as the woman moves, they recreated the concept of what stockings can do. (Of course, they still had to look good when they delivered these additives!)

Managers love to invoke the cliché "think outside the box" (perhaps to silent groans from their employees), but when it comes to customer insights, perhaps it's not enough to do this. Don't just think outside the box—throw the whole box away.

Market segmentation is still valuable, just not as much

Yes, market segmentation is still valuable today and it's still widely employed. However, two crucial issues in our postmodern era render it less valuable than it used to be:

STRATEGISTS THINK IN TERMS OF DICHOTOMIES. CONSUMERS DON'T. Marketing strategy is largely about this or that: Male or female. Introvert or extrovert. Light user or heavy user. Black or white. OK, sometimes we'll see more than two options like age groups that break into Gen Z, Millennials, Gen X, and so on. But even then, we love to divide the entire world into a few manageable categories.

Still, these either/or groupings leave no room for shades of gray (much less 50 shades!). Thus, we might classify someone as a

Millennial if she was born in the year 2000, while her roommate who entered the world in 2001 would be labeled a Gen Z-er. Do we really expect to see a big difference between these two people?

As we'll see throughout this book, those convenient yet rather arbitrary groupings simply don't capture the nuanced ways we all (even marketing strategists!) define ourselves.

TECHNOLOGICAL ADVANCES LARGELY ELIMINATE THE NEED TO DEAL WITH LARGE, HOMOGENEOUS MARKET SEGMENTS

Efficiency is at the heart of traditional market segmentation strategies. The idea is to identify a sizable number of customers whom we can reach in the same way. No need to develop a separate, customized message or product for each person so we can take advantage of economies of scale.

That approach made a lot of sense when we had just a few TV networks and most people read the same mass-circulation magazines. In fact, that's what broadcasting is all about. But today we live in a narrowcasting world. Although it might have seemed crazy to think of even 15 or 20 years ago, the fact is that marketers now have the tools at their disposal to work with markets of literally one. You can potentially track their every move online—and tailor your messages accordingly.

Markets of one

The ability to serve "markets of one" gets more finely honed every day. Now, the explosion of Big Data applications even allows the most sophisticated organizations to send you stuff before you know you want it! Those ubiquitous "cookies" they plant in your Web browser allow them to track you just about everywhere you go online, and that capability exists for mobile phones as well. And our new "guardian angels" Siri, Alexa, and so on help them to stay on top of us in our kitchens, living rooms, and even our bedrooms.

These tech advances (as fraught as they are ethically) get better all the time, and artificial intelligence gets smarter every day. Amazon is rolling out "anticipatory shipping" capabilities that allow the e-commerce behemoth to predict your orders based upon your past orders (again, past behavior is the best predictor of future behavior) and send those items to your local warehouse where they can rest comfortably until you realize what Amazon knew all along and you place your order.[31]

My colleagues who teach Business Intelligence love to cite the classic story about the time that the retail chain Target "outed" a pregnant teenager. Way back in 2012, an analyst realized that pregnant women tend to order a cluster of items that didn't show up in their baskets until they were fairly well along, such as unscented lotion, supplements like calcium, magnesium and zinc, and extra-big bags of cotton balls. He was able to assign customers a "pregnancy prediction score" that allowed Target to identify a woman's likely due date, and then send her coupons for items she'd be likely to crave. Supposedly an indignant father accosted a Target manager because the store was sending these coupons to his innocent teenage daughter. He later had to apologize because it turns out—you guessed it—his little angel was indeed expecting.[32] That incident happened about a decade ago—imagine what data analysts can do today!

PRODUCTS OF ONE

It's not just the marketing message that we can tailor to each individual. Advances in mass customization and 3D printing are revolutionizing our ability to make something unique for each person as well.

Levi Strauss was a pioneer in mass customization. Company researchers found that 80 percent of women around the world fall into three distinct body shapes, so it's physically impossible to offer a one-size-fits-all product. The Levi's CURVE ID program employs an interactive custom fit experience to tell a customer whether she should buy a Slight Curve, Demi Curve, or Bold Curve version of the jeans.[33] And Adidas launched the first mass-produced 3D printable shoe, the Futurecraft 4D, which customizes the size to the customer's foot—perhaps traditional shoe sizes will become a thing of the past?[34]

USE A CRM!

One of my favorite admonitions to my students (and managers as well): it's far more expensive to acquire a new customer than to keep an old one.

You should think in terms of lifetime customer value, rather than in terms of discrete transactions. Follow up after the sale and continue to vigorously court your customers. No matter how much they like you today, there are a lot of other potential suitors out there just waiting for you to drop the ball. Customer relationship management (CRM) databases and strategies that "mind the store" even when you don't are crucial to keep the ball rolling.

This "markets of one" approach is at the heart of the process many marketers follow now when they adopt a CRM system. This allows them to systematically track consumers' preferences and behaviors over time to tailor the value proposition as closely as possible to each individual's unique wants and needs. CRM allows firms to talk to individual customers and to adjust elements of their marketing programs in light of how each customer reacts. The process works in a series of steps:[35]

1 Identify customers and get to know them in as much detail as possible.

2 Differentiate among these customers in terms of both their needs and their value to the company.

3 Interact with customers and find ways to improve cost efficiency and the effectiveness of the interaction.

4 Customize some aspect of the goods or services that you offer to each customer. This means treating each customer differently based on what the organization has learned about him or her through prior interactions.

CHAPTER TAKEAWAYS

- Marketing managers tend to assume they "know" their customers, but they often think about the customer they *want to have* rather than the one they've got.

- The labels we use to define what business we are in derive from cultural categories that may no longer be as relevant as they used to be.

- Revisit the structures you rely upon to organize your business. Your customers don't necessarily speak your "tech" language. Explore how they assign meaning to your products by doing a deep dive into tagging sites like Pinterest that give users the flexibility to provide their own labels.

- Tried-and-true consumer insights methodologies need to be complemented by other techniques that paint a more vivid picture of the buyer's lived experience.

- In a fragmented culture, it often makes sense to think in terms of markets of one rather than homogeneous market segments.

- If you look only within your familiar vertical for new product opportunities, you will miss out on the options that lie in wait between existing verticals.

- It's far more expensive to acquire a new customer than to keep an old one.

Endnotes

1 Grant McCracken, "Culture and Consumption: A Theoretical Account of the Structure and Movement of the Cultural Meaning of Consumer Goods," *Journal of Consumer Research* 13 (June 1986): 71–84.

2 Steph Fraser, "How to Write a Romance Novel [in 12 Steps]," *Squibler,* May 12, 2019, https://www.squibler.io/blog/write-romance-novel/ (archived at https://perma.cc/LFQ8-XWMK).

3   Adapted from Arthur A. Berger, *Signs in Contemporary Culture: An Introduction to Semiotics* (New York: Longman, 1984): 86.

4   Adapted from Tracy Tuten and Michael R. Solomon, *Social Media Marketing*, 3rd ed. (London: SAGE, 2019).

5   Amy Plitt, "20 Awesome Things People Saw at the 1964 World's Fair," *Mental Floss,* April 22, 2014, https://www.mentalfloss.com/article/56322/20-awesome-things-people-saw-1964-worlds-fair (archived at https://perma.cc/VD6M-FYZ2).

6   Michael R. Solomon, Greg W. Marshall, and Elnora Stuart, *Marketing: Real People, Real Choices*, 10th ed. (Hoboken, NJ: Pearson Education, 2019).

7   Robert M. McMath, "Image Counts," *American Demographics* (May 1998): 64.

8   Brian Wansink, James Painter, and Koert van Ittersum, "Descriptive Menu Labels' Effect on Sales," *Cornell Hotel & Restaurant Administration Quarterly* (December 2001): 68–72.

9   Xiaoyan Deng and Barbara E. Kahn, "Is Your Product on the Right Side? The 'Location Effect' on Perceived Product Heaviness and Package Evaluation," *Journal of Marketing Research* 46, no. 6 (December 2009): 725–38.

10   Kevin Lane Keller, "Memory Factors in Advertising: The Effect of Advertising Retrieval Cues on Brand Evaluations," *Journal of Consumer Research* 14 (December 1987): 316–33. For a discussion of processing operations that occur during brand choice, see Gabriel Biehal and Dipankar Chakravarti, "Consumers' Use of Memory and External Information in Choice: Macro and Micro Perspectives," *Journal of Consumer Research* 12 (March 1986): 382–405.

11   Skip Wollenberg, "Pepsi Expands Freshness Dating on Diet Drinks," *AP News,* March 29, 1994, https://apnews.com/46ce27f9014489712 e1a567017dac9a5 (archived at https://perma.cc/G9KA-A95W).

12   Henri Tajfel and John C. Turner, "The Social Identity Theory of Intergroup Behaviour," in *Psychology of Intergroup Relations*, eds. S. Worchel and W. G. Austin (Chicago, IL: Nelson-Hall, 1986): 7–24.

13   Ethan Jakob Craft, "5 Key Takeaways from the Edelman Brand Trust Survey," *Ad Age,* June 18, 2019, https://adage.com/article/digital/5-key-takeaways-2019-edelman-brand-trust-survey/2178646 (archived at https://perma.cc/9847-9QN7).

14   Joe Mandese, "Consumers See Existential Role For Brands, Say They're Meeting It Better Than Government," *Media Post,* March 31,

2020, https://www.mediapost.com/publications/article/349262/ consumers-see-existential-role-for-brands-say-the.html (archived at https://perma.cc/7KT6-TZH3).

15 Geoffrey James, "33 Encouraging Quotes for Times of Crisis," *Inc.,* March 10, 2020, https://www.inc.com/geoffrey-james/33-encouraging-quotes-for-times-of-crisis.html (archived at https://perma.cc/3MTX-3LPC).

16 Beth LaMontagne Hall, "Buyer Personas: What They Are and Why You Need Them," *Raka Creative,* July 26, 2019, https://www.rakacreative.com/blog/inbound-marketing/what-is-a-buyer-persona/ (archived at https://perma.cc/RN3Q-QL7S).

17 Amy Wallace, "Chip Wilson, Lululemon Guru, Is Moving On," *New York Times Magazine,* February 2, 2015, http://www.nytimes.com/2015/02/08/magazine/lululemons-guru-is-moving-on.html?smid=nytcore-iphone-share&smprod=nytcore-iphone&_r=0 (archived at https://perma.cc/SG3B-F7YY).

18 Stephen J. Hoch, "Who Do We Know: Predicting the Interests and Opinions of the American Consumer," *Journal of Consumer Research* 15, no. 3 (December 1988): 315–24, https://www.jstor.org/stable/2489466 (archived at https://perma.cc/2XUV-7NBQ); Basil G. Englis and Michael R. Solomon, "To Be and Not to Be: Reference Group Stereotyping and the Clustering of America," *Journal of Advertising* 24, no.1 (Spring 1995): 13–28.

19 Douglas Coupland, *Generation X: Tales for an Accelerated Culture* (New York: St. Martin's Griffin, 1991).

20 David Glen Mick, Susan M. Broniarczyk, and Jonathan Haidt, "Choose, Choose, Choose, Choose, Choose, Choose, Choose: Emerging and Prospective Research on the Deleterious Effects of Living in Consumer Hyperchoice," *Journal of Business Ethics* 52 no. 2: 207–11, DOI: 10.1023/B:BUSI.0000035906.74034.d4.

21 "Grocery Stores Carry 40,000 More Items Than They Did in the 1990s," *NutriFusion,* https://nutrifusion.com/grocery-stores-carry-40000-items-1990s/ (archived at https://perma.cc/8M5X-7DGK).

22 "Number of TV Channels in Europe Still Growing, Driven by HD Simulcast," *cineEuropa,* May 4, 2016, https://cineuropa.org/en/newsdetail/307002/ (archived at https://perma.cc/3Z5C-B87P).

23 Lauren Cover, "11 Pinterest Facts Marketers Must Know in 2020," *SproutSocial,* January 28, 2020, https://sproutsocial.com/insights/pinterest-statistics/ (archived at https://perma.cc/R9B2-XZAL).

24 Alladi Venkatesh, "Postmodernism, Poststructuralism and Marketing," paper presented at the American Marketing Association Winter Theory Conference, San Antonio, Texas (February 1992); see also Stella Proctor, Ioanna Papasolomou-Doukakis, and Tony Proctor, "What Are Television Advertisements Really Trying to Tell Us? A Postmodern Perspective," *Journal of Consumer Behavior* 1 (February 2002): 246–55; A. F Firat, "The Consumer in Postmodernity," in *NA: Advances in Consumer Research* 18, eds. Rebecca H. Holman and Michael R. Solomon (Provo, UT: Association for Consumer Research, 1991): 70–76.

25 Miriam Jordan, "India Decides to Put Its Own Spin on Popular Rock, Rap and Reggae," *Wall Street Journal,* January 5, 2000, https://www.wsj.com/articles/SB947024752884533726 (archived at https://perma.cc/K6N2-ZSHR); Rasul Bailay, "Coca-Cola Recruits Paraplegics for 'Cola War' in India," *Wall Street Journal*, June 10, 1997.

26 Russell W. Belk, *Third World Consumer Culture: Research in Marketing* (Greenwich, CT: JAI Press, 1998): 103–27.

27 Rick Wartzman, "When You Translate 'Got Milk' for Latinos, What Do You Get?," *Wall Street Journal,* June 3, 1999.

28 Russell W. Belk, *Third World Consumer Culture: Research in Marketing* (Greenwich, CT: JAI Press, 1998): 103–27.

29 Hazel Markus and Paula Nurius, "Possible Selves," *American Psychologist* 41, no. 9 (1986): 954–69.

30 Vanessa Friedman, "The Mask," *New York Times,* March 17, 2020, https://www.nytimes.com/2020/03/17/style/face-mask-coronavirus.html (archived at https://perma.cc/AF7F-5WMB).

31 Megan Ray Nichols, "Amazon Wants to Use Predictive Analytics to Offer Anticipatory Shipping," *Smartdatacollective,* January 16, 2018, https://www.smartdatacollective.com/amazon-wants-predictive-analytics-offer-anticipatory-shipping/ (archived at https://perma.cc/T6VM-LSDS).

32 Kashmir Hill, "How Target Figured Out a Teen Girl Was Pregnant Before Her Father Did," *Forbes,* February 16, 2012, https://www.forbes.com/sites/kashmirhill/2012/02/16/how-target-figured-out-a-teen-girl-was-pregnant-before-her-father-did/#59f639906668 (archived at https://perma.cc/K8AW-PK5A).

33 http://www.levis.com.au/curve-id (archived at https://perma.cc/B4JC-E392).

34 Brett Hershman, "Mass Customization Is the Future of Retail," *Benzinga,* May 25, 2017, www.benzinga.com/news/17/05/9507644/ mass-customization-is-the-future-of-retail (archived at https://perma.cc/ 8GBU-MEMY).

35 "A Crash Course in Customer Relationship Management," Harvard Management Update, March 2000 (Harvard Business School reprint U003B); Nahshon Wingard, "CRM Definition—Customer-Centered Philosophy," *ezine articles*, October 26, 2009, https://ezinearticles.com/ ?CRM-Definition---Customer-Centered-Philosophy&id=933109 (archived at https://perma.cc/5SCB-PA8B); Don Peppers and Martha Rogers, *The One-to-One Future* (New York: Doubleday, 1996); Don Peppers, Martha Rogers, and Bob Dorf, "Is Your Company Ready for One-to-One Marketing?" *Harvard Business Review*, January–February 1999: 151–60.

02

Consumers who defy demographic labels

Many of the distinctions and labels marketers use to describe consumers no longer serve the purpose they used to. In this chapter, I will look at a few of the most basic and pervasive ones and explain why they are no longer relevant for the new chameleon consumer.

Like any other classification scheme, market segmentation is about keeping some people in—and others out. This perspective stems from the insightful recognition that it's very difficult to sell a one-size-fits-all product or service. That approach may suffice when, as in Henry Ford's case when he first started to crank out automobiles, it's my way or the highway.

But once the basic platform becomes widely available, competitors succeed when they identify points of differentiation from the dominant player. They gamble that they can meet or hopefully exceed the original offering because they possess some kind of specialized capability that will attract some members of a market. We call this path to success distinctive competency.

That is the path General Motors took when the company recognized that some drivers were willing to pay a premium for an enhanced product. And it didn't hurt that many of these more affluent drivers wanted a status vehicle as well as a transportation vehicle to be sure others knew they had additional resources to spend. Indeed, in many product categories a major motivation to buy is that not everyone else can. That's one of the foundations of luxury marketing.

And so, in the adolescent years of modern marketing the race was on to provide points of distinction. Income was a logical first step, but certainly there are additional dimensions that we use to show how we are similar to some people and not to others. Indeed, the dual drive to affiliate with our own kind and distance from alien kinds is one of the most basic characteristics of many species, humans included. A herd of antelopes survives by distancing itself from predators like lions. We two-legged creatures may take pains to ensure that only the right people qualify for admission to our exclusive country club.

As production efficiencies grew in the twentieth century, it became easier and easier for manufacturers to create new points of differentiation, including race and gender. A disproportionate number of African American smokers prefer menthol cigarettes, largely because the tobacco industry carefully cultivated them as young and hip in ad messages targeted to these consumers in the 1960s.[1] Several firearms manufacturers offer pink handguns for women.[2]

Do familiar demographic market segments still matter?

Simple demographic categories are the most obvious targets for marketers who want to put their customers into convenient cages.

To be sure, these segmentation categories can be very useful. It makes a lot of sense to assume that Baby Boomers are attractive candidates for Botox procedures, or that women who live in Florida are less likely to buy fur coats than are their counterparts in New York.

The danger comes when these categories outlive their usefulness, but marketers stubbornly insist on applying them. Then they become stereotypes that persist even in the face of conflicting evidence that we may dismiss as "fake news."

Our consumer chameleons revel in defying many of these labels. They believe that today, "sixty is the new forty." They, or perhaps others they know, don't necessarily feel the need to identify as male or female. Perhaps they're proud of the multiple ethnicities that populate their family tree. Maybe they're transplanted New Yorkers who still love to brag about their Brooklyn roots even though they now reside in rural Wyoming or even the British Midlands.

While demographic categories—such as age, race, etc.—represent what marketers see, individual consumers are increasingly shedding these distinctions when they perceive themselves. This is not to that say that labels aren't important, or that they will ever disappear. Indeed, they won't—as we saw in the previous chapter, the process of labeling people is just something our brains like to do.

But it's vitally important for marketers to recognize that the broad-brush categories they use —maybe because they just always have—may no longer be relevant. It's better to identify the newer ones that their customers use and to recognize that even these will probably change in the near future.

As we've seen, demographic segmentation requires the marketer to identify a reasonably large segment of people they can reliably place into an observable category. They may use a tried-and-true dimension like age, ethnicity, religion, income, education level, geography, or gender.

But these familiar labels aren't so easy to apply today. A society in flux constantly redefines these basic categories to the point where we don't all fit into the convenient little boxes that demographers want to place us in. Let's consider a few of the most widely used demographic classification schemes and look at why these distinctions are becoming increasingly irrelevant in our postmodern world.

Haves vs. have nots

Sociologists describe divisions of society in terms of people's relative social and economic resources. Marketers borrow those demarcations when they segment their customers. Some of these divisions involve political power, whereas others revolve around purely economic distinctions.

Karl Marx, the nineteenth-century economic theorist, argued that a person's relationship to the means of production determined his position in a society. The Haves control resources, and they use the labor of others to preserve their privileged positions. The Have-nots depend on their own labor for survival, so these people have the most to gain if they change the system. The German sociologist Max Weber showed that the rankings people develop are not one-dimensional. Some involve prestige or "social honor" (he called these status groups), some rankings focus on power (or party), and some revolve around wealth and property (class).[3]

Whether rewards go to the "best and the brightest" or to someone who happens to be related to the boss, allocations are rarely equal within a social group. Most groups exhibit a structure, or status hierarchy, in which some members are better off than others. They may have more authority or power, or other members simply like or respect them. And those lucky folks are likely to engage in a process that philosophers call Othering, where they assign those who don't make the grade as the Other.[4]

What's more, "birds of a feather do flock together." We tend to marry people in a social class similar to our own, a tendency that sociologists call homogamy or assortative mating. Well more than 90 percent of married high school dropouts marry someone who also dropped out or who has only a high school diploma. On the other side of the spectrum, less than one percent of the most highly educated Americans have a spouse who did not complete high school.[5]

Indeed, in virtually every context some people rank higher than others—even if they just have a larger number of Twitter followers. Patterns of social arrangements evolve whereby some members get more resources than others by virtue of their relative standing, power, or control in the group.[6] The process of social stratification refers to this creation of artificial divisions, where we distribute resources unequally to members according to their relative rankings in a group.[7]

Luxury marketing targets the "haves"

Luxury marketing is largely about exclusivity. If everyone has it, it's not luxury. The popular bumper-sticker slogan, "He who dies with the most toys, wins," summarizes the desire to accumulate these badges of achievement.

Many marketers try to target affluent, upscale buyers. This makes sense, because these consumers obviously have the resources to spend on costly products that command higher profit margins. And our current economic system tends to encourage the accumulation of wealth among the relatively few: the 80 richest people in the world are worth $1.9 trillion. This is about the same amount shared by the 3.5 billion people who are in the bottom half of the world's income. The most affluent one percent of people worldwide control more than half the globe's total wealth.[8]

So, even in dire economic times we'll continue to see elite products and services that only the well-off can afford. For example, if you go to school in London and you happen to have "a few pounds" to rub together, you can join The Luxury Student. This is a subscription service designed for affluent students; it's "a truly unique service for those who seek the finer things in life." Members get a "VIP" student experience that includes a free Nespresso machine, a blogger photoshoot, surprise luxury gifts, and access to Quintessentially Travel, a "luxury lifestyle travel management company."[9] Who says college has to be about living on ramen noodles? How dreary...

The market continues to roll out ever-pricier luxury goods and services, from $12,000 mother–baby diamond tennis bracelet sets to $600 jeans, $800 haircuts, and $400 bottles of wine. Although it seems that almost everyone can flaunt a designer handbag (or at least a counterfeit version with a convincing logo), America's wealthiest consumers employ 9,000 personal chefs, visit plastic surgeons, and send their children to $400-an-hour math tutors.

A luxury brand is a complex platform that conveys messages about quality, lineage, status, and taste. It often encompasses a set of visual icons, such as a distinctive logo, monograms, patterns, and images. A good example is Bottega Veneta, whose leather goods display no visible symbols or logo. Those who are "in the know" recognize them by their distinctive weaved pattern. [10]

Compare a discreet luxury brand like this to, say, the very prominent repeating logo pattern you might find on a Louis Vuitton bag or perhaps a pair of sunglasses emblazoned with a very large Dolce and Gabbana label that runs across the front.[11] This contrast demonstrates that luxury brands vary in the type of status signaling they employ. As a rule, those who are wealthier and don't have a high need for status rely on "quiet signals" and likely will be put off by excessive displays. Luxury brand marketers need to understand these distinctions, because their customers may or may not value products with explicit logos and other highly visible cues that signal conspicuous consumption.

Segmentation even within the "haves"

How do we know whether customers value loud signals or eschew them? At the least it's useful to focus on another familiar dichotomy: old money vs. new money. People who have had money for a long time tend to use their fortunes a lot differently. Old money families (e.g., the Rockefellers, du Ponts, Fords, etc.) live primarily on inherited funds. One commentator called this group "the class in hiding."[12]

Following the Great Depression of the 1930s, moneyed American families became more discreet about exhibiting their wealth. Many fled from mansions such as those we still find in Manhattan (the renovated Vanderbilt mansion now is Ralph Lauren's flagship store) to hideaways in Virginia, Connecticut, and New Jersey.

Mere wealth is not sufficient to achieve social prominence in these circles. You also need to demonstrate a family history of public service and philanthropy, and tangible markers of these contributions often enable donors to achieve a kind of immortality (e.g., Rockefeller University, Carnegie Hall, or the Whitney Museum).[13] "Old money" consumers distinguish among themselves in terms of ancestry and lineage rather than wealth.[14] Furthermore, they're secure in their status. In a sense, they have trained their whole lives to be rich.

In contrast to people with old money, today there are many people—including high-profile billionaires such as Bill Gates, Mark Zuckerberg, and Sir Richard Branson—who are "the working wealthy."[15] The Horatio Alger myth, where a person goes from "rags to riches" through hard work and a bit of luck, is still a powerful force in our society. That's why a commercial that showed the actual garage where the two co-founders of Hewlett-Packard first worked struck a chord in so many.

Although many people do in fact become "self-made millionaires," they often encounter a problem (although not the worst problem one could think of!) after they have become wealthy and change their social status. The label *nouveau riche* describes a consumer who recently achieved their wealth and who don't have the benefit of years of training to learn how to spend it.

Pity the poor *nouveaux riches*; many suffer from status anxiety. They monitor the cultural environment to ensure that they do the "right" thing, wear the "right" clothes, get seen at the "right" places, use the "right" caterer, and so on.[16] In major Chinese cities such as Shanghai, some people wear pajamas in public as a way to flaunt their newfound wealth. As one consumer explained, "Only people in cities can afford clothes like this. In farming villages, they still have to wear old work clothes to bed."[17]

Obviously, income is the way many of us "keep score" in our consumer society. Even a person's credit score sometimes doubles as an admission card when dating sites like Datemycreditscore.com use it to screen potential suitors.

The new chameleon "haves"

When we take a closer look at the basic Haves vs. Have Nots dichotomy, it's not that difficult to identify counterexamples that illustrate just how permeable these categories can be:

- The abdication of Edward III to marry the commoner Wallis Simpson in 1936, and more recently the "stepping back" of

Meghan Markle and Prince Harry as they transitioned from Royals to Commoners.

- The practice of parody display, whereby affluent consumers deliberately adopt symbols we associate with people who don't have such deep pockets, such as ripped jeans and trucker hats.

- Historically, people associated tattoos with social outcasts. For example, authorities in sixth-century Japan tattooed the faces and arms of criminals to identify them, and these markings served the same purpose in nineteenth-century prisons and twentieth-century concentration camps. Marginal groups, such as bikers or Japanese *yakuza* (gang members), often use these emblems to express group identity and solidarity. Today in contrast a tattoo is a fairly risk-free way to express an adventurous side of the self—even when that self belongs to a middle-class adolescent. Getting inked is commonplace around the world; according to one survey Italy leads the pack with 48 percent of respondents claiming to have at least one tattoo.[18] Hardly marginal, right?

Organizations that target "the rich" may fall into the trap of assuming that all affluent consumers are the same. Despite our stereotype of rich people who just party all day long, one study found that the typical millionaire is a 57-year-old man who is self-employed, earns a median household income of $131,000, has been married to the same wife for most of his adult life, has children, has never spent more than $399 on a suit or more than $140 on a pair of shoes, and drives a Ford Explorer (the humble billionaire investor Warren Buffett comes to mind).

Indeed, many affluent people don't consider themselves to be rich. One tendency researchers notice is that these people indulge in luxury goods while they pinch pennies on everyday items; they buy shoes at Neiman Marcus and deodorant at Walmart, for example.[19]

These revelations at the least remind us that the simple dichotomy of Haves vs Have Nots deserves more nuance and probably some psychographic work as well. In fact, SRI Consulting Business Intelligence divides consumers into three groups based on their attitudes toward luxury:

1 **Luxury is functional.** These consumers use their money to buy things that will last and have enduring value. They conduct extensive prepurchase research and make logical decisions rather than emotional or impulsive choices.

2 **Luxury is a reward.** These consumers tend to be younger than the first group but older than the third group. They use luxury goods to say, "I've made it." The desire to be successful and to demonstrate their success to others motivates these consumers to purchase conspicuous luxury items, such as high-end automobiles and homes in exclusive communities.

3 **Luxury is indulgence.** This group is the smallest of the three and tends to include younger consumers and slightly more males than the other two groups. To these consumers, the purpose of owning luxury is to be extremely lavish and self-indulgent. This group is willing to pay a premium for goods that express their individuality and make others take notice. They have a more emotional approach to luxury spending and are more likely than the other two groups to make impulse purchases.[20]

Young vs. old

"Sixty is the new forty!" "You're only as old as you feel." "Youth is wasted on the young." We live in a youth-oriented society that is reinventing the concept of aging. This means that many of us who are getting on in years still have a much younger attitude than our parents did at the same age.

That means that the traditional dichotomy of Young vs. Old doesn't always work anymore. When Honda launched its boxy Element SUV it was going after young men—but to the company's surprise a lot of middle-aged women also bought the vehicle. Based on that experience, Honda deliberately went after two age groups at once with its Fit subcompact. It placed ads in youth-oriented niche publications such as *Filter* music magazine while running others in *Time*. TV commercials included cartoon characters such as a "speedy demon" monster that appealed to youth but who also resembled creatures you might find in 1970s comic books. Similarly, the Scion tC that the company sold until 2016 screamed youth—but in reality, its buyers' median age was 49. It turns out people in their 50s and 60s liked the car's low floor height because it's easy to step into![21]

Age remains a valid demographic dimension that is still useful to sell some products and services such as 55+ retirement communities, perhaps. But it doesn't always coincide with how people think about themselves. Marketers rely heavily on broad age categories such as Gen X, Gen Y, and Gen Z as they devise new products and messaging campaigns. But when elementary school girls wear jewelry and high heels to imitate their Barbie dolls and octogenarians run marathons, it might be time to reconsider whether these long-standing categories are still accurate.

Segmentation by generation

True, the era in which you grow up bonds you with the millions of others who came of age during the same time period. We identify with those of the same generation with whom we share a common age as well as a similar evolution in our needs and preferences. It seems fair to say that we are more likely to share likes and dislikes with people our own age than with those younger or older. Each generation is shaped by common experiences, large and small.

Some events define an era, whether the Vietnam War, 9/11, or the Covid-19 virus. Other markers like popular celebrities and hit songs aren't so cataclysmic, but nonetheless a broad swath of people of roughly the same age cherish their memories. It turns out that a good predictor of whether people will like a specific song is how old they were when that song was popular. On average, we are most likely to favor songs that were popular when we were 23.5 years old. Our preferences for fashion models peak at age 33, and we tend to like movie stars who were popular when we were 26 or 27 years old.[22] American Baby Boomers may reminisce about old favorites like Tang, Pop Rocks, Teem soda, and Quisp cereal, while perhaps their British counterparts smile at the mention of Sainsbury's stem ginger, Vesta instant meals, or anything with quince.

THE AGE YOU ARE VS. THE AGE YOU FEEL

However, that certainly doesn't mean that members of an age cohort are monolithic! Indeed, research confirms that age is more a state of mind than of body. If you're going to segment your customers based upon age, do it by how they *feel* rather than what it says on their birth certificates.

One study investigated what the authors call consumer identity renaissance, which refers to the redefinition process people undergo when they retire. The research identified two different types of identity renaissance: revived (revitalization of previous identities) or emergent (pursuit of entirely new life projects). Even though retirees often have to deal with loss of professional identity, spouses, and so on, many of them focus on moving forward. They engage in a host of strategies to do this, including affiliation, where they reconnect with family members and friends (in many cases online), and self-expression. This latter strategy may involve revisiting an activity they never had time to adequately pursue when they were younger, learning new skills, or perhaps moving into an urban area to re-engage with cultural activities.[23] If you happen to be in a business that provides these services, think carefully about whom you target, and how you speak to them.

Simply put, a person's mental outlook and activity level have a lot more to do with longevity and quality of life than with their chronological age. Age categories are a social construction; every culture creates structures it uses to classify people and events. Perceived age, or how old a person feels, is a better measure of age. Researchers measure perceived age on several dimensions, including "feel-age" (i.e., how old a person feels) and "look-age" (i.e., how old a person looks). They report that the older consumers get, the younger they feel relative to their actual age.[24]

The new chameleon boomers

Let's start at the more "mature" end of the age spectrum. Baby Boomers are a very sizeable age group that has helped to define our culture for decades. Some years ago, a commercial for VH1, the music video network that caters to those who are a bit too old for MTV, pointed out, "The generation that dropped acid to escape reality... is the generation that drops antacid to cope with it."[25]

But again, these consumers who are now at or near retirement age continue to defy efforts to herd them into a monolithic cage—especially one that treats them as if they are on the verge of senility. After all, older adults control more than 50 percent of discretionary income. They are finished with many of the financial obligations that siphon off the income of younger consumers. Eighty percent of consumers older than age 65 own their own homes. In addition, child-rearing costs are over, hence the popular bumper sticker we may spy on sports cars and pricey RVs: "We're Spending Our Children's Inheritance."

Even at the starting gate, the broad brush marketers use to categorize Boomers is inaccurate. Demographers in fact distinguish between two subgroups of Baby Boomers. Leading-Edge Boomers born between 1946 and 1955, grew up during the Vietnam War and Civil Rights eras. Trailing-Edge Boomers, who were born between 1956 and 1964, came of age after Vietnam and the Watergate scandal.[26]

While they may show a few grey hairs, Boomers aren't ready for the rocking chair quite yet. They are 6 percent more likely than the national average to engage in some kind of sports activity.[27] Nielsen estimates that only 5 percent of advertising dollars are currently targeted toward adults 35 to 64 years old, but Boomers spend 38.5 percent of CPG (consumer packaged goods) dollars.

In fact, Nielsen's research reveals that Boomers dominate 1,023 out of 1,083 CPG (consumer packaged goods) categories, and they watch 9.34 hours of video per day—more than any other segment. They also constitute a third of all TV viewers, online users, social media users, and Twitter users, and are significantly more likely to have broadband internet. As a Nielsen executive observed:

> Marketers have this tendency to think the Baby Boom—getting closer to retirement—will just be calm and peaceful as they move ahead, and that's not true. Everything we see with our behavioral data says

these people are going to be active consumers for much longer. They are going to be in better health, and despite the ugliness around the retirement stuff now, they are still going to be more affluent. They are going to be an important segment for a long time.[28]

Boomers are living longer and healthier lives because of more wholesome lifestyles, improved medical diagnoses and treatment, and changing cultural expectations about appropriate behaviors for the elderly. Nearly 60 percent engage in volunteer activities, one in four seniors aged 65 to 72 still works, and more than 14 million provide care for their grandchildren.[29]

As I noted earlier, we need to fight the temptation to go after the customer we want to have rather than the one we do have—or could get. While many marketers shovel promotional dollars into campaigns that will reach Millennials or Gen Xers, they may be missing the boat when it comes to identifying opportunities to expand their clientele. These include, for example, "how-to" books and university courses that offer enhanced learning opportunities, cosmetic surgery and skin treatments, tourism, and exercise facilities.

A few innovative universities like Arizona State and SUNY-Purchase, that like all schools confront declining enrollments among college-age students (especially after the pandemic), have redoubled efforts to lure "lifelong independent learners" (a.k.a. older people) to campus where they can buy housing in pricey adjacent communities. They encourage these "cash cows" to take courses and participate in campus life (we'll see how many beer bongs show up at weekly social receptions).[30]

The new chameleon teenagers

And now to the other end of the life cycle. Labeling the time between childhood and adulthood as the "teenage" years is a relatively new concept—and yet another social construction. Throughout most of history, the teenage years were considered part of childhood. When boys reached puberty, they typically underwent a rite-of-passage ritual such as venturing into the jungle alone to kill a wild beast and bring it home, and then their status morphed into adult virtually overnight. Young girls who reached menarche might be sequestered in a separate location and then married off. Just like that, no more childhood. Remember, Shakespeare's Juliet was only 13 when she died as a "star-crossed lover."

Things began to change in the mid-twentieth century as the transitional category of "teenager" began to develop. This social construction evolved into a "formative" period of several years when young people were neither children nor adults. Indeed, for many middle-class kids the "college experience" provided a safe haven from adult responsibilities as students prepared themselves for "the real world" and "found themselves" (and sobered up). We also see this transition today in Europe as many teens opt for a "gap year" of traveling before they attend university.

The US magazine *Seventeen* helped to pioneer this construction as a separate and distinct transitional period for young people. Founded in 1944 after World War II, the magazine emerged just as the teenage conflict between rebellion and conformity unfolded. But it wasn't until 1956 that the label teenager entered the general vocabulary. Frankie Lymon and the Teenagers became the first pop group to identify themselves with this new subculture.

And then the floodgates opened as an emerging youth culture that celebrated the slicked hair and suggestive dance moves of Elvis Presley found itself at odds with the wholesome white bucks and whiter teeth of Pat Boone. And of course, the British Invasion offered both wholesome role models like the Beatles (at least in their early years) and Herman's Hermits as well as insubordinate rockers including the Rolling Stones (whose rebellious image was carefully choreographed by the band's manager to contrast with the Mop Tops).[31]

As anyone who has lived through the adventures of raising children can attest, even this category is highly fluid. At the turn of the twentieth century, the average age for an American girl to get her period was 16 or 17. Today, that number hovers closer to 12 or 13.

Societal pressures for kids to adopt "grownup" products like cosmetics (not to mention drugs and alcohol) kick in much earlier as well.[32] One research study reported that 43 percent of six- to nine-year-olds use lipstick or lip gloss, and 38 percent use hair-styling products.[33] More than half of American kids own their own smartphone by age 11.[34]

There's even an intermediate category lurking among the posters of rap idols and tubes of acne cream. Marketers refer to kids aged 8 to 14 as tweens because they exhibit characteristics of both children and teenagers. These avid consumers certainly don't self-identify as kids. Marketers spend about $43 billion annually marketing to these "teens in training," who are keen to experiment with products that make them appear older, even though they may not be psychologically or physically ready.

And the line between childhood and adolescence continues to blur. Good luck to the marketers who try to figure out when kids become tweens, become teens, or when teens morph into young adults.

The new chameleon parents

A previous generation warned, "Never trust anyone over 30." Yet today, parents are no longer the enemy. Many Millennials are very tight with their parents and think of them as friends. In fact, over half view them as their best friends![35] When Mom or Dad consult their kids about new music or even share hot new clothing items with them, they may not self-identify with their expected role of stern authority figure. This new trend works both ways; parents want to be friends with their kids as well.

Well, all that chumminess is nice—but it does take some of the "fun" out of being an annoying parent. A classic study conducted in 1972 revealed what researchers called the "Romeo and Juliet Effect"; like Shakespeare's characters, increases in parental interference made it *more* likely that kids would persevere in a romantic relationship and even marry.

At that time, parents were authority figures, and so their attempts at meddling were destined to boomerang. A replication attempt over 40 years later that examined this question among couples of various ages failed to reproduce this relationship.[36] It seems that in the intervening decades offspring had become less likely to rebel and perhaps more likely to take seriously their parents' sage advice. This is at least one indication of a more "cooperative" relationship between parents and offspring. A kinder, more gentle relationship between what used to be warring parties perhaps erodes the need for marketers to think in terms of traditional parent/offspring segments.

Marketers and merchants can do much more to celebrate and incentivize parent/child activities. I've heard from several retailers—and have experienced it firsthand in my own family—that mother-daughter shopping expeditions are very common. Daughters no longer seem to have the desire to dress differently in order to rebel against their mothers. Quite the opposite: now the resort wear retailer Lilly Pulitzer is one of numerous companies that devotes an entire section of its catalog to Mother Daughter Matching Outfits.[37]

This new category just scratches the surface of what marketers might do to cater to what may be a new surge in parent-child togetherness—especially after the pandemic turned "quality time" into "just another day time," and families found themselves engaging in a lot more activities together. Companies that sell hobby supplies, games, cooking kits, and many other products may benefit as well as those that offer clothing, shoes, and jewelry to mom/daughter teams.

My race/ethnicity vs. whatever you are

The rapidly growing diversity of US culture is one of the most important drivers of change in this century. As of 2015, the majority of babies born in the United States are non-Caucasian. Over the next 45 years, the US Census Bureau expects the Hispanic population to more than double; by 2060 almost one in three Americans will identify as Hispanic. The Asian population will double during the same time period.

It's easy to point to companies that have prospered by developing offerings that appeal to distinct racial/ethnic subcultures. These include BET (Black Entertainment Television), Goya Foods' line of Hispanic products, or Huy Fong's Sriracha dipping sauce (rooster sauce), which originated in Vietnam.

Even within a "pure" subcultural category there are in fact many gradations. At one extreme we might find people who are "hard core"; perhaps they speak only their native language, buy products only from stores that carry products from their homeland, and rarely even communicate with those who aren't part of their closed circle. In some sections of Miami like Hialeah, a newcomer would swear she's arrived at an outpost of Cuba. Virtually everyone is happily conversing in Spanish, perhaps making moves in a game of dominoes between bites of *arroz con pollo*, *boliche*, and *dulce de leche*. At the other end of the spectrum lie those whose identities are only loosely linked to the same group. Maybe they celebrate a few cultural events like a friend's daughter's *quinceañera*, and know only a few juicy expletives in Spanish that they picked up from their parents.

The new multicultural chameleon

In late 2017, the singer Rihanna launched her cosmetics brand Fenty Beauty. The line offered 40 shades of foundation that covered the skin tone spectrum from albino white to dark chocolate. It was a huge success, and other companies scrambled to follow this example as 40 shades became the new industry standard almost overnight.[38]

Rihanna didn't introduce a new cosmetics line just for black women. Fenty Beauty exploded partly because the company offered something for everyone, regardless of their skin tone. This is the kind of multicultural flexibility that enables brands today to capture the allegiance of consumers across a broad spectrum of racial/ethnic identities.

It's when subcultural favorites slip into the mainstream that the action happens. A great example is one of my favorite trivia questions that I love to ask my students: what US city produces the most bagels per year? When everyone screams out, New York! I gleefully tell them the answer is Cincinnati, the home of Lender's frozen bagels. To make things a bit more convoluted, the Mexican bakery company Grupo Bimbo now owns Lender's.

Even if you want to target only members of a racial/ethnic subculture, it's becoming increasingly hard to do so. One reason is that traditional subcultural categories are breaking down. The Census Bureau predicts that by 2050, people who identify themselves as multiracial will make up almost 4 percent of the US population. Among US children, the multiracial population has increased almost 50 percent, to 4.2 million, since 2000, making it the fastest-growing youth group in the country. The number of people of all ages who identified themselves as both white and black has soared by 134 percent since 2000 to 1.8 million people.[39] The United States truly is a "melting pot" of people who belong to many different racial and ethnic subcultures. That helps to explain why about 6 percent of people who filled out the last Census didn't select one of the race categories on the form provided.[40]

In the US, Europe, and elsewhere, immigrants typically undergo an assimilation process that involves a complex tradeoff between adopting new ways and retaining old ones. Thus, for example, a Dutch teenager with Turkish parents may create her own consumption "pastiche" as she watches TV on a local Turkish network and buys gifts for *bayram* (religious holidays), while she develops a passion for *drop* (Dutch licorice) and listens to "Western" music in Amsterdam's clubs.[41]

Acculturation is the process of movement and adaptation to one country's cultural environment by a person from another country.[42] This is an important issue for marketers due to our increasingly global society. As people move from place to place, they may quickly assimilate to their new homes, or they may resist this blending process and choose to insulate themselves from the mainstream culture. It's typical for a new arrival in the United States, for example, to feel ambivalence or conflict about relinquishing old ways (and consumer behaviors) for new ones. The retail chain Home Depot segments its campaigns when the retailer speaks to the Hispanic market; it creates different ads for "acculturated Hispanics" (second- or third-generation Americans) than it shows to consumers who almost always speak Spanish.[43]

The progressive learning model helps us to understand the acculturation process. This perspective assumes that people gradually learn a new culture as they increasingly come in contact with it. Thus, we expect that when people acculturate, they will mix the practices of their original culture with those of their new or host culture.[44]

Research that examines such factors as shopping orientation, the importance people place on various product attributes, media preference, and brand loyalty generally supports this pattern.[45] When researchers take into account the intensity of ethnic identification, they find that consumers who retain a strong ethnic identification differ from their more assimilated counterparts in these ways:[46]

- they have a more negative attitude toward business in general (probably caused by frustration due to relatively low income levels);
- they access more media that's in their native language;
- they are more brand loyal;
- they are more likely to prefer brands with prestige labels;
- they are more likely to buy brands that specifically advertise to their ethnic group.

We can see how the process of acculturation slowly but steadily tends to erode identification with a person's original culture as they assimilate into their host culture when we look at how Hispanics in the United States think about their identities. A high intermarriage rate and a declining number of immigrants from Latin America reduce the likelihood that younger people call themselves Hispanic or Latinx. While 93 percent of immigrant Hispanics have a Hispanic spouse, only 35 percent of third-generation Hispanics do. Roughly 10 percent of US adults with Hispanic ancestry do not even consider themselves members of this subculture. Today, 40 million people in the United States say they speak Spanish in their home, but that number is dropping.[47] Many Hispanics just don't think of themselves as distinctly Latinx or American, but rather somewhere in the middle or ambicultural.[48]

So much for that Latinx label. Marketers who try to talk to them by assuming they will "get" whatever ethnic references they include in their messaging or by appealing to their sense of ethnic pride may find their tactics falling on deaf ears. They may wish to temper their approach by painting a more realistic picture of everyday life; for example, by echoing the hybrid "Spanglish" idiom that these people may speak.

Well over 25 million Europeans belong to an ethnic subgroup, and in several European countries such as France, Belgium, and Germany, they collectively account for around 10 percent of the total population. In the UK, the ethnic communities represented are forecast to double in population to over six million within the next 30 years.[49]

The European Union projects an inflow of 40 million people by 2050, while simultaneously aging populations in Western countries will increase the relative proportion of immigrants in these populations.[50] A recent study by Lloyds reported that representation of black, Asian, and minority ethnic groups in British advertising has doubled from 12 percent to 25 percent since 2015. However, only 7 percent of lead roles in ads are played by someone from a minority group.[51] Marketers in this region may wish to cast a wider net when it comes to casting practices, to say the least.

In the United States until fairly recently, advertisers focused exclusively on white consumers, who were their so-called "general market." When they referenced minorities, this often took the form of derogatory stereotypes. In fact, it wasn't until the Black Lives Matter movement erupted in 2020 that PepsiCo's Quaker Oats company got around to eliminating the Aunt Jemima brand.[52]

It took some simple financial data to wake up much of the business world to the overlooked economic clout of non-Caucasian consumers. The combined buying power of minority groups in the United States was close to $4 trillion in 2019.[53] In the UK, the BAME community (black, Asian, and minority ethnic people) accounts for 12 percent of the population and has purchasing power of £300 billion per year and rising.[54]

Predictably, as the word got out, advertising agencies began to fall all over themselves to develop or acquire multicultural specialists who could talk to nonwhite consumers. Soon US consumers were blanketed with targeted ads, shows, and products that spoke exclusively to African Americans or Hispanics. Minority consumers were deluged with advertising messages that contained unique subcultural advertising references and images of people who looked like them. Suddenly there were a lot of categories to contend with. Each segment was put it into its own tidy little silo and pursued by specialized agencies.

However, it seems that many US consumers—even minorities who were ignored before—are growing weary of the silos in which the marketing industry has placed them. Although the broader representation is a positive, marketers may be overcompensating when they go to great lengths to feature nonwhite families or other social groups. A recent study that surveyed over 2,000 people reported that 80 percent of parents like to see *diverse* families in advertisements. Sixty-six percent said that brands showing reverence for all kinds of families was an important factor when they chose among competing options.[55]

We can see how minority/majority categories are merging when we look at the trajectory of a fairly new category in fashion: streetwear. For example, the breakthrough company Supreme is valued at about $1 billion. That's impressive for a brand that sells hoodies and nunchucks. But Supreme's success is part of a larger story that involves the dissolution of a wall between marginalized hip-hop culture and the mainstream market.[56] The fashion cage opens even wider when we look at the recent collaboration the company announced with none other than the luxury brand Louis Vuitton.[57]

CHAPTER TAKEAWAYS

- Perceived age is more important than chronological age.

- Parents are no longer the enemy. Incentivize parent/child shopping and consumption, and consider multigenerational marketing strategies.

- Consumers increasingly regard themselves as members of multiple ethnic groups. There is huge potential for mainstream niche products as more of us hunger to experience new offerings that lie outside of the cage in which we've been placed.

Endnotes

1   Phillip S. Gardiner, "The African Americanization of Menthol Cigarette
    Use in the United States," *Nicotine & Tobacco Research* 6, Supplement 1
    (February 2004): S55–S65. http://www.acbhcs.org/tobacco/docs/2017/
    African_Americanization.pdf (archived at https://perma.cc/SZQ5-BZM7).

2   For example, https://www.tzarmory.com/hand-guns/pink-duracoat-
    handguns/ (archived at https://perma.cc/8W9C-J8BG).

3   Jonathan H. Turner, *Sociology: Studying the Human System*,
    2nd ed. (Santa Monica, CA: Goodyear, 1981).

4   "Othering," *The New Fontana Dictionary of Modern Thought*,
    3rd ed. (HarperCollins, 1999), 620.

5   Rebecca Gardyn, "The Mating Game," *American Demographics*
    (July–August 2002): 33–34.

6   Richard Coleman, Kent McClelland, and Lee Rainwater, *Social
    Standing in America* (New York: Basic Books, 1978).

7   Jonathan H. Turner, *Sociology: Studying the Human System*, 2nd ed.
    (Goodyear, 1981).

8   Patricia Cohen, "Oxfam Study Finds Richest 1% Is Likely to Control
    Half of Global Wealth by 2016," *New York Times*, January 19, 2015,
    http://www.nytimes.com/2015/01/19/business/richest-1-percent-
    likely-to-control-half-of-global-wealth-by-2016-study-finds.
    html?smid=nytcore-iphone-share&smprod=nytcore-iphone&_r=1
    (archived at https://perma.cc/DNG7-RZ53).

9   https://www.luxurystudent.com/ (archived at https://perma.cc/
    AL5T-4ANL).

10 https://www.bottegaveneta.com/gb (archived at https://perma.cc/
    9BYL-XXDA).

11 https://www.therealreal.com/products/women/handbags/totes/
    louis-vuitton-monogram-giant-onthego-gm-
    6u0zq?sid=pxogmz&utm_source=Google&utm_
    medium=shopping&cvosrc=cse.google.google&cvo_crid=337846446
    371&gclid=EAIaIQobChMI7-CPndOE6gIVAwiICR1HAA_
    TEAQYByABEgJPT_D_BwE (archived at https://perma.cc/
    Y9Y2-ZWM4); https://www.ezcontacts.com/product/
    sunglasses/612259-612260/dolce-and-gabbana-dg2233?gclid=
    EAIaIQobChMIgc-03NKE6gIVCk2GCh2nOgJDEAkYAiABEgKa
    hfD_BwE (archived at https://perma.cc/FHA4-UUFP).

12 Paul Fussell, *Class: A Guide Through the American Status System*
    (New York: Summit Books, 1983), 29.

13   Elizabeth C. Hirschman, "Secular Immortality and the American Ideology of Affluence," *Journal of Consumer Research* 17 (June 1990): 31–42.

14   Richard C. Coleman and Lee Rainwater, *Social Standing in America: New Dimensions of Class* (New York: Basic Books, 1978), 150.

15   Kerry A. Dolan, "The World's Working Rich," *Forbes,* July 3, 2000, 162.

16   Jason DeParle, "Spy Anxiety: The Smart Magazine That Makes Smart People Nervous About Their Standing," *Washingtonian Monthly* (February 1989): 10.

17   Martin Fackler, "Pajamas: Not Just for Sleep Anymore," *Opelika-Auburn News,* September 13, 2002, 7A.

18   https://www.newsweek.com/which-country-most-people-tattoos-943104 (archived at https://perma.cc/2Z6W-XS9Z).

19   Shelly Reese, "The Many Faces of Affluence," *Marketing Tools* (November–December 1997): 44–48.

20   Rebecca Gardyn, "Oh, the Good Life," *American Demographics* (November 2002): 34.

21   Gina Chon, "Car Makers Court Two Generations," *Wall Street Journal,* May 9, 2006, B1.

22   Robert M. Schindler and Morris B. Holbrook, "Nostalgia for Early Experience as a Determinant of Consumer Preferences," *Psychology & Marketing* 20, no. 4 (April 2003): 275–302; Morris B. Holbrook and Robert M. Schindler, "Some Exploratory Findings on the Development of Musical Tastes," *Journal of Consumer Research* 16 (June 1989): 119–24; Morris B. Holbrook and Robert M. Schindler, "Market Segmentation Based on Age and Attitude Toward the Past: Concepts, Methods, and Findings Concerning Nostalgic Influences on Consumer Tastes," *Journal of Business Research* 37, no. 1 (September 1996): 27–40.

23   Hope Jensen Schau, Mary C. Gilly, and Mary Wolfinbarger, "Consumer Identity Renaissance: The Resurgence of Identity-Inspired Consumption in Retirement," *Journal of Consumer Research* 36 (August 2009): 255–76; cf. also Michelle Barnhart and Lisa Peñaloza, "Who Are You Calling Old? Negotiating Old Age Identity in the Elderly Consumption Ensemble," *Journal of Consumer Research* 39, no. 6 (April 2013): 1133–53.

24   Benny Barak and Leon G. Schiffman, "Cognitive Age: A Nonchronological Age Variable," in *Advances in Consumer Research 8,*

ed. Kent B. Monroe (Provo, UT: Association for Consumer Research, 1981): 602–6.

25 Jeremy Gerard, "An MTV for Grown-Ups Is Seeking Its Audience," *New York Times,* August 7, 1989, https://www.nytimes.com/ 1989/08/07/arts/an-mtv-for-grown-ups-is-seeking-its-audience.html (archived at https://perma.cc/2XZH-ABR2).

26 John H. Fleming, "Baby Boomers Are Opening Their Wallets," *Gallup Business Journal,* January 30, 2015, http://www.gallup.com/ businessjournal/181367/baby-boomers-opening-wallets.aspx (archived at https://perma.cc/TB5G-NFU9).

27 Angel Jennings, "Contests, YouTube and Commercials Converge for Skin Product," *New York Times*, July 26, 2007, https://www.nytimes.com/2007/07/26/business/media/26adco.html (archived at https://perma.cc/KH8G-B85X).

28 Quoted in Sarah Mahoney, "Nielsen: Time to Recommit to Boomers," *Marketing Daily,* July 21, 2010, http://www.mediapost.com/ publications/article/132364/nielsen-time-to-recommit-to-boomers .html?edition= (archived at https://perma.cc/425Q-2N4X).

29 Rick Adler, "Stereotypes Won't Work with Seniors Anymore," *Advertising Age*, November 11, 1996, 32.

30 Anemona Hartocollis, "At Colleges, What's Old Is New: Retirees Living on Campus," *New York Times*, September 10, 2019, https://www.nytimes.com/2019/09/10/us/college-university- retirement-communities.html (archived at https://perma.cc/ B8EZ-9KCA).

31 "Image Is Everything: Was Marketing Key to Success of the Rolling Stones?" *University of Rochester Newscenter*, March 12, 2015, https://www.rochester.edu/newscenter/image-is-everything-was- marketing-key-to-the-success-of-the-rolling-stones-93212/ (archived at https://perma.cc/CYX9-GB5C).

32 Dominic Hernandez, "The Decreasing Age of Puberty," *Vital Record* (Texas A&M Health) January 10, 2018, https://vitalrecord.tamhsc.edu/ decreasing-age-puberty/ (archived at https://perma.cc/7S2S-MU3F).

33 Jessica Bennett, "Are we Turning Tweens into 'Generation Diva'?" *Newsweek*, March 29, 2009, https://www.newsweek.com/are-we- turning-tweens-generation-diva-76425 (archived at https://perma.cc/ EQP2-PSXT).

34 Anya Kamenetz, "It's a Smartphone Life: More Than Half of U.S. Children Now Have One," *NPR*, October 31, 2019,

https://www.npr.org/2019/10/31/774838891/its-a-smartphone-life-more-than-half-of-u-s-children-now-have-one (archived at https://perma.cc/T4YV-F9BU).

35 Catey Hill, "More Than Half of Millennials Say Their Parents Are Their Best Friends," Marketwatch, May 10, 2017, https://www.marketwatch.com/story/more-than-half-of-millennials-say-their-parents-are-their-best-friends-2017-05-10-11883834 (archived at https://perma.cc/S3XR-LTXS).

36 Driscoll, R., Davis, K. E., and Lipetz, M. E., "Parental Interference and Romantic Love: The Romeo and Juliet Effect," *Journal of Personality and Social Psychology 24*, no. 1 (1972): 1–10; H. Colleen Sinclair, Kristina B. Hood, and Brittany L. Wright, "Revisiting the Romeo and Juliet Effect (Driscoll, Davis, and Lipetz, 1972): Reexamining the Links Between Social Network Opinions and Romantic Relationship Outcomes," *Social Psychology 45*, no. 3 (2014): 170–78.

37 https://www.lillypulitzer.com/womens-girls-matching-outfits/?71700000060611896;s.a=GOOGLE;p.a=71700000060611896;as.a=58700005487904586;c.n=Search-NB-W-DSA-All-X;p.n=Search-NB-W-DSA-All-X;as.n=DSA-All;qpb=1bidkw=DYNAMIC+SEARCH+ADS&dvc=c&gclid=EAIaIQobChMIlpv9vsjU6QIVCb7ACh31dQ0fEAAYAiAAEg KcxPD_BwE&gclsrc=aw.ds (archived at https://perma.cc/8BCG-N7QU).

38 "SJC Insights: The Importance of Inclusive Marketing in 2019," *SJC*, January 22, 2019, https://stjoseph.com/insight/importance-inclusive-marketing-2019/ (archived at https://perma.cc/2AQ3-WPDB)].

39 Kendra Yoshinaga, "Babies of Color Are Now the Majority, Census Says," *NPR*, July 1, 2016, https://www.npr.org/sections/ed/2016/07/01/484325664/babies-of-color-are-now-the-majority-census-says (archived at https://perma.cc/8K8Q-7HSH).

40 Jens Manuel Krogstad and D'vera Cohn, "U.S. Census Looking at Big Changes in How It Asks About Race and Ethnicity," *Pew Research*, March 14, 2014, http://www.pewresearch.org/fact-tank/2014/03/14/u-s-census-looking-at-big-changes-in-how-it-asks-about-race-and-ethnicity/ (archived at https://perma.cc/H6YD-5DUG).

41 Gokcen Coskuner and Ozlem Sandikci, "New Clothing: Meanings and Practices," in *Advances in Consumer Research 31*, eds. Barbara E. Kahn and Mary Frances Luce (Valdosta, GA: Association for Consumer Research, 2004): 285–90.

42 See Lisa Peñaloza, "*Atravesando Fronteras*/Border Crossings: A Critical Ethnographic Exploration of the Consumer Acculturation of Mexican Immigrants," *Journal of Consumer Research* 21 (June 1994): 32–54; Lisa Peñaloza and Mary C. Gilly, "Marketer Acculturation: The Changer and the Changed," *Journal of Marketing* 63 (July 1999): 84–104; Carol Kaufman-Scarborough, "Eat Bitter Food and Give Birth to a Girl; Eat Sweet Things and Give Birth to a Cavalryman: Multicultural Health Care Issues for Consumer Behavior," *Advances in Consumer Research* 32, no.1 (2005): 226–69; Søren Askegaard, Eric J. Arnould, and Dannie Kjeldgaard, "Postassimilationist Ethnic Consumer Research: Qualifications and Extensions," *Journal of Consumer Research* 32, no. 1 (2005): 160.

43 Stuart Elliott, "1,200 Marketers Can't Be Wrong: The Future Is in Consumer Behavior," *New York Times,* October 15, 2007, https://www.nytimes.com/2007/10/15/business/media/15adcol.html (archived at https://perma.cc/4UKZ-4Z8E).

44 Melanie Wallendorf and Michael D. Reilly, "Ethnic Migration, Assimilation, and Consumption," *Journal of Consumer Research* 10, no. 3 (December 1983): 292–302.

45 Ronald J. Faber, Thomas C. O'Guinn, and John A. McCarty, "Ethnicity, Accessed Ulturation and the Importance of Product Attributes," *Psychology & Marketing* 4 (Summer 1987): 121–34; Humberto Valencia, "Developing an Index to Measure Hispanicness," in *Advances in Consumer Research 12*, eds. Elizabeth C. Hirschman and Morris B. Holbrook (Provo, UT: Association for Consumer Research, 1985): 118–21.

46 Rohit Deshpandé, Wayne D. Hoyer, and Naveen Donthu, "The Intensity of Ethnic Affiliation: A Study of the Sociology of Hispanic Consumption," *Journal of Consumer Research* 13 (September 1986): 214–20.

47 Mark Hugo Lopez, Ana Gonzalez-Barrera, and Gustavo López, "Hispanic Identity Fades Across Generations as Immigrant Connections Fall Away," *Pew Research Center*, December 20, 2017, http://www.pewhispanic.org/2017/12/20/hispanic-identity-fades-across-generations-as-immigrant-connections-fall-away/?utm_source=pew+research+center&utm_campaign=3d0eb798a6-email_campaign_2017_12_14&utm_medium=email&utm_term=0_3e953b9b70-3d0eb798a6-399653965 (archived at https://perma.cc/BWV4-SP2L).

48 Karl Greenberg, "More Latinos See Themselves as Bicultural," *Marketing Daily*, February 20, 2013, http://www.mediapost.com/publications/article/193900/more-latinos-see-themselves-as-bicultural.html?edition=56909#axzz2LyoalJqc (archived at https://perma.cc/RER5-EDYJ).

49 *Demographic Statistics 1997: Population and Social Conditions Series* (Luxembourg: Office for Official Publications of the European Communities, 1997); "Colour Blind," *Marketing Week*, June 21, 1996, 38–40.

50 "Regions 2020: Demographic Challenges for European Regions," Commission of the European Communities, November 2008, https://ec.europa.eu/regional_policy/sources/docoffic/working/regions2020/pdf/regions2020_demographic.pdf (archived at https://perma.cc/EUB2-9L65).

51 "Ethnicity in Advertising: Reflecting Modern Britain in 2018," Lloyds Banking Group, https://www.lloydsbankinggroup.com/our-group/responsible-business/inclusion-and-diversity/ethinicity-in-advertising/ (archived at https://perma.cc/C3C5-5AAC).

52 Ben Kesslen, "Aunt Jemima Brand to Change Name, Remove Image That Quaker Says Is 'Based on a Racial Stereotype,'" NBC News, June 17, 2020 https://www.nbcnews.com/news/us-news/aunt-jemima-brand-will-change-name-remove-image-quaker-says-n1231260 (archived at https://perma.cc/XK5L-GA9X).

53 "Minority Markets Have $3.9 Trillion Buying Power," The University of Georgia, March 21, 2019, https://www.newswise.com/articles/minority-markets-have-3-9-trillion-buying-power (archived at https://perma.cc/T8LM-THCD).

54 Lydia Amoah, "To Tap into the 'Black Pound,' Brands Must Embrace Cultural Transformation, Campaign, October 23, 2018 https://www.campaignlive.co.uk/article/tap-black-pound-brands-embrace-cultural-transformation/1496325 (archived at https://perma.cc/T3CH-T5UR).

55 Michelle Castillo, "Study: Americans Want More Diversity in Ads," March 7, 2016, https://www.cnbc.com/2016/03/07/study-americans-want-more-diversity-in-ads.html (archived at https://perma.cc/R5YF-7LQD).

56 https://qz.com/1032714/beyonce-and-kendrick-lamar-dominate-the-charts-because-hip-hop-is-now-officially-bigger-than-rock-music/ (archived at https://perma.cc/4VDB-ESWQ).

57 https://www.authenticsupreme.com/supreme-collaboration-list (archived at https://perma.cc/K9CP-SMLV)

03

Consumers who defy traditional purchasing behavior

1967: Mary is so excited. Biff just called and asked her to be his date at the senior prom! The second she hangs up with him, she dials her best friend Jane to share the news. Jane tells Mary that she's just been downtown, where she saw a "to-die-for" dress in the window of Gimbel's. Without hesitating, Mary grabs the keys to her Chevy Impala, picks up Jane and two other friends, and heads straight to the store. She tries on a pile of dresses for her girlfriends to critique in the dressing room. This process takes a couple of hours, but at the end her friends render their decision: the dress that Jane spied is the one after all. Mary carefully counts out bills in her purse she's been saving from her allowance and heads home with her find. The prom comes and goes, and six weeks later she picks up the roll of film she dropped off to be developed that she'll mail to her proud family members.

2020: Madison, Mary's granddaughter, sits in her history class idly scrolling through some of her favorite fashion blogs; just a typical Wednesday in high school. It's May, and so many of her clothing gurus are chatting about the latest trends in prom styles. On a whim, Madison texts Silas to see if he and his bros are going to the senior prom. Silas replies yes, and he asks her to come to the dance with them as well as to the overnight after-party. Madison immediately posts gossip on Facebook about who will be at the uber-cool after-party on, and she texts Mary with the news. As she sits in algebra class later that day, she googles "senior prom wear." She starts to pin dresses to several of her Pinterest boards, which she shares with her Facebook friends. An hour later, Madison receives a Pinterest "Fashion Boards Outfits" notification on her iPhone. She reads what others have posted about the outfits; many seem to like a few she pinned from the Revolve.com website. As she sits in her Prius before driving home from school, Madison visits Revolve, and creates her personal virtual model to try on some dresses.

When Madison shares screenshots with her friends online, she's disappointed to see that most of them give the highest number of stars to one dress that's a bit out of her price range. On a hunch she goes on her *Gilt* app, and sure enough that exact dress is 60 percent off! Of course, there's a catch: there are only 25 in stock, and then the offer is over. Her heart pounds as she sees on the real-time message board that 15 dresses have been sold in the last hour. Madison jumps on the deal—she pays with her mom's PayPal account and figures she will be fine with that since she found such a bargain.

Two days later, UPS delivers the dress in the three sizes Madison ordered. Sure enough, the size 10 fits like a glove, and she returns the other two. On prom night, Madison takes a selfie, posts it to Instagram and shares it on Facebook, Twitter, and Tumblr, where she receives many likes and comments. The next day, Madison links the previous comments to her photos, and she recommends the brand. She also writes a positive review on the brand's Facebook page. Lastly, she browses the brand's website and creates additional looks, which she uploads to Pinterest to ease the way for others who will face the same dilemma. Hooking up with Silas was okay, but the important thing is that she snagged a great deal and earned the respect of her fashionista network. And, her grandma Mary will be thrilled to see her looking so grown up—if she can finally teach her how to log on to her Facebook page.[1]

How we buy: linear decision making

The high school prom is an American invention that has endured for over 50 years—often to the chagrin of worried parents. It's increasing in popularity in Europe as well. And Mary's 1967 prom story conforms to over 50 years of consumer behavior research that shows people engage in a systematic, linear sequence as they process information prior to purchase. But her granddaughter's 2020 experience shreds this fundamental assumption. Young shoppers like Madison force us to tear up much of what we know about how people decide what to buy.

But let's take a step back. Before we can illustrate how things are changing, it helps to know a bit more about the conventional wisdom. Just what do we (think) we know about how consumers decide what to buy? Our saga begins in 1968, when three academic researchers formalized and published a decision-making model that has guided a lot of explorations into how people choose one brand over others.[2] There are five separate stages in this classic conceptualization:

1 Problem recognition

2 Information search

3 Evaluation of alternatives

4 Purchase

5 Post-purchase evaluation

This process typically starts with a consumer's conscious recognition of an unsatisfied need, whether for a new dress, a carton of milk, or a college education. It's grounded in the idea of a solitary, rational decision maker who systematically accesses and sifts through information to maximize utility (that's economist-speak for "arrive at the best possible choice").

The stages of consumer decision making

When we can count on a reliable sequence of decision-making steps, it's fairly easy to leverage this knowledge in order to successfully court your customers. That's because we "unpack" what looks like a simple yes/no activity into a more extended set of decisions, each of which present challenges and opportunities. If you know where your prospect sits in the sequence, you can tailor your messages to move the needle that's specific to that stage. Let's take a closer look at these traditional stages, and how they're changing faster than you can swipe right on your phone.

STAGE 1: PROBLEM RECOGNITION

Mary's decision-making process triggers when she's asked to the prom. This invitation prompts her to recognize an unmet need—a new dress for the event.

Problem recognition starts when the consumer perceives some gap between where she is now and where she wants or needs to be. That gap can be functional: I've run out of milk for my cereal, and I have cereal with milk for breakfast for every morning. Or, the disparity can be psychological: I can no longer fit into my pants and I need to find new ones that still make me look good.

Old-school advertising messages often help us to recognize these gaps. They show us images of "happy, shiny people" who seem to be in a state of near ecstasy because their toilets are clean, or they receive admiring looks from passers-by.

Sometimes they even "helpfully" invent gaps or at least shine a light on them. For example, Gerald Lambert, the son of the owner of a pharmaceutical company, stumbled upon the term "halitosis" in a medical journal; it's an old Latin word for bad breath. The Listerine brand appropriated the label because it sounded scientific. Its advertising included vignettes of unfortunates who would never recover from the dreaded condition, such as this one: "Enter Edna, a beautiful young woman with all of the charm and social graces that made her desirable, except for one fatal flaw—Edna suffered from halitosis. What made it worse was that she didn't even know it! Not even her closest friends would tell her and so poor Edna, despite all of her charms, was 'always the bridesmaid and never the bride.'" Listerine's annual sales climbed from a little over $100,000 in 1921 to more than $4 million annually in 1927.[3] Apparently a lot of consumers never knew they had the problem until the company helpfully pointed it out to them.

Part of the challenge at this stage of decision making is to antici-pate just when your customers will think about a new purchase.

When Ford wanted to plug its new Fusion hybrid model, the company targeted what the auto industry terms the "upper funnel," or potential buyers down the road. To create desire where none yet existed, visitors to a special website entered to win a trip and a new Fusion. Ford publicized the sweepstakes on Twitter and Facebook; during the first two weeks of the promotion, almost 70,000 people requested more information about the car.[4]

STAGE 2: INFORMATION SEARCH

Once we've recognized a gap between where we are and where we want to be, we begin to scan for solutions. Of course, the extent to which we work at this depends upon a variety of factors such as the urgency of the need. But in general, we consult two broad sources: internal and external.

First, we review our knowledge of what actions we may have taken in the past and if they worked. Thus, a person who confronts an "I'm out of milk again because my #$@!$# roommate finished the carton and didn't replace it" problem may simply add the item to today's shopping list.

But many gaps are new ones to us, so we may not have a precedent to fall back upon. Or, perhaps the last response wasn't satisfactory. Now we have to go farther afield. We may choose to consult friends or experts, or perhaps look at specialized magazines or other sources. Mary figured out right away what she had to do: she rang up her friend, whom she knew was the kind of person who stays on top of pressing items like dress styles.

STAGE 3: EVALUATION OF ALTERNATIVES

At this stage, the decision maker identifies a set of feasible options. Now the task is to whittle these down and choose one. Again, depending upon the importance of the decision, there are different cognitive strategies we use to do this. Some of these resemble sophisticated algorithms that involve meticulously weighing the plusses and minuses of each option. Others are much more casual; we may grab a candy bar from the rack just because we like the package or because it brings back fond memories.

If you ask someone to list all the brands he or she can think of in a category, they will probably quickly reel off several, and then reflect before they add a few more (try it). This list is actually pretty important, especially if your brand isn't on it! We call the alternatives a consumer actively considers his or her evoked set.[5]

For obvious reasons, a marketer who finds that his brand is not in his target market's evoked set has cause to worry. You often don't get a second chance to make a good first impression; a consumer isn't likely to place a product in his evoked set after he has already considered it and rejected it. Indeed, we're more likely to add a new brand to the evoked set than one that we previously considered but passed over, even after a marketer has provided additional positive information about it.[6]

Mary quickly limited her evoked set because she chose one store to act as a "curator" that defined her choices much more narrowly. Then she selected a small number of dresses that were physically in inventory and selected one winner from the pile.

STAGE 4: PURCHASE

Once we assemble and evaluate the relevant options in a category, eventually we have to choose one.[7] Recall that the decision rules that guide our choices range from simple and quick strategies to complicated processes that require a lot of attention and cognitive processing.[8] Mary systematically evaluated each dress option using criteria such as fit and price, and proudly marched her selection to the cash register.

STAGE 5: POST-PURCHASE EVALUATION

Savvy "relationship marketers" have known for a long time that the purchase usually isn't the end of the process at all. The real destination is post-purchase evaluation, which helps to determine whether the company has a shot to create a brand-loyal customer down the road. They understand that it's far more expensive to acquire a new customer than to keep an old one, so you can't just rest on your laurels after the sale.

In the traditional model, the consumer receives feedback in the form of compliments (such as oohs and aahs from Mary's adoring grandparents when they get her prom photos in the mail), an electric shock, a stomach ache, a clearer TV picture, and so on, that validates or negates her choice. This choice feedback plays a key role in the learning process. Very simply, positive feedback makes it more likely the person will choose the same solution the next time the problem arises, while negative results steer them into the arms of a competitor. And organizations that have figured this out will intermittently solicit their own feedback, in the form of surveys and other customer insights tools, to keep tabs on how they are doing post-sale.

How we buy today: nonlinear decision making

Madison's decision-making odyssey looks quite different from her grandmother's. It doesn't follow a predictable, comfortably linear path from problem recognition to purchase and post-purchase evaluation. Instead, the teenager's purchase decision seems to emerge almost randomly from a 24/7 barrage of inputs from her social networks, combined with her outputs in the form of ongoing Web and social media platform queries. Although Madison still experiences all the traditional elements of decision making, the process is no longer so neat and tidy. In fact, it looks more like an organic, constant mutation than a series of steps we can isolate in real time.

Rather than a predictable slow march toward a purchase decision, today we witness a steady stream of interactions with marketers, including:

- native marketing executions that blur the lines between editorial and commercial messages;
- applications linked to the "Internet of Things" that enable companies to monitor our physical and mental well-being (and automatically restock us with medicine and food as necessary);
- encounters with digital avatars and holographs;

- smartphone alerts that let us know when a price we're watching drops.

And there are many more. The always-on shopper no longer distinguishes between consuming and nonconsuming states of being. They are open for business 24/7. No more Buying vs. Not Buying.

Let's do a quick recap of some of Madison's behaviors vis-à-vis the components of the decision-making model. It no longer makes as much sense to call them stages, so let's refer to them as elements instead.

Element 1: Problem recognition

We're all too familiar with the eerie experience of people walking by us with their heads bent over their phones, oblivious to everything but what they view in their devices. Madison is immersed in her network, so she's constantly exposed to new "problems," i.e. needs and wants she didn't know she had until her network alerted her.

Today's consumers are constantly exposed to people's challenges and accomplishments that contribute to the ubiquitous state of anxiety that others are more popular, beautiful, or accomplished. This condition even has a name: *FOMO (fear of missing out)*. Many of us are always on high alert to meet the next social challenge as we troll the internet to anticipate problems before they find us.

This vigilance takes its toll; several studies report that heavy usage of social media platforms like Facebook links to feelings of unhappiness, loneliness, and envy.[9] In a sense, problem recognition has morphed into an ongoing Google search as users ask, "How can I know what I want until I read what other people say?"

Element 2: Information search

Information search is big business. No kidding! Globally, in 2019 companies spent about $140 billion in search advertising (Google pockets about 80 percent of that revenue).[10] But the real story isn't just how much we search. *It's whom we ask.*

When Mary was a teen, it was easy for her to consult the "bibles" of fashion like *Vogue* to find out what was officially "in" or not. Her granddaughter may check out a fashion mag or two, but she's more likely to consult the new oracles, including Instagram stars like Olja Ryzevski, Claire Most, and Sylvie Mus, and of course her network.[11]

And, Madison's search is increasingly more visual than text based. The growth of image banks like Pinterest, coupled with image recognition technology, means that consumers can search for visual markers of a product rather than trying to describe it in words. Just as the Shazam app (now owned by Apple) can tell you the name of a song that's playing right now on your radio, new software products from startups such as Snap Fashion allow shoppers to take a picture of a garment on their smartphones and then link to a retailer where they can buy that piece or something similar.[12]

Element 3: Evaluation of alternatives

One of the most formidable challenges consumers face today is very much a "First World Problem:" we have far too many choices. While it's surely good to have options, at least in the developed world, ironically we suffer from an abundance of riches.

In the last chapter we called this problem hyperchoice. This condition unfortunately means that we have too much of a good thing. Numerous studies show that consumers actually make dumber decisions—and feel frustrated and angry—when they have a lot of choices than when they have relatively few.

The internet enables us to turn on a fire hose of information whenever we request it. Now we urgently need some strong valves to manage this overwhelming flow of information,[13] lest we get swept away. In other words, today we need help just to filter the vast river of options into a manageable choice set. We have never needed editors more than we do today.

Hence the growth of powerful new tools such as comparison matrices, filters, and ranking and scoring programs that allow us to customize our informational environment so that we only see a small fraction of the choices out there. The downside: just as with the news, we tend only to "discover" what we already know, and we don't learn about novel options. We are likely to inhabit what the internet activist Eli Pariser famously calls a filter bubble.[14]

Element 4: Purchase

Madison may never set foot in a bricks-and-mortar structure to buy her dress. Eight in ten Americans shop online today, over half have purchased something from their phones, and 15 percent bought something after they clicked through on a link shared on social media.[15] Similarly, the EU reports that in 2019 about 71 percent of internet users purchased something online.[16]

And, as chains like the US retailer Best Buy have discovered, showrooming shoppers may come to regard the store as more of a convenient venue to test out a product before they buy it cheaper online. And as we adjust to life after the pandemic, it remains to be seen whether the massive shift to ordering items online during the crisis will be a habit that stays with us.

WHO MOVED MY ZMOT?

This sea change illustrates a crucial point about the breakdown of the traditional linear decision-making model. Let's take a look at how Google thinks about this. Google is obsessed with something the company calls *ZMOT*. Here's how they define it:

> It's a new decision-making moment that takes place a hundred million times a day on mobile phones, laptops and wired devices of all kinds. It's a moment where marketing happens, where information happens, and where consumers make choices that affect the success and failure of nearly every brand in the world. At Google, we call this the Zero Moment of Truth, or simply ZMOT ("ZEE-mot").[17]

Google is right to fixate on ZMOT, because its survival and prosperity depends on understanding how people search for information and how they use this to decide what to buy.

This idea is especially important because the answer to "what is the ZMOT?" has changed radically. Google knows that today ZMOT is probably not going to happen in an online or physical store, which is where we usually assume it will. In fact, it's just as or more likely to happen when the shopper is browsing at home or work, or even driving around (hopefully not in the driver's seat).

In the old days, marketers viewed the in-store transaction as being when the customer magically throws down their credit card as the final stop on the road to a purchase. Thus, many traditional selling strategies view the transaction as a way to seal the deal that has been forged previously via the steps of problem recognition, information search, and evaluation of alternatives.

The purchase environment is the last chance to sway the customer, and increasingly marketers divert resources from traditional advertising and toward point-of-purchase messaging to make the sale in the store. This strategy still works well for small impulse purchases—who can pass up that alluring candy bar that's calling your name at the cash register?

Fast forward to today's moving ZMOT: it's increasingly common for shoppers to decide what they plan to buy before they even exit from their cars. Surveys report that fully eight in ten shoppers now do online research before they buy.[18]

Thus, Madison chose to search online bargain sites rather than purchase the dress she first encountered. Retailers, take note: because your shoppers are "always on," you have to be, too. Gone are the days when you could just turn on the charm when the customer walked through your door. Now you need to do whatever you can to engage and interact with them much earlier in the process. ZMOT has come and gone.

IT'S ALL ABOUT THE PAIN POINTS

In Mary's day, a bricks-and-mortar retailer (with a few exceptions such as TV sales, there was no other kind) competed with other physical stores for her business. She just didn't have a lot of other options. Of course, that's no longer the case.

For this reason, an important component of this step is the purchase modality the customer chooses to obtain the product. This element cuts to the heart of the issues many companies grapple with, especially as they transition from physical stores to e-commerce. After all, the reality is that for a large majority of items the customer has a multiplicity of purchase options, from in-store to a few clicks to phone sales, etc.

A primary goal is to minimize the number of pain points during the purchase process. We want to make this as frictionless as possible, because if the customer encounters too many bumps in the road they may abandon the process and seek an alternative. This happens more often than we usually assume, both in physical stores and online. In fact, studies of e-commerce businesses estimate that so-called shopping cart abandonment occurs in anywhere from 50 percent to as much as 80 percent of transactions. This costs merchants between about $2–4 trillion per year. There are many reasons for this high rate, including slow websites, the need to create an account, unanticipated fees tacked on at the end, a lack of security, and site glitches.[19]

There are some strategies that reduce this problem, such as allowing customers to create guest accounts, following up with email reminders to check out, and even "exit-intent pop-ups"—last-ditch efforts to save the sale by offering the shopper additional incentives to see things through.[20] But clearly the steady rise of cart abandonment points to the need to double down on reducing the friction that increasingly impatient consumers may encounter.

Element 5: Post-purchase evaluation

Mary had to wait six weeks to see how radiant she looked in her prom dress. In contrast, Madison lives in a world of constant feedback. She and her peeps spend each day posting virtually everything for evaluation by their social network. These posts include the infamous selfie, endless details about routine activities, even the meals she eats. Indeed, the fascination with sharing glamorized photos of what's on our plates before we dig in has led to a craze popularly known as food porn. It's gotten so out of control that some New York restaurants have banned the taking of selfies at their tables.[21]

This accelerated feedback loop is part of the new ZMOT story. It's a really, really profound change that just about every organization needs to grasp. That's because these new ZMOTs blow a big, gaping hole in the traditional linear decision-making model.[22]

The new chameleon buys by committee

The new chameleon is very, very busy. It seems like she spends hours and hours in meetings. That's because today it's a "committee" rather than the individual that processes the information and decides what to do.

The traditional decision-making model, while acknowledging that we consult external sources, nonetheless tends to depict the decision maker as a lone wolf. Sure, after she buys she avidly solicits feedback from others to validate her choice. But that doesn't happen so much as it used to, because the new "always-on" consumer asks for validation from her social network *before* she chooses.

Ironically, though the internet was supposed to make our lives easier, it seems that shoppers often work a lot harder than they used to. They are far more likely to painstakingly research even the most minor purchases, and this process often includes one or more consultations with others before they pull the trigger.

This frenetic consultation dramatically alters our picture of that lone wolf. It almost seems that these decisions look a lot more like what researchers observe in industrial buying situations. In these settings, members of a buying center (not a physical place!) collaborate to coordinate the information flow, investigate the pros and cons of each option, and (of course!) find out what other buyers have to say about them. As we saw with Madison's process, today it seems that "it takes a village" to buy a prom dress!

Let's think of this as the new age of participatory consumption, where many of us are loath to make a move before we get buy-in from our networks and we can validate our decisions. Indeed, a Pew Research Center survey found that 40 percent of Americans say they almost always consult online reviews before they buy something new.[23]

So, yesterday's lone wolf becomes today's corporate procurement manager. She relies upon her "peeps" to play different roles during the process, just as a company's "buying center" works as a team.

The emergence of social shopping

The massive need for curation in marketplaces brings us back full circle to the obituary for traditional, linear decision making. The early years of e-commerce cast doubt on the viability of the online channel, because clicking at home on a computer can't replicate the experience of trying on an item, receiving feedback from shopping partners, or even the thrill of wearing the new garment home.

That criticism is almost moot today and likely will be ancient history within a few years. New technologies are coming to the fore that marry the convenience of online shopping with the "warm and fuzzy" experience of shopping with your BFF in a fancy store. These applications bridge the gap between digital and IRL (in real life) in several ways:[24]

- Scrapbooking sites like vi.sualize.us and Pinterest allow shoppers to collect a bunch of options as they surf the web, just as an in-store shopper might accumulate a pile of pants to lug into the dressing room. Members of the community submit their outfit ideas for others to use.

- Virtual try-on sites like My Virtual Model and Joy of Clothes allow shoppers to superimpose outfits over a photo or avatar of themselves. In some cases, the user can customize the model's body dimensions to yield a more accurate representation.

- Pre-purchase feedback sites like Instagram solicit reactions from a user's social network and other fashionistas.

- Recommendation sites like ClosetSpace and Cladwell consider variables such as weather and occasion to generate suggestions for outfits the user can purchase on sponsoring websites.

- Augmented reality applications create an immersive, interactive experience either at home or in-store. Companies including Converse, Uniqlo, and IKEA have successfully deployed AR platforms that enhance the bricks-and-mortar customer experience.

Madison's prom shopping journey incorporated some of this new tech. Recall that she created her own personal virtual model to try on dresses. Now compare this process to the "old days" of picking items out of an online catalog without having any idea of what they would actually look like when they arrived. Madison also shared photos of dresses with her friends online, and she didn't make a move until they weighed in on each. Just as her grandma Mary was able to audition her choices in front of her three friends in a store dressing room, Madison now accesses others' feedback before rather than after the sale. Same task, different ZMOT.

Let's refer to these emerging platforms collectively as social shopping. As more of us turn to online options to shop, we still yearn for the stimulation of browsing the racks. New technologies may not fully replicate that experience, but they are getting closer to the real thing. At the least, they allow the shopper to garner others' thumbs up or down as they (virtually) look at one item after another.

Maybe it's time for marketers to go shopping as well—for new models that explain the wild, wild world of today's nonlinear, always-on decision maker.

The cages we have built over the years to partition the different stages of decision making just have to open. Let's take a quick look at how the traditional stages of problem solving are changing— even as you read this.

THE GROUP CALLS THE SHOTS

As decision making shifts from a solo exercise to one that involves others in our networks, it's crucial for marketers to appreciate how this dynamic alters the very nature of the process.

It's a truism to state that the (perceived) presence of others exerts a huge influence on an individual's choices—but just in case, we have about 75 years of solid research evidence to back that up. Even many laymen are familiar with classic studies like the Milgram Experiment, where ordinary people were persuaded to deliver severe electric shocks to another person (actually a confederate of the experimenter, fortunately) when they were pressured to do so.

We also know that when we join a group, our tolerance for risk often increases. Social psychologists call this tendency the risky shift. This effect is well documented, and it should make retailers and other marketers pay attention because one ramification is that our purse strings tend to loosen when we shop with others. For that reason (social distancing excepted) it's a smart move to encourage shoppers to move around in packs. There are probably some clever yet simple ways to do this, such as running "pop-up sales" for customers who can claim the goodies with, say, three or more friends. However, I've yet to see any retailers that incentivize group shopping.

THE GROUP ISN'T ALWAYS RIGHT

Is the customer always right? Not anymore. There's another aspect of social scoring, albeit largely overlooked, that has the potential to be a game-changer in retailing and customer service. While we're busily documenting our interactions with salespeople and other service providers, they're returning the favor. People who work in small businesses have always been aware of problem customers who drop in periodically to torment them. But now, at least in theory, a salesperson or other service provider at any kind of organization large or small can grade your behavior. And the icing on the cake is that they can share these scores with others. It's no longer only Santa who knows if you've been naughty or nice.

At platforms like Airbnb and Uber, users get a rating each time they patronize the service. It's no surprise that according to Lyft and Uber drivers, failure to leave a tip is a surefire road to a dismal evaluation. For what it's worth, other routes to disaster apparently include puking in the car or being rude (or both I assume).[25] This is not just FYI stuff; a bad rating can prevent you from booking rooms or rides down the road.

This new kind of "scoreboard" may have huge implications for the traditional power disparity between buyer and seller. Suddenly, it's not just the service provider who has to play nice. The shoe is on the other foot, as the customer also has to play nice and think about how today's nasty behavior will influence tomorrow's reputation. So much for "the customer is always right."

So far it doesn't seem that service businesses have thought much about the potential impact of this reverse rating process, but it could be just a matter of time before overly demanding patients need to locate doctors who will agree to put up with them, customers who like to yell at repairmen have no one to fix their leaking toilets, and perhaps even students who email their professor at 2:00 a.m. with urgent questions about assignments that were due two weeks ago get banned from registering for classes (OK, that last one is a fantasy of mine that I just threw in there). We are just beginning to feel the rumblings of this cage opening, but it could be a big one.

Social shopping creates the hive mind

The hive mind is a large digital community of people who share their knowledge and opinions to keep members engaged in a constant feedback loop. This results in collective intelligence and concentric rings of group affinity that rely upon one another for validation of their choices.

In stark contrast to the sequential paradigm of the old-school linear model, a hive mind is constantly buzzing—and constantly acting. We've morphed into an endless state of polysynchronous consumption: a nonstop blending of multiple channels of asynchronous online and synchronous online communication that we access in tandem with our other activities via mobile phones and other devices.

Back in the day, young people used to proudly proclaim, "Do your own thing." Today a more common refrain is, "What do my peeps think?" A constant immersion in social media creates a hive mind. As we've seen, it seems that before the consumer commits to a choice, decisions large and small—where to eat, what to wear, who to like—first need to be voted upon by his or her social network.

In many cases, the consumer makes a selection, but it doesn't "count" until they post a photo to officially seal the deal. Anecdotally, many of my students have told me they didn't know the person they were dating broke up with them until they noticed s/he changed their relationship status on Facebook!

And then the process repeats again for the next choice—the hive hums 24/7. Indeed, a hardcore *Star Trek* fan is tempted to think of the Borg; an army of drones plugged into the "Collective" (or, coincidentally, the "Hive") that relentlessly assimilates technology from other species and absorbs them into its net. For marketers at least, the Borg's battle cry resonates: "Resistance is futile."

The constant barrage of reactions to almost anything we say, buy, or do propels us into a perpetual feedback loop. Our own satisfaction seems to largely be determined by what others in our social graph decree to be a good or bad choice.[26] Consumers seem to ask, "How can I know if I'm satisfied until I hear what other people say?"

Social scoring: you are what you post

A corollary to the social shopping boom is that consumers increasingly submit *themselves* and their choices to scrutiny by the collective. The hive mind works both ways: shoppers hunger for intelligence about others' choices, but they also welcome others to comment on their own. Indeed, some of us go to great lengths to carefully stage-manage these impressions. The quest to present the most upbeat, impressive image has created a cottage industry for "personal brand managers" who meticulously curate a client's photos and posts.[27]

Why do people post so many photos that document silly pet costumes, a "selfie" at the dry cleaner, or the poké bowl they had for lunch? Because they can. The smartphone has turned each of us into a documentary filmmaker—and an artiste who is obsessed with how the "critics" will review the movie of his or her life. We've reached the point where reporting the activity seems to be more important than the activity itself. Many seem to hunger for this online validation, so they post videos of themselves in search of evaluations and perhaps eagerly count the number of likes they've received from prior posts. Researchers call this ongoing documentation social scoring.

THE CURSE OF FOMO

The constant quest to describe a "perfect" lifestyle, complete with pictures of glamorous friends or perhaps visits to exotic locales, fuels a never-ending game of FOMO (fear of missing out) as people ruefully compare their own lives to these stylized images.

Consumers who are susceptible to FOMO seem to always be on high alert to meet the next social challenge, as they troll the internet to anticipate problems before problems find *them*. This almost constant vigilance means that you as a marketer need to stay in touch on a more constant basis rather than just dropping into your customers' lives intermittently with a pithy message or two. Like your shopper, your digital assets need to be "always on" to be sure that customers can tune into up-to-the minute info when *they* are ready for it. At will. And as I've seen over and over in college classrooms, we've taught people to expect instant gratification—and this means their attention spans seem to get shorter every semester!

YOU: THE BRAND

It's exhausting to always be on Red Alert! Small wonder that numerous studies link social media usage to myriad mental health problems including depression, anxiety, and decreased self-esteem.[28] Mea culpa: ever since I published the first edition of my Principles of Marketing textbook in the early 1990s, we have included a section we call "Brand You" that emphasizes to students the importance of carefully cultivating their image for professional success.[29] I didn't realize at the time just how big a topic "personal branding" would become in the age of the selfie.

But even if we don't shell out for a professional identity manager, many of us seem to spend a huge amount of time documenting our daily existence. It's almost as if your friends believe you're desperate to know that you picked up your dry cleaning today.

In a typical day, people upload 350 million photos to Facebook. They share 1.3 million pieces of content on Facebook every minute of every day. On top of that, they send 500 million tweets in a day, pin 14 million items on Pinterest, post 85 million videos and photos on Instagram, and still find time to view 25 million LinkedIn profiles.[30]

Whew! That's quite a busy day! This digital obsession helps to explain the findings of one jaw-dropping survey: one in three smartphone owners would rather give up sex than their phones![31]

For marketers, the new omnichannel consumer is a mixed blessing. On the one hand, they have to contend with a loss of control over where their customers search for information. That's why it's crucial to—as much as possible—track where your consumers tend to go during their daily journeys so you can do your best to be there when they return.

On the other hand, perhaps many of our marketing predecessors would have been thrilled to have such an engaged customer! They don't just suddenly turn on when they have to solve an immediate problem; they're more likely to be in information-gathering mode for a long period of time. Thus, it's important to ask the question, "When does my customer's problem become my opportunity?"

THE INFLUENCER ECONOMY

Just about anyone with access to an iPhone can—and probably will—tap into our evolving, video-driven culture when they document their own purchase experiences in painstaking detail. Indeed, so-called haul videos have become so popular they have become their own subgenre on YouTube. They're part of a slightly broader category (there's that word again!) of unpacking videos that show you exactly how to remove a product from a box and put it together. Today, influencers are the new prophets of commerce. Their incessant posts steadily accumulate online social capital— basically, "street cred" from posting videos and enticing others to watch them—that in time may escalate into (minor) celebrity status. By cleverly promoting their online product evaluations, bloggers and vloggers can gain a large following and generate revenue from views and endorsements. If successful, they can create their own personal brands as they amass power and legitimacy in online marketplaces.

But as the internet's span of attention grows ever shorter, these moments of fame are short-lived. Before too long, our focus turns to the next microcelebrity. Many bloggers who aspire to be the next Perez Hilton or Kim Kardashian would be quite grateful for the "fifteen minutes of fame" Andy Warhol promised each of us almost 50 years ago. Certainly, former microstars such as Katy Perry's bumbling Left Shark in the 2017 Super Bowl show or the British YouTube star Sophie Hannah Richardson would agree.

On auction sites like eBay, the knowledge that others are interested in acquiring that Elvis figurine or used Rolex heightens your own interest and spurs bidders to offer amounts they might not consider spending in a traditional retail environment. Similarly, when Groupon (or Gilt in Madison's case) shares how many others have purchased a deal in the last 24 hours this fosters an illusion of scarcity and also validates the urge to jump on the bandwagon.

When Robert Putnam published his controversial book *Bowling Alone: The Collapse and Revival of American Community* in 2001, he bemoaned the disintegration of traditional social institutions as large numbers of us gravitated instead toward solitary pursuits both offline and online.[32]

How things have changed since then! In the twenty years since Putnam's book came out, millions of us have discovered the sticking power of social media. At least in a digital sense, most of us are far from alone. Like the new shopper who cherishes her network, many of us no longer seem to be bowling alone. Is it possible to bowl by committee?

If anything, many of us (even when we're sequestered in a pandemic) suffer from too much (digital) love. Concerns about "social networking addiction disorder" continue to grow.[33] The South Korean government estimates that 20 percent of its population is in danger of addiction, and it sends some of its younger "addicts" to special camps where they can safely detox.[34] Some universities sponsor "social media detox" events. I ask my students to go 48 hours without social media and to write a report about their experiences. Invariably, they thank me for forcing them to live through this harrowing experience because they realize how dependent they are. Not that they give it up permanently, of course.

Marketing to the hive mind

Madison's prom shopping adventure shouldn't be shrugged off as just another example of the younger generation's limited attention span or a sign that civilization as we know it will soon be over. Her constant movement between the borders that separate the online and offline worlds illustrates the challenges and opportunities that organizations face in an environment where the familiar, linear model of consumer decision making rapidly recedes in the rearview mirror. The "always on" landscape upends many of our cherished assumptions about where, when, and why customers engage with the marketplace.

According to one estimate, the average human brain receives about 34 GB of information per day. That's enough to overwhelm a laptop within a week.[35] We saw earlier that hyperchoice is not a good thing, because the quality of our decisions diminishes when there are just too many options.

The futurist Stewart Brand famously observed, "information wants to be free," in defense of an unfettered internet. However, what's not as well-known is that he went on to say, "information [also] wants to be expensive" because it's so valuable.[36] The paradox he was noting is that the value of all this amazing content is lost if we can't use it.

As the amount of information available to all of us cascades, the need for editors, curators, gatekeepers, whatever you'd like to call them, to sift the wheat from the chaff grows as well. The hive mind can be overwhelmed by a surplus of choices. Sure, information wants to be free, but anarchy just doesn't work when you're trying to find that perfect outfit.

CURATION STREAMLINES DECISION MAKING

What does this information avalanche mean for marketers? Very simply, *content curation is as, or more, important than content creation.*

For example, there are more than 60 million sales consultants worldwide who work as distributors in the multi-level marketing (MLM) industry.[37] They represent hundreds of companies (many rep for more than one) who use a direct selling model to sell products that range from storage solutions (Tupperware) to cleaning products (Amway) to dietary supplements and skincare (Modere), and even sex toys (Intimate Tickles). Within each vertical, the distributor needs to compete for the customer's preferences with other direct selling companies as well as similar ones that sell through stores.

But today's consumer, as we've seen, is overwhelmed by choices; they lack the will or even the cognitive capacity to explore the numerous options and make intelligent decisions. Therefore, the new role of the successful MLM representative is to become more of a category expert who is able to sift through the vast mountain of information and make an informed recommendation that is tailored to the needs of each client. That role is especially crucial in growing verticals like supplements that require some degree of technical expertise to be sure that products do not cause harmful side effects.

This curation function also is golden to consumers who are desperate to simplify their lives. Lifestyle gurus like Marie Kondo preach the virtues of decluttering. Countless articles and YouTube videos demonstrate "hacks" or shortcuts to minimize the time we spend on our to-do lists. Magazines and blogs publish "Top 10" lists of the best restaurants, employers, roller coasters, and just about anything else you can imagine. Ironically, as our access to better and better data about our lives increases, so too does our need for editors to make sense of all of it.

Influencers accumulate online social capital that in time may even escalate into (minor) celebrity status. By cleverly promoting their online product evaluations, bloggers and vloggers can gain a large following and generate revenue from views and endorsements. You can be proactive by courting these intermediaries but caution: if these attempts are too overt, they will backfire.

The primacy of content curation also elevates the traditional salesperson to be more of a trusted consultant that the customer can turn to for advice. And especially post-pandemic, when the nature of shopping for many products is profoundly changed, we can expect to see salespeople across the board to become more important as even fewer of us flock to stores and experience our ZMOT at the shelf.

The flip side is that companies need to rethink how they identify, train, and compensate these curators. One of the great ironies of traditional retailing is that most multimillion-dollar businesses rely upon the quality of their least-paid employees to nurture the shopper experience. That simply has to change as the salesperson's role becomes more important. We saw some baby steps in this direction in the months after the pandemic hit, as retailers including CVS, Target, and Walmart started to provide modest raises and enhanced benefits to their workers.[38] Remember, one of the few competitive advantages a traditional retailer can still offer vis-à-vis an online store is the value-add of a trusted salesperson to guide the shopper through the labyrinth. That is, at least until AI technology gets a bit more advanced.

MARKETERS ARE CURATORS

As we know all too well, not all products succeed. In fact, the large majority never make it past the cutting room floor. It's literally impossible for every clothing label, new album, potato chip flavor, or lamp design to thrive. Consumers simply don't have the time, bandwidth, or money to buy everything that gets thrown at them (much as some may valiantly try). They need agents in the system to winnow down the options for them, lest the hyperchoice tsunami sweeps over them. Think of this vast ocean of options pouring into a giant funnel—only a (relatively) small proportion of these choices trickle out at the other end for shoppers to consider.

The need for these gatekeepers illustrates why, for example, amateur bloggers and "influencers" have become such a force to be reckoned with in industries as diverse as apparel, tech products, and wine. Contrary to what some observers proclaim, we still need "experts" to sift through the ocean of options for us. What has changed is that the potential pool of expertise is no longer confined to the people and institutions, such as "intellectual elites" (unfortunately perhaps including college professors) and legacy publications like *Vogue*, that traditionally held the reins of power.

Ding ding ding! That's where marketing agents enter to provide value as curators. Many of these individuals, whom we can think of as cultural gatekeepers or tastemakers in addition to their other job titles, have a big say in the products we consider. They filter the overflow of information as it travels down the funnel. Gatekeepers include movie, restaurant, and car reviewers; interior designers; disc jockeys; brand managers; retail buyers; magazine editors; and increasingly a fan base that obsessively follows and shares the latest gossip, styles, TV and film plots, and other pieces of popular culture. Sociologists call this set of agents the "throughput sector."[39]

CURATORS CONFER CREDIBILITY

But here's a twist: today many of the new gatekeepers are algorithms, as AI (artificial intelligence) applications take center stage to sift through reams of data and recommend choices to us. For example, startups like We Are Travel Girls, aimed at women travelers, learn clients' preferences over time, so they can customize travel recommendations for discerning vacationers.[40]

This sea change presents both a challenge to traditional centers of expertise and a golden opportunity to newcomers. Today there is

huge market value in credentialing, i.e., demonstrating that according to some standard one is in fact eligible to opine on the "correct"
clothing styles, the best wines, the most cutting-edge tech, etc.

One illustration of this battle for credibility is the trend toward
the awarding of microdegrees (or nanodegrees) in the tech space.
These credentials, offered by online education disruptors such as
Coursera and Udacity, do an end run around legacy higher education agents. Microdegrees certify expertise in a specific skill set that
employers desire without the price tag of an entire degree program.[41]
Online platforms got a huge push from the pandemic, as hordes of
people scrambled to retool themselves or perhaps just to learn
about new things to take a break from Netflix binge-watching. The
big ones saw enrollment increases of over 400 percent in the months
following lockdown.[42]

Similar "guild issues" regarding the consensus about who is an
expert—and thus qualified to curate consumers' choices—are roil-
ing fields as diverse as physical conditioning (e.g., the National
Strength and Conditioning Association versus "upstart" regimens
like CrossFit), psychiatrists versus social workers, and even the
right of Orthodox rabbis versus those in other branches of Judaism
to certify who is a Jew. There will be winners and losers for sure,
but we can count on a growing demand for agents to provide these
services—and many opportunities wait for companies that recognize this need and move to fill the gaps in this growing market.

Curation also is crucial to make sense of the barrage of marketing communications that everyday consumers post. The two-way
interactivity of Web 2.0 transformed an entire generation of passive
internet consumers into proactive internet producers. These amateur
content creators upload vast amounts of "stuff" 24/7. Today almost
anyone can film their own commercial for a favorite product, or
even worse upload a diatribe or parody of a brand they don't like.

This opening of the dikes worries a lot of people in the advertising business. They see the tidal wave of consumer-generated content
that's about to engulf them and fret that they'll be out of a job very
soon. Who needs copywriters and art directors, when amateurs can

shoot their own crowd-pleasing commercial that logs thousands of views on YouTube?

Doritos' success with this amateur model shows why the pros are worried. The brand's crowdsourced "Crash the Super Bowl" initiative was a huge win during its ten-year run. This campaign allowed individuals to submit their own Doritos commercials. The winning spots aired during precious ad time at the Super Bowl, the Mecca of broadcast advertising.

Why worry about juvenile spots that novices film on shoestring budgets? Very simple—the winning spots earned top-five rankings on the *USA Today* Ad Meter every year in which they aired, and they claimed the #1 ranking four times.

But take a deep breath: even a campaign like "Crash the Super Bowl" required the input of many professionals, who helped to find the few pearls in the thousands of oysters that everyday people submitted to the contest. As the CMO of the National Football League noted about the Doritos spots:

> One reason that crowdsourcing is no longer as threatening to agencies is because shops still play a role... You still need people to organize it. Crash didn't happen because consumers decided to do it. This program happened because somebody had the idea, organized it, made it happen, provided the vehicles... The agency world is as relevant as ever, if not arguably more relevant, as more crowdsourced individual ideas have come to pass.[43]

The upshot: marketing professionals don't make all the rules any longer, but you still get to decide who plays the game. The tsunami of information faced by every consumer creates the need for individuals and organizations to filter out 99 percent of the noise (on a good day). Like it or not, there's a lot of mind-numbing stuff out there, and even the most brain-dead among us can look at only so many cute kitty videos.

All hail the marketing curator!

CHAPTER TAKEAWAYS

- A constant barrage of information creates an always-on shopper who no longer makes most decisions in a systematic, linear way.

- Consumers *think* they want more choices. They really want fewer, but better, ones.

- Today we see a lot more "buying by committee," as younger consumers tune into a hive mind composed of a large digital community of people who share their knowledge and opinions to keep members engaged in a constant feedback loop.

- Purchase decisions are less likely to be made at the store shelf or on an e-commerce site, as consumers conduct a lot more research about their options and often decide on one before they ever visit the place where they will buy it.

- The most compelling offer can implode if the customer encounters pain points during the decision-making and purchase process; the large majority of online sales never happen because the shopper abandons their cart. It's imperative to identify these and do whatever you can to reduce friction.

- A consumer's tolerance for risk changes when they are part of a group. Encourage your customers to shop in groups by promoting social activities and offering other kinds of rewards.

- As customer and business rating services start to take off, both parties to a transaction will feel more pressure to behave or deliver good service.

- The democratization of the internet ironically amplifies the need for professionals to select and curate worthy content. That's why it's important to appreciate the role of curator YOU play in the vast marketplace ecosystem.

Endnotes

1 Some of this content has been adapted from R. Ashman, M. R. Solomon, and J. Wolny, "An Old Model for a New Age: Applying the EKB in Today's Participatory Culture," *Journal of Customer Behaviour* 14, no. 2 (2015): 127–46.

2 James Engel, David Kollat, and Roger Blackwell, *Consumer Behavior* (New York: Holt, Rinehart and Winston, 1968).

3 Quoted in "The Surprising History of Halitosis," *Dental Depot*, December 7, 2018, https://dentaldepot.net/history-of-halitosis/ (archived at https://perma.cc/BUJ7-DGVK).

4 Jean Halliday, "With Fusion Campaign, Ford Targets 'Upper Funnel' Car Buyers: $60M to $80M Ad Blitz Aimed at Consumers Not Yet Ready to Buy New Vehicle," *Advertising Age*, March 2, 2009, https://adage.com/article/news/ford-fusion-campaign-targets-upper-funnel-car-buyers/134986 (archived at https://perma.cc/H36D-XMDY).

5 Mary Frances Luce, James R. Bettman, and John W. Payne, "Choice Processing in Emotionally Difficult Decisions," *Journal of Experimental Psychology: Learning, Memory, & Cognition*, 23 (March 1997): 384–405; example provided by Professor James Bettman, personal communication (December 17, 1997).

6 John R. Hauser and Birger Wernerfelt, "An Evaluation Cost Model of Consideration Sets," *Journal of Consumer Research* 16 (March 1990): 393–408.

7 Mita Sujan and James R. Bettman, "The Effects of Brand Positioning Strategies on Consumers' Brand and Category Perceptions: Some Insights from Schema Research," *Journal of Marketing Research* 26 (November 1989): 454–67.

8 See William P. Putsis, Jr., and Narasimhan Srinivasan, "Buying or Just Browsing? The Duration of Purchase Deliberation," *Journal of Marketing Research* 31 (August 1994): 393–402.

9 Maria Konnikova, "How Facebook Makes Us Unhappy," *The New Yorker*, September 10, 2013, http://www.newyorker.com/tech/elements/how-facebook-makes-us-unhappy (archived at https://perma.cc/BFY4-G9KB).

10 "Search Advertising Spending Worldwide from 2009–2019, *Statista*, https://www.statista.com/statistics/267056/paid-search-advertising-expenditure-worldwide/ (archived at https://perma.cc/DZB7-HL2Y);

Ginny Marvin, "Report: Google Earns 78% Of $36.7B US Search Ad Revenues, Soon to be 80%," *Search Engine Land*, March 14, 2017.

11 "The Most Stylish Instagrams to Follow Now," *Harpers Bazaar*, April 30, 2020, https://www.harpersbazaar.com/fashion/street-style/g3957/best-blogger-instagrams/ (archived at https://perma.cc/Y9LC-WGP2).

12 Shane Hickey, "Fashion Retailers Eye Up Image-Recognition Apps for Smartphones," *The Guardian*, April 20, 2014, https://www.theguardian.com/business/2014/apr/20/fashion-retailers-image-recognition-apps-smartphones (archived at https://perma.cc/Z8AV-Q5QS).

13 Alina Tugend, "The Paralyzing Problem of Too Many Choices: A Problem That Can Paralyze," *The New York Times*, February 26, 2010, https://www.nytimes.com/2010/02/27/your-money/27shortcuts.html (archived at https://perma.cc/59XG-Z9M8).

14 Eli Pariser, *The Filter Bubble: How the New Personalized Web Is Changing What We Read and How We Think* (New York: Penguin Books, 2012).

15 Sarah Perez, "79 Percent of Americans Now Shop Online, But It's Cost More than Convenience That Sways Them," *Techcrunch*, December 19, 2016, https://techcrunch.com/2016/12/19/79-percent-of-americans-now-shop-online-but-its-cost-more-than-convenience-that-sways-them/ (archived at https://perma.cc/C9SH-9FQP).

16 "E-commerce Statistics for Individuals," Eurostat, January 30, 2020, https://ec.europa.eu/eurostat/statistics-explained/index.php/E-commerce_statistics_for_individuals (archived at https://perma.cc/UK2D-B6FT).

17 Quoted from Jim Lecinski, *Winning the Zero Moment of Truth* (Google, 2011) https://www.thinkwithgoogle.com/marketing-resources/micro-moments/2011-winning-zmot-ebook/ (archived at https://perma.cc/5L23-QTL5).

18 Kimberlee Morrison, "81% of Shoppers Conduct Online Research Before Buying," *Adweek*, November 28, 2014, http://www.adweek.com/digital/81-shoppers-conduct-online-research-making-purchase-infographic/ (archived at https://perma.cc/76T3-QWHG).

19 Grace Miller, "31 Shopping Cart Abandonment Statistics For 2018," *Annex Cloud*, https://www.annexcloud.com/blog/31-shopping-cart-abandonment-statistics-for-2018/#:~:text=The%20phenomenon%20of%20a%20customer,from%2050%25%20to%2080%25 (archived at https://perma.cc/PL4S-58NC).

20 Grace Miller, "5 Shopping Cart Abandonment Solutions That Really Work," *Annex Cloud*, https://www.annexcloud.com/blog/shopping-cart-abandonment-solutions/ (archived at https://perma.cc/9HHZ-U5BY).

21 Christian Jarrett "How Food Porn Hijacks Your Brain," *New York Times Magazine*, October 20, 2015, http://nymag.com/scienceofus/2015/10/how-food-porn-hijacks-your-brain.html (archived at https://perma.cc/DN6Y-WR9D).

22 For one recent, somewhat similar perspective cf. J. Turner, R. Shah, and V. Jain, "How Brands Are Using Nonlinear Marketing to Connect with Customers in the Post-Advertising Era," *60 Second Marketer*, Atlanta (2018).

23 Aaron Smith and Monica Anderson, "Online Shopping and E-Commerce," Pew Research Center, December 19, 2016, http://www.pewInternet.org/2016/12/19/online-shopping-and-e-commerce/ (archived at https://perma.cc/BJ2U-SE82).

24 Adapted from Rachel Ashman, Kristhy Salazar, and Michael Solomon, "Let's Go Social Shopping! Social Shopping in a Researcher's Paradise," Institute of Direct and Digital Marketing, Google UK, January 2014.

25 Quoted from Rachel Gillete, "17 Uber and Lyft Drivers Reveal How They Rate Their Passengers," *Business Insider*, October 29, 2016, http://www.businessinsider.com/how-uber-and-lyft-drivers-decide-your-passenger-rating-2016-10 (archived at https://perma.cc/ZKK2-DSEW).

26 Tracy Tuten and Michael R. Solomon, *Social Media Marketing*, 3rd ed. (London: Sage, 2019).

27 "10 Steps to Building Your Personal Brand on Social Media," Direct Marketing Institute, https://digitalmarketinginstitute.com/en-us/blog/10-steps-to-building-your-personal-brand-on-social-media (archived at https://perma.cc/2NEF-RVDM).

28 Gigen Mammoser, "The FOMO Is Real: How Social Media Increases Depression and Loneliness" *Healthline*, December 9, 2018, https://www.healthline.com/health-news/social-media-use-increases-depression-and-loneliness (archived at https://perma.cc/N7H9-S2R7).

29 Michael R. Solomon and Elnora Stuart, *Marketing: Real People, Real Choices* (Englewood Cliffs, NJ: Prentice Hall, 1991). This text is now in its 11th edition.

30 Jimit Bagadiya, "309 Social Media Statistics You Should Know in 2020," *Social Pilot*, 2020, https://www.socialpilot.co/blog/social-media-statistics#fb-usage-stats (archived at https://perma.cc/P3H3-WQUS).

31 Bob Greene, "Late-Night Gadget Use Damages Your Sleep Cycle," *Mashable*, November 19, 2012 http://mashable.com/2012/11/19/gadgets-sleep/ (archived at https://perma.cc/A959-E4VR).

32 Robert Putnam, *Bowling Alone: The Collapse and Revival of American Community* (New York: Touchstone Books, 2001).

33 Leslie Walker, "What Is Social Networking Addiction?" *Lifewire*, December 16, 2019, https://www.lifewire.com/what-is-social-networking-addiction-2655246 (archived at https://perma.cc/75ZH-ABVT).

34 Michael Sullivan, "Hooked on the Internet, South Korean Teens Go into Digital Detox," NPR, August 13, 2019, https://www.npr.org/2019/08/13/748299817/hooked-on-the-internet-south-korean-teens-go-into-digital-detox (archived at https://perma.cc/XC6C-ERGD).

35 "The Human Brain Is Loaded Daily with 34 GB of Information," *Tech 21 Century*, http://www.tech21century.com/the-human-brain-is-loaded-daily-with-34-gb-of-information/ (archived at https://perma.cc/34FG-4SKP).

36 Jennifer Lai, "Information Wants to be Free… and Expensive," *Forbes*, July 20, 2009, http://fortune.com/2009/07/20/information-wants-to-be-free-and-expensive/ (archived at https://perma.cc/4MQU-3W6X).

37 Nikhil Ravindran, "100+ MLM Statistics You Need to Know in 2019!" July 8, 2019, https://www.epixelmlmsoftware.com/blog/100-mlm-statistics-2019 (archived at https://perma.cc/6F7V-G8FM).

38 Bailey Aldridge, "Hazard Pay? Stores Staying Open Amid Coronavirus Outbreak Increase Pay for Employees," *Miami Herald*, March 23, 2020, https://www.miamiherald.com/news/coronavirus/article241431236.html (archived at https://perma.cc/3WQZ-887J).

39 Paul M. Hirsch, "Processing Fads and Fashions: An Organizational Set Analysis of Cultural Industry Systems," *American Journal of Sociology* 77, no. 4 (1972): 639–59; Russell Lynes, *The Tastemakers* (New York: Harper & Brothers, 1954); Michael Solomon, "The Missing Link: Surrogate Consumers in the Marketing Chain," *Journal of Marketing* 50 (October 1986): 208–19.

40 https://wearetravelgirls.com/ (archived at https://perma.cc/W4J3-GG6D).

41 Stuart M. Butler, "How Google and Coursera May Upend the Traditional College Degree," *Brookings*, October 23, 2015. https://www.brookings.edu/blog/techtank/2015/02/23/how-google-and-coursera-may-upend-the-traditional-college-degree/ (archived at https://perma.cc/CZ75-FX2H).

42 Paul Sawers, "Udemy: Online Course Enrollment Surged 425% Amid Lockdowns," *Venture Beat*, April 30, 2020, https://venturebeat.com/2020/04/30/udemy-online-course-enrollment-surged-425-amid-lockdowns/ (archived at https://perma.cc/65WV-AHJ8).

43 Quoted in E. J. Schultz, "How 'Crash the Super Bowl' Changed Advertising," *Advertising Age*, January 4, 2016, http://adage.com/article/special-report-super-bowl/crash-super-bowl-changed-advertising/301966/ (archived at https://perma.cc/UPB6-2TFH).

04

Consumers who defy
the bricks vs. clicks debate

Almost as soon as the world decided the internet wasn't just a fad, marketers began to explore this tantalizing new domain. Most proceeded with caution. This was wise, considering the limited capabilities back in the day when we still had to dial in to secure a cranky modem connection (my students can't grasp that idea). At that time internet marketing meant you were cool enough to have your own domain name.

As the Web got faster, access grew much broader to encompass billions of people worldwide, and—most importantly—it's now a two-way interchange where we can interact with companies. But as online purchasing began to take off, many retailers fretted that physical stores would soon be consigned to museums. The discussion evolved from determining *whether* a store should branch into e-commerce, to *how much* time and money to devote to e-commerce versus bricks-and-mortar, to *whether* e-commerce activity would cannibalize bricks-and-mortar sales.

And today (especially after the pandemic further disrupted shopping habits) for some the debate has come full circle: should we even bother to have an offline presence? More recently we've seen the emergence of many pure play retailers that don't maintain any physical storefronts, such as ASOS, Warby Parker, Birchbox, Zalando (in Germany), eBay, and many others. But even in some of these cases (such as Warby Parker and Birchbox) the pure players are dipping a toe into the waters as they experiment with physical stores. Even the behemoth pure player Amazon is playing around with bricks-and-mortar formats.

The always-on digital native

This bricks vs. clicks debate will no doubt continue, but it's based on a false dichotomy. The reason is that today's chameleon consumer stopped making the distinction between offline and online years ago.

Starting in the primitive days when it took a fair amount of effort and a ton of patience to secure that noisy modem connection and then wait minutes for a screen to load, online pioneers (that's any of us over the age of 30 or so) made the conscious decision to "go online." Some of us intrepid souls went online and offline (often involuntarily when we lost the connection) numerous times in a day. But no matter how often we attempted this perilous journey, we were always aware of our condition: we were either offline or online.

That's no longer the case.

This revelation came to me because I'm a frustrated grandparent. My three lovely little granddaughters live in LA, while we live in Philadelphia. That makes regular visits to spoil them a bit difficult. However, my wife and I often "FaceTime," so they are quite used to seeing us onscreen. That's certainly a different experience from the disembodied voice I heard over the phone every now and then, when I was growing up far away from my own grandparents.

On one occasion as I was on one of these video calls (a technology that was first unveiled at the 1964 World's Fair, by the way), it came to me. I realized that the kids had always had access to the ability to see us on a screen. To them there was nothing particularly gee-whiz about it. Sometimes they saw my wife and me on a screen and other times face-to-face. No big deal.

Today's Digital Natives seamlessly cross the boundaries between offline and online, pretty much all day and all night. Often, they inhabit both spaces at once; they multitask while they watch TV, post on Facebook, listen to streaming music, and occasionally even do their homework. They don't regard their physical and digital personas as separate identities. In a 2019 survey, roughly half of 18- to 29-year-olds (48 percent) said they go online almost constantly, and 46 percent go online multiple times per day. That percentage rose nine points from just the year before, so you can see where we're heading.[1]

The rest of us still log a respectable amount of time—the average adult devotes almost two hours to social media every day, which translates to a total of five years and four months spent over a lifetime. For what it's worth, you can fly to the moon and back 32 times in the same time, or, if you prefer, walk your dog about 93,000 times (probably while you listen to XM Radio on your smartphone).

We still put in more time in front of the television (an average of seven years and eight months watching TV in a lifetime), but given current trajectories it won't be long before social media overtakes television (especially as more cord cutters actually consume their TV content on mobile devices).[2] And, these figures don't include the time we spend on e-commerce sites, Wikipedia, or other informational or transactional websites.

From brick vs. clicks to bricks and clicks

But, enough about my grandchildren (unless you want to see some pictures?). What does this minor revelation tell us about decisions to invest in a bricks-and-mortar strategy and/or a clicks strategy? After all, even before the pandemic rocked our world, we heard a lot of talk about the so-called retail apocalypse that would lead to widespread shuttering of many familiar store chains and shopping malls. The virus was indeed the proverbial straw that broke the back of many venerable retailers that were teetering anyway. As we slowly recover, it remains to be seen whether shoppers will double down on their online buying habits or instead flock back into the surviving stores, masks and all.

I don't believe that physical retailing is dead, even though certainly won't look the same as it did pre-pandemic. But this is not a new story. For decades we've taught our students about the so-called "wheel of retailing," which shows that merchandising formats evolve over time and new ones displace older ones. Department stores replaced general stores. Off-price stores diminished the clout of department stores. Category killers wiped out a lot of specialty stores. Kiosks and pop-up stores contributed to the carnage. It's evolution with sales tags instead of dinosaur fossils.

There will always be a role for stores because of the added value they can provide—although our definition of what constitutes a store may change. At least in the near future, the shopping experience people get at M&M World, the American Girl Store, or at an REI climbing wall can't be totally replicated online.

Shopping satisfies a multitude of needs, including socialization and tactile stimulation. Younger shoppers actually prefer shopping in stores versus digitally by a wide margin (even though they may eventually order the merchandise online).[3] Indeed, I envision that physical shopping for nonessentials will become more of a luxury experience. Most consumers won't be able to afford to retain the services of salespeople who have transformed into higher-paid shopping consultants that wait on customers by appointment at the stores still left standing.

But my point here makes that beside the point. The new hybrid chameleon consumer renders the bricks-and-mortar vs. e-commerce debate obsolete. It no longer makes sense to draw a line between offline and online shopping (or dating, learning, and many other activities). Simply put, most of us no longer "go" online. We are online all day and sometimes all night, just as we are offline for much of the same time. That means the shopping experience has to become a hybrid one that *combines* physical and digital experiences.

A traditional storefront business needs to provide an environment that Digital Natives expect. This means integrating digital technology into store aisles, such as touchscreens, beacons, and perhaps even holographic salespeople. Certainly, a lot of retailers today recognize the importance of a multichannel strategy that allows their customers to purchase what they sell in multiple formats such as in-store, online, by phone, etc.[4]

However, with a few notable exceptions, they don't tend to apply this logic to the shopping experience as well. Their fulfillment operations are planted firmly in the twenty-first century, while their merchandising processes may be stuck in the nineteenth century.

The ability to seamlessly transition back and forth, back and forth, between the physical and digital worlds is a hallmark of today's technological environment. Just ask any professor who tries to deliver in-class lectures as his students listen with one ear while they check their social media posts—or for that matter all those people who were introduced to the wonders of Zoom and Google Hangouts when in quarantine.

The tech company Intel refers to these digital expansions of our literal, physical existence as connected visual computing. I simply view it as a challenge to see what I can possibly do to get my students to look up from their devices. Tap dancing and serving free beer have been considered.

Instead of thinking about offline/online as an either/or dichotomy, let's get with the program and paint a more realistic picture: visualize a consumer who spends a typical day moving in and out of these environments—and often existing simultaneously within them. Then our job is to better understand what these consumer experiences look like, and to think carefully about how to deploy our resources to be sure our brand is adequately represented *wherever* our customer happens to be at any given time.

Marketers who want to speak to young people in particular need to be "reality agnostic"; they have to follow these consumers as they move back and forth between physical and digital identities many times during the day. This means being sure you project a consistent presence across all platforms and that you integrate these experiences. For example, Nordstrom ran a promotion in its shoe departments: employees tagged the merchandise that received the most pins on Pinterest.[5]

If we can adjust our thinking a bit, we'll be following the lead of some of the most successful digital companies on the planet. Three fairly recent strategic acquisitions make it look pretty obvious how these organizations think about the future:

- Minecraft is a hugely popular Swedish online gaming site. Microsoft paid $2.5 billion for it.

- Twitch is a live video game streaming site with more than 55 million users that's like a YouTube for video games. Amazon paid $970 million for it (in cash, thank you very much).

- Oculus VR is a startup that makes virtual reality headsets. Facebook shelled out $2 billion for the company.

In addition to rocking the worlds of some very happy entrepreneurs with these huge paydays, these purchases provide a strong hint of how our worlds as consumers are going to change as well. Each deal indicates how these companies plan to expand and transform our connections to digital environments as they add rich new visual interfaces.

The multichannel chameleon is ready to go. Are you?

Reaching the online/offline consumer in digital environments

If you recognize that your customers are just as—or more—likely to be checking you out online as they are offline, you're off to a good start. But it's just not that simple. The fact is, they think about themselves and act differently when they're focusing more on their real-world or digital identities. For example, an introverted shopper in the physical world may morph into a risk-taker when she cruises around online. She may even "hide" behind different identities that even her closest "meat world" friends don't know about. That's why it is important to develop those personas we've been talking about that take these multiple "realities" into account.

Your consumer has a unique online identity

Our wired world takes the process of strategic self-presentation to a new level.[6] We may still need a trained surgeon to reshape a troublesome nose, but we can undertake other makeovers on our own. This is especially true when it comes to the identity we express on digital platforms.

The digital self is a crucial concept for marketers to understand, even though it might seem like a strange one. As the number of hours we spend in our online worlds continues to escalate, so too do our online identities become more central to how we think about ourselves.

We know from a multitude of studies spanning decades that the way we feel about ourselves and the ways we choose to present ourselves to others (a process sociologists call "impression management") exerts a massive impact on what we buy or avoid. Now, whether a person frets about just the right photo to use as a Facebook profile photo while another carefully chooses a digital avatar to represent them when they interact with others online, those decisions and their ramifications follow us into online territories.

In the old days, a woman might get a "makeover" at a department store, or perhaps sit for a Glamour Shots photo session that temporarily transformed her into a beauty queen. The late Hugh Hefner owed a big chunk of his fortune to the abilities of his staff, who photographed *Playboy*'s centerfolds beginning with Marilyn Monroe in the 1950s. These airbrushed women literally *do not exist*, at least as they appear in the magazine.

As I conducted several research studies at major fashion modeling agencies in Manhattan, I was often struck by the appearance of the various "supermodels" I would encounter in the hallways. Attractive women, to be sure—but nothing close to what they looked like after a photo shoot had gone into "post-production."

Today, techie teenagers can effortlessly produce the same before/after results with Photoshop or even Snapchat filters. Such transformations are possible because we have access to online "post-production" tools that give us the ability to create our *own* makeovers.

These free or inexpensive applications allow virtually anyone to dramatically alter their digital self at will. We carefully "modify" the profile photos we post on Facebook or the descriptions we share on online dating sites. Retailers can help us along on the path of self-delusion as well—sometimes it's as simple as adding a slight curvature to a dressing room mirror to make the reflected image look thinner.[7]

New virtual makeover technologies make it even easier for each of us to involve the digital self as we choose products to adorn our physical selves. These platforms allow the shopper to superimpose images on their faces or bodies. Then they can quickly and easily see how products would alter their appearance, without taking the risk of actually buying the item first. The online glasses merchant Warby Parker allows consumers to upload a picture of themselves and try on frames virtually. Other apps such as Perfect365 and Facetune let you touch up your photo so you can remove a pimple, a wrinkle, or even a few pounds before you post it on Instagram or Facebook for others to admire. Companies including Sephora and Mary Kay provide simulators that allow women to see how their brands will look on their faces before they buy.[8]

Your customers are online—playing games

Who knows? Maybe the mild-mannered customer or employee you know as Emma or Bob is, at this very moment, playing the character of Banshee or Renegade in the popular *Fortnite* video game or a High Prophet in *Halo*. There's a lot of "normal" people out there who love to search for alien artifacts or shoot orcs in their spare time (or when they're at work, but that's a story for a later chapter).

By one estimate there are more than two billion (yes, billion) video game players worldwide. While Asia is the epicenter of gaming, here in the United States we are pretty well represented. In fact, in about six in ten US households at least one person plays these games at least three hours per week. And, throw out that tired stereotype of the gamer as a complexion-challenged teenage boy huddled in the basement surrounded by a pile of old pizza boxes.

The average game player is 35 years old, and about one quarter are over 50.

It also may come as a surprise that about 40 percent of these players are female.[9] That explains why mainstream brands including Dunkin' Donuts, Mercedes-Benz, Pillsbury, and Huggies actively advertise on these platforms. Marketers like to reach people in these environments, because they feel consumers are more relaxed, happier, and less stressed out when they play mobile games than while they do any other activity on mobile devices.[10] Next to social networking, game play is the most popular reason that consumers use their phones—they average 537 minutes per month in play.

Some traditionalists may view video gaming as antisocial. Perhaps this is because players seem to "get lost" in their own worlds, or because some of the games challenge participants to brutally kill as many "bad guys" as they can. However, the reality is that online gaming is very much a social activity. Games are interactive and typically involve multiple players (sometimes hundreds or even thousands!). There are defined rules of engagement and a community of enthusiasts that encourage one another to keep playing (which helps to explain why revenues from social games are expected to top $196 billion by 2022).[11]

Role-playing games (RPGs) are the epitome of digital social interaction. Whether *Dungeons and Dragons*, *World of Warcraft*, *League of Legends*, or many others, these games propel players into a fantasy world where each takes on a specific role. And many of these games boast literally millions of players worldwide, earning them the unwieldy label MMORPG—Massive Multiplayer Online Role-Playing Games.

That doesn't count the burgeoning e-sports industry, where rapt spectators watch *other people* play competitive video games, often in large stadiums. The fascination with viewing a bunch of gamers manipulate digital warriors on huge screens escapes me personally, but clearly it's seducing a lot of aficionados: revenue for e-sports teams from marketing spends in 2020 is projected at $465 million, and the global audience for e-sports is about $385 million and climbing.[12] Almost overnight, "geeks" with sharp minds and nimble fingers are turning into sports idols, complete with groupies and lucrative endorsement deals.

To many marketers the idea of integrating their brands with the stories that games tell is still a well-kept secret. Others, including Axe, Mini Cooper, and Burger King, have figured it out: they create game narratives that immerse players in the action. Online travel site Orbitz offers playable banner games that result in the highest click-through rate of any kind of advertising they do. In the video game *Crazy Taxi*, you can pull into a KFC for a quick bucket. A version of the popular game *Doom*, known as *Chex Quest*, dialed down the violence level but increased sales of Chex cereal by over 200 percent. The characters in *Mario Kart 8* drive Mercedes cars.[13]

The future is bright for advergaming, where online games merge with interactive advertisements that let companies target specific types of consumers. These placements can be short exposures such as a billboard that appears around a racetrack, or they can take the form of branded entertainment and integrate the brand directly into the action. The mushrooming popularity of user-generated videos on YouTube and other sites creates a growing market to link ads to these sources as well. This strategy is growing so rapidly that there's even a (trademarked) term for it: Plinking™ is the act of embedding a product or service link in a video.

Why is this new medium so hot?[14]

- Compared to a 30-second TV spot, advertisers can get viewers' attention for a much longer time. Players spend an average of five to seven minutes on an advergaming site.

- Physiological measures confirm that players are highly focused and stimulated when they play a game.

- Marketers can tailor the nature of the game and the products in it to the profiles of different users. They can direct strategy games to upscale, educated users, while they gear action games to younger users.

- The format gives advertisers great flexibility because game makers now ship PC video games with blank spaces in them to insert virtual ads. This allows advertisers to change messages on the fly and pay only for the number of game players that actually see them. Sony Corporation now allows clients to directly insert online ads into PlayStation 3 video games; the in-game ads change over time through a user's internet connection.

- There's great potential to track usage and conduct marketing research. For example, an inaudible audio signal coded into Activision's *Tony Hawk's Underground 2* skating game on PCs alerts a Nielsen monitoring system each time the test game players view Jeep product placements within the game.

Your customers are in virtual worlds

In 2009, director James Cameron's hit movie *Avatar* popularized the idea of humans who could take on the appearance of another life form and exist in a different world (in this case, a 10-foot-tall blue humanoid who lives on the planet Pandora). *Avatar* is a Hindu word that means a manifestation of a deity or released soul in bodily form on earth, but in the computing world it refers to a digital representation of a person.

Well before the movie's release, it turns out that millions of people around the world were already creating avatars and spending countless hours in alternative worlds right here on Earth. Indeed, way back in 2006, *Business Week* ran a cover story about so-called virtual worlds like *Second Life*. The article highlighted the amount of real money players were making as they bought and sold virtual items to dress their avatars and furnish their digital residences. *Second Life* generated $500 million in that year alone, and many major marketing organizations including Apple, H&R Block, and Reebok set up advertising or retailing operations in this virtual world.[15]

WELCOME TO THE METAVERSE
Fast forward to today. Literally millions of people interact in digital environments. Their experiences dissolve the false dichotomy of

reality vs. fantasy. Current and emerging technologies allow many of your customers to live their "unrealities," as they role-play other identities, no matter how much these may diverge from their physical characteristics (that's why they call them fantasies).

Some of your customers may just dabble with new (or "edited" identities), like people who just happen to post a 20-year-old photo of themselves on a dating site. But others take on identities you can only start to imagine. That shy 50-year-old woman may stroll around a virtual world in the form of a buxom starlet. The teenage boy who wrestles with the challenges of puberty in the real world may look a lot like her as well (it's common for teens to experiment with their online sexual identities by taking on the form of the opposite gender in a virtual environment). A man in his thirties may look like a fearsome dragon. The possibilities are virtually endless. But these permutations are important for you to understand if you are going to devise goods or services that will attract them.

Welcome to the metaverse.

Way back in 1999, *The Matrix* captivated our imaginations. The movie depicted a future where most humans live in a simulated reality created by intelligent machines. Today, as artificial intelligence (AI) applications like IBM's Watson become more sophisticated, the notion that machines will soon run our lives isn't so far-fetched.

This pioneering movie (trilogy, actually) didn't invent the scenario of people who inhabit a digital environment apart from their corporeal bodies. That honor goes to the sci-fi author Neal Stephenson, who developed the metaverse concept in his seminal 1992 novel *Snow Crash*. He conceived this as a collective virtual space inhabited by our digital doppelgängers. Essentially, it's a vision of the future internet on steroids, where we interact with our "friends" as avatars and live parallel lives in cyberspace. In Stephenson's initial vision, a humble pizza delivery boy in the "meat world" transforms into a sword-wielding hero when he enters the metaverse.

The allure of virtual worlds such as *Second Life*, *Kaneva*, *Whyville*, *Habbo*, and others has faded, especially as new virtual reality technologies begin to surface (more on this shortly). However, even today many popular virtual worlds especially targeted to kids and tweens abound, such as *Poptropica, Toontown*, and *Bin Weevils*. Linden Labs, the creator of *Second Life*, launched its new *Sansar* platform in 2017 to enable developers to create and monetize their own virtual worlds.[16]

Virtual worlds still hold promise as platforms to facilitate marketing activities as diverse as enterprise training, new product development, trade shows, advertising, and shopping. They are a scalable way to encourage employees and consumers to interact in a nonthreatening environment on a global level. These immersive environments are an ideal, low-cost testing ground for new styles and product modifications. Many thousands of consumers post their own product designs virtually; these represent an invaluable source of marketing intelligence if you know where to look.

Examples of harnessing the power of virtual worlds abound, but I'll just share just one here. The screenshot in Figure 4.1 is taken from a virtual world my colleagues and I created for Avon's younger Mark brand. The company has thousands of distributors who have very limited opportunities to interact with one another (unless they pay to attend the raucous annual convention). Sales leaders typically connect with these women online or on an impersonal monthly conference call that can include hundreds of participants.

As an alternative that would allow individual distributors to interact one-on-one with others in their region, we built a virtual meeting venue—complete with Mark's real-world brand color palette. Each woman entered the room as an avatar. She could talk to other individuals and also watch an audiovisual presentation by Mark's people. Results were very encouraging, to say the least. Many participants told us they really appreciated the opportunity to make a more personal connection with their peers. The typical distributor is relatively young and usually a novice when it comes to selling or managing a business. It's a huge advantage to network with others who are in the same boat—kind of like a digital version of the Mastermind groups that are all the rage today.[17]

FIGURE 4.1   Our virtual distributor meeting venue for Avon's Mark brand

Too beautiful to be real?

The fashion and beauty industry is being pulled in two conflicting directions right now. On the one hand, there is the tsunami of "body positivity" that rebels against overly idealized images of Photoshopped models in favor of "real people" who model for companies like Aerie and Third Love, warts and all. We'll take a deeper dive on that important trend in a later chapter.

But on the other hand, we also see digitally created models who are even more perfect than a Photoshopped flesh-and-blood person. There is even a modeling agency that specializes in digital creations. Several companies like the Japanese AI firm DataGrid create models that are extremely realistic.[18] Because these systems can create virtually any face and body, they have the potential to cut costs enormously—but also to put a lot of models out of work.

The AI wave has already washed over the high-end fashion world. Balmain features a "Balmain Army" that includes CGI models Margot, Shudu, and Zhi who showcase the latest designs from its BBox line. The world's first digital supermodel, Shudu, has thousands of Instagram followers. And the model Miquela might be the most successful of all: In 2018 "she" collaborated with Prada for Milan Fashion Week, by posting 3D-generated GIFs of herself at the Milan show venue. And on the luxury firm's Instagram account, she gave followers a mini tour of the space. Miquela was featured in the pages of *V Magazine* wearing Balenciaga and Kenzo, and she's even released a record. *Time* named her one of the most influential people on the internet.[19]

Private vs. public: fair game online?

Believe it or not, there was a time when even the private lives of celebrities and public figures were sacrosanct. Whispered rumors may have spread about JFK's supposed dalliance with Marilyn Monroe and other women, but the news media dutifully ignored them. Fast forward to 1998, and we were spared no details about Bill Clinton's affair with Monica Lewinsky—down to the famous stained blue dress.[20]

So, now we take it for granted that celebs are fair game—and there's a live market in bootlegged sex tapes to prove it.[21] But more has changed. Now, it seems that not even ordinary citizens carry a reasonable expectation of privacy, that there is a barrier between what they do in their "off time" versus "on time."

Widespread access to reams of data by just about anyone who can game the system also highlights the steady crumbling of yet another barrier as our private lives become public. A country song used to proclaim, "no one knows what goes on behind closed doors." You can delete that one from your playlist.

Today there's some evidence that our "guardian angels" like Siri and Alexa vacuum up our "secret" behaviors and desires and send them back to HQ.[22]

Way back in 1999, the CEO of Sun Microsystems caused a stir when he told a group of reporters and analysts, "You have zero privacy anyway. Get over it."[23] Fast forward two decades, and it seems many of us have.

The traditional boundary between our private and public lives is eroding quickly. In some cases, the average person is unaware of just how much the government and data brokerage firms know about them. In others, we willingly supply this information as millions of us gleefully post selfies, Instagram photos, and intimate blogs that reveal many aspects of our private lives that used to be, well, private.

To be sure, we're not going down without a fight. Clearly concerns about the erosion of privacy are top-of-mind to many, even when they resign themselves to losing much of their own. The Pew Research Center reports that over 90 percent of Americans "agree" or "strongly agree" that people have lost control over their personal information. About the same proportion say they do not trust the government, social media platforms, or other external entities to safeguard their data.[24]

But at the same time, it seems that a steady erosion of this once formidable wall has conditioned a new generation of consumers to accept this as inevitable. Anecdotally, I can report that I routinely ask my students to talk about their concerns regarding online privacy. The most typical response I get goes something like this: "Anyone who goes on the internet knows that what they post isn't private. If you don't want others to know about you, get off of social media." Perhaps for a generation that introduced the practice of "sexting" where people send one another selfies of their private parts, this shouldn't surprise us.

The author Shoshana Zuboff describes our current condition as "surveillance capitalism." She observes, "This new market form declares that serving the genuine needs of people is less lucrative, and therefore less important, than selling predictions of their behavior." The tradeoff is simple, albeit tacit: we agree to give up the pretense that we have private lives that will remain private, and in exchange we benefit from convenience and connections with others.[25] Zuboff provides many examples of tech companies that buy access to our innermost thoughts and desires; for example, she notes a document Facebook sent to advertisers that claimed the platform could identify exactly when a young user would be receptive to a "confidence boost."

Reaching the online/offline consumer in physical environments

The Proteus Effect

As we spend more and more of our time in digital reality, it's inevitable that some of the things we do online will return with us when we transition back to offline mode. My colleague Jeremy Bailenson at Stanford refers to this as the Proteus Effect (Proteus was a shape-changing Greek god). Our experiences in virtual environments change the way we think and act after we return to our physical state.[26]

When people in a study observed an avatar that looked like them engaging in exercise, for example, they were more likely to boost their level of physical activity in the real world at a later point.[27] In another study, college males who entered the virtual world of *Second Life* as handsome avatars were more likely to act confidently and assertively when they encountered an attractive female student (a confederate of the experimenter) upon returning to their offline environment.[28]

The Proteus Effect holds some interesting ramifications for marketers. For one, it calls our attention to the idea that brand-related interactions in virtual worlds can shape the way we think about those products when we come back to our physical selves. Recalling our discussion of advergaming and the impact of marketing communications and product placement in video games, the same logic applies here. It may make sense to allocate part of a promotional budget to these virtual environments. After all, it's a lot cheaper to air a commercial in one of these interfaces than on a real-world broadcasting network.

A new world for the disabled

Consider this: disabled people are the largest minority market in the United States. One in five US adults lives with a disability that interferes with daily life. The Census Bureau reports that there are 54 million adults with disabilities who spend almost $200 billion annually, yet companies pay remarkably little attention to the unique needs of this vast group. Fully 11 million US adults have a condition that makes it difficult for them to leave home to shop, so they rely almost exclusively on catalogs and the internet to purchase products.

Many people have limited mobility and are unable to gain easy access to stores, entertainment venues, educational institutions, and other locations. Bodily limitations or disfigurements result in real or imagined stigmatization, so self-concept and interpersonal relationships may be problematic. People who rely on wheelchairs for mobility often encounter barriers when they try to enter stores, move around the aisles, or enter dressing rooms that are too narrow to accommodate a chair. Others have mental illnesses, such as excessive anxiety in public places.

The early evidence that our virtual encounters shape our "real world" self-concepts also holds promising therapeutic and marketing implications for specialized populations like this that are more difficult to reach in their corporeal states.

A virtual environment can be a life-changer for a disabled person, a veteran who suffers from PTSD, or anyone whose mobility is impaired in their offline world. Consider for example the potential to elevate the self-esteem and quality of life of the thousands of disabled people who currently patronize virtual worlds like *Second Life* at designated gathering spots.

When they take the form of an avatar that is able to walk, suddenly individuals who suffer from cerebral palsy and other debilitating conditions in their offline lives can easily talk, flirt, run, and even dance. Take advantage of virtual technologies that remove the walls keeping these people from interacting with other consumers and with companies. You'll improve a lot of lives, but also your bottom line.

Reaching the online/offline consumer using augmented reality

Imagine a flight attendant who knows what you want even before you hit that call light. Air New Zealand is issuing its crew headsets that allow them to see holograms alongside the physical world. When a flight attendant looks at a passenger, the headset displays personal details including their preferred meal and why they're travelling. The device can display a range of personal details, including how long it's been since the person had their last drink. The airline hopes that staff may even be able to detect a passenger's emotional state from cues including facial expressions or heart rate.[29] This is a novel application of augmented reality (AR).

The term augmented reality refers to media that superimpose one or more digital layers of data, images, or video over a physical object. Although I've been touting the benefits of AR to marketers for years (mostly to puzzled gazes), it's been a lot easier to make this point since the explosion of the Pokémon Go fad a few summers ago. Suddenly everyone seems to "get" how AR works when it relates to finding furry creatures that lurk in familiar places.

But you don't even have to know how to use your smartphone to launch a Poké Ball in order to grasp the power of AR: if you've seen that yellow line in an NFL game that shows the first down marker, you've also encountered AR in a simple form (hint: that line doesn't actually exist on the field). IKEA has been an early mover in this space; its AR-enabled catalogs allow shoppers to "see" how the store's items would actually look in a living space.[30]

Immersive digital environments present huge opportunities for organizations to create inexpensive, scalable venues that can bring together employees, suppliers, and customers. These platforms have the potential to transform education, enterprise training, trade shows, new product development, and customer insights. It's hard, for example, to oversell the promise of AR for a range of marketing applications. For one, think about your package as a true sales tool.

A mascara box can morph into a tutorial about how to apply the makeup. A pill bottle can bring up a physician who walks you through potentially harmful interactions with your other prescriptions. A box of linguini shows you how to use the contents to prepare the best scampi your family has ever tasted.

Over the next few years you'll experience AR through your smartphone or tablet. New apps like Google Goggles (for Android phones) and Layar (for Android and Apple devices) impose a layer of words and pictures on whatever you see in your phone's viewer. The Microsoft HoloLens technology used by Air New Zealand blends holograms with what you see in your physical space so that you can actually manipulate digital images. Thus, a user who wants to assemble a piece of furniture or fix a broken sink can actually "see" where each part connects to the next through their goggles.[31]

Augmented reality apps open new worlds of information—and have the potential to revolutionize marketing communications. Would you like to know more about the singer you saw on a CD cover? Or maybe who painted that cool mural in your local bar? How much did that house you were looking at last month actually sell for? Just point your smartphone at each and the information will be superimposed on your screen.[32] AR is about to be big business: the global augmented reality market size is projected to reach $3665 million by 2026, up from $849 million in 2019.[33]

Facebook CEO Mark Zuckerberg said that he thinks AR could replace anything in your life with a screen, including your TV. Even sooner than that, many tech experts think AR could one day replace your smartphone. After all, why carry a separate phone if your emails, texts, calls, and spreadsheets are projected straight into your field of view?[34]

Reaching the online/offline consumer using virtual reality

Virtual reality (VR) technology vividly demonstrates that the familiar dichotomy of "In Here vs. Out There" no longer applies. A VR application immerses the user in a completely simulated environment via a special headset—often as a 360-degree experience.

If you've never tried a VR application, do it! You'll immediately understand how the simulated world that Neo and his compatriots in *The Matrix* movies inhabited could be so realistic.

The revenue from the global VR market is projected to hit $26.89 billion by 2022.[35] Not surprisingly, the big initial successes are in the gaming industry, where the potential to transform the entire experience is both obvious and profound.[36] Shooting an orc on your screen is one thing; getting up close and personal with that same orc in a totally immersive environment is quite another.

The commercially available Oculus headset (that little startup Facebook bought) was just the first step in what promises to be an avalanche of consumer-oriented VR technology from major companies including Samsung, Sony, and Google.[37] The apparatus is still a bit clunky, but it's a good bet that before we know it Silicon Valley companies that smell the money will find ways to shrink the tech into our eyeglasses.

VR platforms hold a lot of promise for marketers as well as gamers. For example, one VR company created a virtual supermarket for Hershey to measure the impact of various in-store marketing tactics designed to encourage shoppers to throw bags of Kisses and other delights into their carts. Shoppers wore a VR headset and navigated the aisles of a virtual Walmart store. They reacted to different variations of Hershey's product displays that allowed the company to identify specific configurations that increased sales.[38]

VR brings to life both the mundane, such as the trade logistics company DP World's immersive tour of its facilities, and the glamorous, such as Topshop's virtual runway show.[39] And, it's likely that the pandemic's aftershocks will add fuel to the fire as VR provides another way for people who are stuck In Here to get Out There (or at least to feel as if they are).

Other companies are aggressively entering the VR space: In Australia, eBay launched a virtual Myer department store that allows shoppers to view thousands of products without leaving home. Amazon is exploring the idea of creating virtual stores to sell furniture and home appliances like refrigerators that shoppers are reluctant to buy over the internet sight unseen. This platform will allow customers to see how the item will look in their homes without the bother of having it delivered.[40]

VR is, for now, largely a solitary experience, where each user steps into an immersive world and interacts with software designed to take him on a perceptual ride. I experienced this literally when I had the opportunity to try a developer's version of the Oculus headset a few years ago: I suddenly found myself sitting in a pretty realistic roller coaster. The scary ride I took, all while sitting at a desk, clearly showed me the future of media experiences.

The band Queen created a 360-degree virtual reality music video remake of its 1975 hit "Bohemian Rhapsody." Innovators in the music industry see a VR future where bands could essentially jam in a sophisticated chat room with musicians from around the world. They could stream the performance so they wouldn't have to hire an expensive venue for concerts.[41]

This type of shared experience will move us into a new generation of VR—and closer to Stephenson's original vision of the metaverse. Already, MC Entertainment, the world's largest theater chain, has invested $20 million in a company called Dreamscape Immersive that plans to launch what it calls a "virtual-reality multiplex." Instead of showing movies, these venues will offer a variety of virtual reality experiences. Most importantly, its technology will allow up to six people to explore the same environment at once as they interact with the avatars of one another.[42] A baby step toward the metaverse!

The future of the online/offline consumer

Before we leave this important topic, let's briefly consider one dichotomy that still does make sense: AR vs. VR. People often confuse the two applications, but they are actually quite different. As the term "augmented" implies, AR is not a substitute for physical reality. An AR-enabled message instead adds a second layer of data onto the physical world. In contrast, VR does make the complete swap of physical reality for digital reality.

As sexy as VR sounds, I'm putting my money on AR to make a more meaningful—and immediate—impact on the way marketers connect with customers. At least until the tech industry figures out a way to compress that bulky VR headset into a wearable device, these applications are most effective when the consumer can access them in a fixed physical location (and we certainly don't want people wandering around the physical world while they're totally immersed in a fantasy world!).

In contrast, AR tech goes wherever you do; in fact, it usually sits in your smartphone just waiting to be activated. It's mind-boggling to imagine the ways that AR can change the way we experience marketing communications. Think for example of a simple pill bottle that turns into a video presentation about contraindications for the drug inside. Or, how about a book cover sitting in your local Barnes & Noble that transforms into an enticing depiction of one of the scenes nestled in the pages within?

No matter what vehicles you choose to transport you, the offline and online worlds have never been closer neighbors.

CHAPTER TAKEAWAYS

- Many people, especially younger ones, don't regard their physical and digital personas as separate identities.
- The new hybrid consumer renders the bricks-and-mortar vs. e-commerce debate obsolete.
- Consumers create identities and new product ideas when they are online.
- Retailers should envision a hybrid shopping experience where they integrate digital technologies into physical environments.
- Gaming is evolving into a significant social activity for people of all ages. Marketers have only scratched the surface of advergaming possibilities.
- E-sports is poised to take off as the next major sport activity—and as a marketing medium.

- A virtual environment can be a life-changer for a disabled person, a veteran who suffers from PTSD, or anyone whose mobility is impaired in their offline world.

- Augmented reality (AR) opens up staggering new marketing possibilities because it can turn a package, ad, or other static surface into a vibrant communications medium.

- Virtual reality (VR) provides a totally immersive experience that transports the user into an entirely separate 3D environment.

Endnotes

1 Adapted from Andrew Perrin and Madhu Kumar, "About Three-in-Ten U.S. Adults Say They Are 'Almost Constantly' Online," *Pew Research Center*, July 25, 2019, https://www.pewresearch.org/fact-tank/2019/07/25/americans-going-online-almost-constantly/ (archived at https://perma.cc/EAA7-K3MG).

2 Evan Asano, "How Much Time Do People Spend on Social Media?" *Social Media Today*, January 4, 2017, http://www.socialmediatoday.com/marketing/how-much-time-do-people-spend-social-media-infographic (archived at https://perma.cc/5WBR-PUP8).

3 Barbara Thau, "Five Signs That Stores (Not E-Commerce) Are the Future of Retail," *Forbes*, June 27, 2017, https://www.forbes.com/sites/barbarathau/2017/06/27/five-signs-that-stores-not-online-shopping-are-the-future-of-retail/#27d057f04641 (archived at https://perma.cc/A64M-TKJK).

4 Tracey Wallace, "Omni-Channel Retail Report: Generational Consumer Shopping Behavior Comes into Focus + Its Importance in Ecommerce," *Big Commerce*, https://www.bigcommerce.com/blog/omni-channel-retail/#why-us-consumers-shop-where-they-shop (archived at https://perma.cc/8SVZ-LSZZ).

5 John Cook, "Nordstrom Experiments with Pinterest, Showcasing Top 'Pinned' Items in 13 Stores," *Geek Wire*, July 2, 2013, https://www.geekwire.com/2013/nordstrom-experiments-pinterest-showcasing-top-pinned-items-13-stores/ (archived at https://perma.cc/82BK-FJ8P).

6   Adapted from Jagdish N. Sheth and Michael R. Solomon, "Extending the Extended Self in a Digital World," *Journal of Marketing Theory and Practice* 22, no. 2 (2014): 123–32; cf. also Russell W. Belk, "Extended Self in a Digital World," *Journal of Consumer Research* 40, no. 3 (2013): 477–500.

7   Gergana Ivanova, "Why Do Some Mirrors Make Me Look Skinnier than Others?" *The Sun*, February 16, 2017, https://www.thesun.co.uk/fabulous/2651730/why-do-some-mirrors-make-me-look-skinnier-than-others/ (archived at https://perma.cc/A386-VVDQ).

8   https://sephoravirtualartist.com/landing_5.0.php?country=US&lang=en&x=&skintone=&currentModel= (archived at https://perma.cc/8ATE-J4JR); https://www.marykay.co.uk/en-gb/tips-and-trends/makeover-and-beauty-tools/virtual-makeover (archived at https://perma.cc/69L5-JYDE); Hilary Stout, "Mirror, Mirror in the App: What's the Fairest Shade and Shadow of Them All?" *New York Times*, May 14, 2014, http://www.nytimes.com/2014/05/15/business/mirror-mirror-in-the-app-whats-the-fairest-shade-of-all.html?_r=0 (archived at https://perma.cc/UTQ8-7ZJP).

9   Joe Tenebruso, "21 Video Game Stats That Will Blow You Away," *The Motley Fool*, February 25, 2017, https://www.fool.com/investing/2017/02/25/21-video-game-stats-that-will-blow-you-away.aspx (archived at https://perma.cc/DV2Y-GKG3).

10   Susan Borst, "Forecast 2017: Brands to Take a Fresh Look at Game Advertising," *Interactive Advertising Bureau*, November 11, 2016, https://www.iab.com/news/forecast-2017-brands-take-fresh-look-game-advertising/ (archived at https://perma.cc/R6BG-8RDT).

11   Tracy Tuten and Michael R. Solomon, *Social Media Marketing*, 3rd ed. (London: SAGE, 2019); Tom Wijman, "The Global Games Market Will Generate $152.1 Billion in 2019 as the U.S. Overtakes China as the Biggest Market," *Newzoo*, June 18, 2019, https://newzoo.com/insights/articles/the-global-games-market-will-generate-152-1-billion-in-2019-as-the-u-s-overtakes-china-as-the-biggest-market/ (archived at https://perma.cc/A6RV-9UY2).

12   Simon Hattenstone, "The Rise of eSports: Are Addiction and Corruption the Price of Its Success?" *The Guardian*, June 16, 2017, https://www.theguardian.com/sport/2017/jun/16/top-addiction-young-people-gaming-esports (archived at https://perma.cc/QFN2-KDUJ).

13 Zachery Barton, "The Evolution of Advergames: Top 3 Examples of Marketing in Gaming," *Medium*, May 20, 2017, https://medium.com/@zbbarton0706/the-evolution-of-advergames-top-3-examples-of-marketing-in-gaming-3e688aad6884 (archived at https://perma.cc/HT86-KTC7).

14 Nick Wingfield, "Sony's PS3 to Get In-Game Ads," *Wall Street Journal*, June 4, 2008, B7; Jeffrey Bardzell, Shaowen Bardzell and Tyler Pace, "Player Engagement and In-Game Advertising," *t=zero*, November 23, 2008, https://www.academia.edu/2826794/Player_Engagement_and_In_Game_Advertising (archived at https://perma.cc/H94J-VHVF).

15 Natalie Wood, Michael Solomon, and David Allan, "Welcome to the Matrix: E-Learning Gets a Second Life," *Marketing Education Review* 18, no. 2 (2008): 1–7; Natalie Wood et al., "From Interactive to Immersive: Advertising Education Takes a Virtual Leap of Faith," *Journal of Advertising Education* 13, no. 1 (2009): 64–72.

16 Ben Lang, "'Sansar' Will Open to All in First Half of 2017 with a New Approach to Virtual Worlds," *Road to VR*, January 15, 2017, https://www.roadtovr.com/sansar-release-date-preview-virtual-reality-liden-lab/ (archived at https://perma.cc/L3DH-FZ4S).

17 "What Is a Mastermind Group? A Definition and Tutorials" [Blog] *The Success Alliance*, http://www.thesuccessalliance.com/what-is-a-mastermind-group/ (archived at https://perma.cc/M9JR-YT37).

18 Abhimanyu Ghosha, "This AI Generates Ultra-Realistic Fashion Models from Head to Toe," *The Next Web*, May 1, 2019, https://thenextweb.com/artificial-intelligence/2019/05/01/this-ai-generates-ultra-realistic-fashion-models-from-head-to-toe/ (archived at https://perma.cc/Y7R3-NNNW).

19 Jessica Davis, "How Artificial Intelligence Models Are Taking over Your Instagram Feed," *Harper's Bazaar*, August 31, 2008, https://www.harpersbazaar.com/uk/fashion/fashion-news/a22722480/how-artificial-intelligence-models-are-taking-over-your-instagram-feed/ (archived at https://perma.cc/3YTQ-QG68).

20 "Top 10 Mistresses," *Time*, http://content.time.com/time/specials/packages/article/0,28804,1908008_1908007_1907992,00.html (archived at https://perma.cc/M5W3-3LYS); John F. Harris, "'Washington Was About to Explode': The Clinton Scandal, 20 Years Later," *Politico*, January 21, 2018, https://www.politico.com/magazine/story/2018/01/21/clinton-lewinsky-scandal-20-years-later-me-too-216484

(archived at https://perma.cc/K97N-JVFF); https://famous-trials.com/
clinton/889-lewinskydress (archived at https://perma.cc/9CZQ-2DC4).

21   Mehera Bonner, "The Wild Stories of 20 Notorious Celebrity Sex
Tapes," *Marie Claire*, February 7, 2020, https://www.marieclaire.com/
celebrity/a13817385/celebrity-sex-tapes/ (archived at https://perma.cc/
5TS4-M494).

22   "Apple Contractors 'Regularly Hear Confidential Details' on Siri
Recordings," *The Guardian*, July 26, 2019, https://www.theguardian.
com/technology/2019/jul/26/apple-contractors-regularly-hear-
confidential-details-on-siri-recordings (archived at https://perma.cc/
RTW2-NWWY).

23   Polly Sprenger, "Sun on Privacy: 'Get over It,'" *Wired*, January 26,
1999, https://www.wired.com/1999/01/sun-on-privacy-get-over-it/
(archived at https://perma.cc/2VXK-4PJK).

24   Lee Rainie, "Americans' Complicated Feelings About Social Media
in an Era of Privacy Concerns," *Pew Research*, March 27, 2018,
https://www.pewresearch.org/fact-tank/2018/03/27/americans-
complicated-feelings-about-social-media-in-an-era-of-privacy-
concerns/ (archived at https://perma.cc/8MQC-VNF2).

25   Shoshana Zuboff, *The Age of Surveillance Capitalism: The Fight for
a Human Future at the New Frontier of Power* (New York: Public
Affairs, 2019); Jannifer Szalai, "OK Google, How Much Money Have
I Made for You Today?" *New York Times*, January 16, 2019,
https://www.nytimes.com/2019/01/16/books/review-age-of-
surveillance-capitalism-shoshana-zuboff.html (archived at
https://perma.cc/NZ9E-62GB).

26   Cf. for example Jesse Fox, Jeremy N. Bailenson, and Liz Tricase,
"The Embodiment of Sexualized Virtual Selves: The Proteus Effect
and Experiences of Self-Objectification via Avatars," *Computers in
Human Behavior* 29 (2013): 930–38.

27   Jesse Fox and Jeremy N. Bailenson, "Virtual Self-Modeling: The
Effects of Vicarious Reinforcement and Identification on Exercise
Behaviors," *Media Psychology* 12, no. 1 (2009): 1–25.

28   Paul R. Messinger et al., "On the Relationship Between My Avatar
and Myself," *Journal of Virtual Worlds Research* 1, no. 2 (November
2008): 1–17.

29   Daisy Dunne, "Could THIS Improve Inflight Customer Service? Airline
Tests 'Mixed Reality' Hololens Glasses to Attend to Passengers'
Needs," *Daily Mail*, May 25, 2017, http://www.dailymail.co.uk/

sciencetech/article-4540930/Flight-attendants-use-Microsoft-HoloLens-customers.html#ixzz4u6X2dKHr (archived at https://perma.cc/7M4D-4NPJ).

30 "IKEA Augmented Reality Catalogue," Digital Marketing Case Study—IKEA Augmented Reality Catalogue, Digital Training Academy, www.digitaltrainingacademy.com/casestudies/2014/11/ikea_augmented_reality_catalogue.php (archived at https://perma.cc/HN24-NF84).

31 http://www.microsoft.com/microsoft-hololens/en-us (archived at https://perma.cc/DQ7P-M8SK).

32 Gabriel Kahn, "Chinese Characters Are Gaining New Meaning as Corporate Logos," *Wall Street Journal Interactive Edition*, July 18, 2002.

33 "Augmented Reality (AR) Market Size Is Projected to Reach USD 3664.5 Million by 2026—Valuates Reports," *Cision PR Newswire*, July 20, 2020, https://www.prnewswire.com/news-releases/augmented-reality-ar-market-size-is-projected-to-reach-usd-3664-5-million-by-2026---valuates-reports-301096109.html#:~:text=%E2%97%8F%20Augmented%20and%20Virtual%20Reality,63.3%25%20from%202018%20to%202025 (archived at https://perma.cc/U9YR-KDDV).

34 Matt Weinberger, "Augmented Reality Is Already Changing the Way Big Companies Do Business," *Business Insider*, June 26, 2017, http://www.businessinsider.com/augmented-reality-in-the-enterprise-2017-6 (archived at https://perma.cc/FM5P-FKSV).

35 Zion Market Research "Virtual Reality Market Size Revenue to Surge to US\$ 26.89 Billion by 2022," *GlobeNewswire*, July 12, 2016, https://www.globenewswire.com/news-release/2019/07/12/1882002/0/en/Report-Virtual-Reality-VR-Market-Size-Revenue-To-Surge-To-US-26-89-Billion-by-2022.html (archived at https://perma.cc/TA7Y-D4LU).

36 Nadia Kovach, "Virtual Reality in Gaming," *Thinkmobiles*, thinkmobiles.com/blog/virtual-reality-gaming/ (archived at https://perma.cc/DK42-QGTF).

37 Andrew Rosenblum, "2015: The Year Virtual Reality Finally Reaches Living Rooms," *Popular Science*, January 12, 2015, http://www.popsci.com/virtual-reality-meets-its-public (archived at https://perma.cc/5H9R-RK2V).

38 Chuck Martin, "Hershey's Taps VR to Test In-Store Marketing," *Mediapost*, July 10, 2017, https://www.mediapost.com/publications/

article/304046/hersheys-taps-vr-to-test-in-store-marketing.html?utm_
source=newsletter&utm_medium=email&utm_content=
readnow&utm_campaign=104136&hashid=eVVwVNz5JMib0
Noa-eSr9QuVlK0 (archived at https://perma.cc/82PR-9BYK).

39 Braden Becker, "9 VR Marketing Examples That You'll Want to Steal
for 2020," *Hubspot*, September 19, 2018, https://blog.hubspot.com/
marketing/vr-marketing-examples (archived at https://perma.cc/
MQ4H-N8HD).

40 Deniz Ergürel, "Amazon Is Building Virtual and Augmented Reality
Stores," *Haptic.AL*, March 26, 2017, https://haptic.al/amazon-virtual-
store-33c420b5f921 (archived at https://perma.cc/42CK-ZSA7).

41 Nicola K. Smith, "How Virtual Reality Is Shaking Up the Music
Industry," *BBC News*, January 31, 2017, http://www.bbc.com/news/
business-38795190 (archived at https://perma.cc/U32N-MUNM).

42 Brooks Barnes, "Coming Soon to AMC Theaters: Virtual Reality
Experiences," *New York Times*, September 26, 2017,
https://www.nytimes.com/2017/09/26/business/media/amc-theaters-
virtual-reality.html (archived at https://perma.cc/V49Y-EZYX).

05

Consumers who defy
buyers vs. sellers

So, an Apple employee walks into a bar... No, it's not the opening to a bad joke. About a decade ago, an engineer had a few beers in a local bar and mistakenly left behind a disguised prototype of a new iPhone model. Apple scrambled to get it back. A year later, a similar incident occurred in a Mexican restaurant near Apple's California office.[1] The buzz about these rare slipups was intense. Apple is notoriously secretive about its products before they launch, so tech gossips treated these lapses as major scandals. Who needs the escapades of Brad Pitt and Angelina Jolie when you can check out a pirated Apple product still in development?

Apple's efforts to guard its trade secrets are probably a bit extreme, but most companies work pretty hard to keep outsiders away until a new product is absolutely, positively ready to enter the market.

Talk about a process! When a company decides to develop a new product, it often carefully follows a series of steps that start with ideation (idea generation), continue through several phases of concept development and analysis, and then (if it decides to launch) culminates in some test marketing and eventually commercialization.

All of this is done in a "cone of silence," as the organization does whatever it can to keep the idea under wraps until the very last minute. And occasionally these efforts get derailed by competitors if they smell an opportunity to meddle with the process. For years, the manufacturer of venerable Listerine wanted to introduce a mint-flavored version of its classic gold formulation to compete more directly with P&G's pleasant-tasting Scope (it originally introduced this alternative under the brand Listermint). Unfortunately, every time it tried to run a market test, P&G found out, and the rival poured substantial extra advertising and coupons for its Scope brand into the test market cities. This counterattack reduced the usefulness of the test market results for Listerine when its market planners tried to decide whether to introduce Listermint nationwide. Because P&G's aggressive response to Listermint's market tests actually *increased* Scope's market share in the test cities, there was no way to determine how well Listermint would actually do under normal competitive conditions.[2]

Other than divulging intelligence to the competition, there are other reasons that marketers like to keep things under wraps. One is obvious: they don't want a defective product launch to rain on the parade. And especially in the case of new tech products, this can be a reasonable fear. We only need to look back a few years to Samsung's marketing fiascos, when the company launched its Galaxy smartphone models that had a nasty tendency to catch fire, to understand why rival Apple might be spooked about pulling the trigger prematurely.[3]

But there's another reason that's not so obvious. In many industries, the simple truth is that designers and manufacturers prefer to trust their own guesses about what their customers want, rather than going to the trouble to ask them. None other than Apple's legendary founder Steve Jobs famously remarked:

Some people say, "Give the customers what they want." But that's not my approach. Our job is to figure out what they're going to want before they do. I think Henry Ford once said, "If I'd asked customers what they wanted, they would have told me, 'A faster horse!'" People don't know what they want until you show it to them. That's why I never rely on market research. Our task is to read things that are not yet on the page.[4]

Mr. Jobs seemed to confuse the understanding of attributes versus benefits when he made this remark. People in fact often *do* know the underlying benefits they want. They just may not be able to envision the specific new device that will provide those end results.

But more broadly, it's not just tech companies that sometimes suffer from this bias. Even organizations that sell products with a high stylistic or aesthetic component that end consumers buy to express parts of their identities may not collect a lot of input from their intended customers before they go to market. They choose to wait until consumers see what they create, and then vote with their dollars or euros for the company that most closely anticipated their desires.

A peek under the kimono:
use your consumers as co-creators

I discovered this tendency to "ready, shoot, aim" firsthand several decades ago. With the help of funding from the US Commerce Department, my colleague and I had developed one of the first online platforms that was able to put photos of products in front of customers on their home computers to solicit their reactions (this doesn't sound like a big deal today, but trust me it was in the early days of the internet).[5]

We were exhibiting our technology at a meeting that was attended by executives from several major textile manufacturers. One distinguished-looking gentleman stood in front of our booth for quite a while. He seemed transfixed by the images of models wearing different outfits that he saw on the screen. When he finally emerged from his reverie, he exclaimed to us that he could use this system to test consumers' reactions to carpet designs *before* they saw them in stores. It turns out he was in charge of product development at one of the largest manufacturers of carpets and other home products—and up until that time their "marketing research" consisted of recruiting a few people to walk on carpet samples to see how they felt.

We learned that this was pretty much the norm in the massive home furnishings industry, which at least at that time was dominated by a few family-owned firms that didn't feel the need to solicit input from customers at all. For what it's worth, this company became our first client. We went on to work with other apparel and interior design companies as they realized it actually made sense to ask people what they liked *before* they manufactured these products.

The logic is compelling: even if it's difficult to predict the winners, imagine the cost savings when you can identify some of the losers. To use a simple example, suppose that rather than going to market with ten new products or styles, you can weed out even three that your customers don't like very much. Now you can allocate your marketing budget to seven rather than ten contenders.

The "brainstorm" to involve your customers before you go to market seems like a no-brainer, and indeed today we see that many companies buy into this idea. Amazingly, many still don't. The reluctance to let outsiders see what's underneath the kimono is just too baked into their corporate DNA.

But it's really hard to close the cage that separates producers from consumers, once companies wake up to the value of involving their users in the process as early as possible. Ironically, much of the innovation here occurred in B2B contexts, where we might expect concerns about leaking new products to be even more intense.

Instead, some industrial marketers began to buy into the "lead user" approach first proposed by MIT professor Eric von Hippel in 1986. He observed that in industries like aerospace and chemicals it's often a company's biggest customers that discover unfulfilled needs well in advance. Indeed, a majority of new product ideas in industries like chemical products initially come from customers, rather than the companies that supply them.[6]

Finally, forward-looking companies in the B2C sector started to catch on to this idea as well. They understand that it makes a lot of sense to recruit their own customers as product designers. These crowdsourcing techniques can be intimidating to some designers; they fear their expertise will be supplanted by amateurs. But fortunately, many creatives also understand the value of obtaining detailed feedback from users *before* the product goes to market. For example, the founder of the *Into the Gloss* beauty website created an Instagram account before she launched. She used this platform to invite suggestions from thousands of cosmetics fans and then used them as a starting point to build her new company.[7]

Today, this is hardly an isolated occurrence. Consumers are climbing out of their cages and jumping into all sorts of roles they never touched before as the consumer-generated content (CGC) revolution spreads. Let's take a look at the most important ones.

How to engage with chameleons who produce as well as consume

LEGO is one of the leaders in the charge to crowdsource its product design process. The company started an online community it calls LEGO Ideas, which allows members to submit ideas for new LEGO sets and to vote on the concepts others contribute. If an idea earns 10,000 votes, LEGO develops it and sells it around the world. DeWalt runs a platform for over 10,000 people who use its tools and have ideas for new ones—they earn royalties if the company chooses their designs.[8]

These companies get it. But again, many don't. Even at the most basic level of verifying that what you say to customers is what you intend, we sometimes see even the big guys let down their guard. For example, a cardinal rule in marketing is to ensure that your branding matches the language your customers employ. That becomes even more crucial when an organization expands into other markets where customers speak other languages. There are many egregious (and often hilarious) examples of marketing campaigns that forgot this basic principle. Most likely they could have easily avoided their blunders simply by using the technique of back-translation, where a native speaker translates the adapted text back into the original language to be sure it syncs. But apparently, they didn't. Here are a few of my favorite missteps:[9]

- Audi calls its sporty electric car the Etron. Unfortunately, to a French speaker the word *étron* hardly connotes motoring sophistication. Instead, it translates as "excrement."

- Kraft Foods reorganized recently and renamed itself Mondelēz International. *Monde* is French for world, and *delez*, with a long e in the final syllable, is a play on delish. However, to Russians the word sounds like a term for oral sex.

- The Scandinavian company that makes Electrolux vacuum cleaners sold them in the United States with this slogan: "Nothing sucks like an Electrolux."

Use consumer-generated content to develop new products

More and more innovators have decided it's actually a good idea to hand the inmates the keys to the asylum. Another early innovator that sparked a lot of crowdsourcing—especially in the apparel industry—is Threadless, a company that makes graphic t-shirts. On its online platform, aspiring designers submit ideas for new shirts and the community votes on the ones they will buy. Because Threadless only makes the t-shirts that people say they intend to buy, this virtually assures that inventory will always sell out. Other co-creation platforms have since jumped in, including Ssense, Krush, and thousands of individual fashion accounts on Instagram.[10]

The new supremacy of design means that the battle for consumers' hearts, minds, and wallets won't be won in R&D labs (sorry). Sure, shoppers love new gadgets and there's always room for innovation. However, the sad truth is that for the most part consumers don't see that much difference among competing brands—unless they're loyal followers of a cult brand like Apple, Nike, or the Boston Red Sox.

That's why a lot of companies are waking up to the urgent need to design *with* rather than *for* their customers. When you include the users in the creation process, it's easier to bake in elements that will engage them.

Use design thinking to improve customer experience

Empathy. Customer-centric marketing. CX. The service encounter. Customer journeys. No matter what you call it, it's no longer enough to phone it in by conducting a few focus groups in order to guess at what will resonate with buyers. The market moves too fast and product cycles have accelerated too dramatically to afford this luxury. Again, mass-market segmentation no longer makes much sense in a micro-targeted world.

A revolution called Design Thinking is afoot. The fundamental building blocks of this trending philosophy are EDIT: empathize, define, ideate, and test. You can't walk down this road without immersing yourself in your customer's perspective. So, empathy is the first big step. How can organizations truly understand the lived experiences of their customers so they can design new products and services that will resonate with them?

As I suggested early on, one very valuable way to accomplish this is to fish where the fish are: immerse yourself in the worlds in which your customers live, not the ones where you *think* they live. And give them ample opportunities to suggest changes or even a sandbox where they can play around with their own fantasies of what your products should look like or do.

For example, back in the heyday of the virtual world *Second Life* that we discussed in the last chapter, Starwood's aloft Hotels division opened a virtual version of the prototype design to get feedback from the avatar visitors who stopped by. The new chain actually incorporated several changes into the bricks-and-mortar hotels based on feedback from digital guests who hung out in the lobby or checked out the guest rooms. These tweaks included adding radios in the guest room showers, providing additional seating in the lobby, and incorporating artwork created by local artists on the walls in the public areas.[11]

And, despite fears that customers will revolt if they think a company has turned its design process into amateur hour, it turns out that they actually think better of the organization when it listens to its customers. A German company called Red Chili that sells gear for rock climbers gets it. It proclaims in its advertising, "Only climbers know what climbers need."[12] Indeed, one study found that when a company labels its products as "crowdsourced," sales increase by up to 20 percent.[13]

Use crowdsourcing: "None of us is as smart as all of us"

Way back in 2004, James Surowiecki's book *The Wisdom of Crowds* publicized the concept of crowdsourcing.[14] He documented numerous examples where groups of people made better estimates of an outcome than did individuals.

Even Surowiecki admitted that this technique doesn't always work; he identified certain conditions that were required to make the magic happen. For one, the crowd needs to include people with diverse opinions to avoid a "groupthink" mentality. Nonetheless, the crowdsourcing model has been shown to work in a mix of applications that include political forecasting, Hollywood movies (the Hollywood Stock Exchange), and pharmaceutical products.

A crowdsourcing forum is sometimes called a prediction market. Players are drawn from the industry, so they are knowledgeable about the dynamics that make a success or failure. And, it's important to note that they are discouraged from making "safe" or politically correct choices (i.e., the ones their bosses want to hear) because they earn rewards when they guess an outcome correctly.[15]

For example, several pharma companies including Eli Lilly and Hewlett-Packard have tested prediction markets for their employees. Their "traders" place bets on what they think will happen regarding future sales, the success of new products, or how other firms in a distribution channel will behave. Then they receive a cash reward if their "stock picks" pan out. Eli Lilly routinely places multimillion-dollar bets on drug candidates that face overwhelming odds of failure. The relatively few new compounds that do succeed have to make enough money to cover the losses incurred by the others. Obviously, the company will benefit if it can separate the winners from the losers earlier in the process—just as we did with carpet and apparel designs. In one experiment that Lilly ran with about 50 of its employees involved in drug development, including chemists, biologists, and project managers, the traders correctly predicted which candidates out of a set of potential drug products would go on to succeed in the market.[16]

Crowdsourcing for advertising and PR

Just as consumer chameleons love to be a part of what they buy, they also want a say in the messages they see, read, and hear about those products and services. Indeed, a *Harvard Business Review* article in 2013 proclaimed, "The End of Traditional Ad Agencies."[17] Well, that obit for an entire industry was probably a bit premature, but it's hard to ignore how the cage that separates professional advertising creatives and creative amateurs is opening.

In reality, you won't find the real action on Madison Avenue. Ad agencies are still alive and well, thank you. But that hasn't stopped huge numbers of amateurs from creating their own product-related content that they share online. A majority of adult internet users say they regularly create and share photos and videos.[18] Sure, some of it is just the latest funny cat spot on Tik Tok, but a big chunk of these gems directly reference actual brands—for better or worse.

Why do the rest of us pay attention? Maybe because almost no one trusts traditional ads anymore. In one survey of 4,500 active social media users in the US and Europe, a paltry 6 percent of respondents said they have faith in what ads show them, and at the same time over three-quarters said they would rather look at user-generated images than the ones they see in professional executions. What's more, they trust photos that feature "real people" *seven times* more than the pictures they see in traditional advertising. Furthermore, over half of the respondents said they are more likely to click on an ad that features a user-generated photo, and the same amount are more inclined to buy the product after they see this kind of ad.[19]

Top brands are taking note of the many consumers who enthusiastically recommend their favorite products on social media. Many now use branded hashtags to increase visibility and engagement.

Following NYX's #NYXCosmetics campaign, for instance, the company found that customers who interact with UGC have a 93 percent higher average order value and convert to customers at a rate 320 percent higher than those who do not.[20]

As noted earlier, Andy Warhol famously predicted that "In the future, everyone will be world-famous for 15 minutes."[21] Today, it seems more like 15 seconds is accurate.

Consider the legions of everyday folks who turn themselves into online celebrities when their commentary and advice about products goes viral. While the messages are impactful, the messengers are expendable. In the vast majority of cases fame is fleeting, to put it mildly. The spotlight may shine on a self-made celeb for hours, days, weeks, or months when they achieve the microfame that bloggers like Perez Hilton and the singer Tila Tequila found. They are the lucky ones: some analysts propose that microfame has morphed into nanofame, as the glare of the internet spotlight shines brighter and increasingly faster and we cycle through these celeb wannabees at dizzying speed. Here today, gone today.

There's little doubt that these consumers' verdicts about what is hot and what is not rule the day, even when compared to expensive endorsements from established stars companies pay (handsomely) to tout their goods and services. According to one study, nearly nine in ten consumers (84 percent) make purchases after they read about a product or service on a blog. Among consumers between the ages of 18 and 34, blogs ranked as the most important source of information to make buying decisions.[22]

Retailers vs. shoppers

As if traditional retailers didn't have enough problems after the pandemic, they also face mounting competition from their own customers who decide to jump into the game. Say goodbye to the cage that separates retailers and shoppers. Everyday folks are creating their own online stores by the thousands, as P2P (peer-to-peer) commerce grows by leaps and bounds. Consumers manage their own inventories and trade with one another in staggering numbers. One reason for this boom is the emerging P2P payments industry, where platforms including PayPal, Venmo, Square, and Zelle turn each of us into bankers.

eBay alone boasts over one billion live listings and 182 million active buyers.[23] Although eBay seems to have grown out of the homegrown "artisanal" character of its early days as many sellers adopt sophisticated marketing techniques, it's still a platform that allows anyone with used clothing (or memorabilia or just about anything else...), a shipping box, and a dream to become a retailer.

Established retailers will need to try radical solutions to deal with this encroachment. They may even want to consider an "if you can't beat 'em, join 'em" strategy by expanding the scope of their merchandise buying strategies to include individual artisans. Levi Strauss is doing this now. The company recruits indie designers into the fold via its Makers Project. It promotes makers like the Forestbound brand, which sells tote bags made out of salvaged military fabrics. Levi's sells the bags along with other unusual items at boutique stores with a Levi's Makers tag, along with branded videos that extol the independent spirit of the creators. As a Levi's designer observed, "For Levi's, the Makers program celebrates those who are still making things by hand while providing an outlet to tell their stories to inspire others."[24]

"Artisanal fries with that?" The quest for authenticity

Artisanal beer. Artisanal pizza. Artisanal pastry. After the pandemic, we'll probably even find artisanal toilet paper. The term is every-where. It implies that an item isn't mass-produced, and often the maker is a skilled artist who otherwise is "one of us" (i.e., they haven't sold out to a big corporation). The e-commerce site Etsy calls itself "the most beautiful marketplace in the world" and features thousands of unique creations sold by everyday people.

What's behind this quest for All Things Artisanal? I believe it reflects a burning desire for *authenticity*. Consumers are eager to learn about where the things they buy came from. That's why clothing catalogs like that of The J. Peterman Company provide stories about apparel items, and food stores like Whole Foods let us know which farms provided their produce and meat. I actually ate at a seafood restaurant that listed the name of the fisherman who caught each of the menu items! I refer to this thirst to trace the origins of a product as product genealogy.

Authenticity is now a key driver of purchase decisions in many categories, whether food, art, or fashion. Researchers claim that although authenticity can be a hard concept to pin down, it's generally composed of three attributes: heritage, sincerity, and commitment to quality.[25] Many companies like to tout their "authentic" story. New Balance describes its Maine factory like this: "Built in 1945, the Depot Street building is the workplace of almost 400 associates. Each pair of shoes they produce is a proud work of craftsmanship that carries a little bit of the long history that is the town and its people."[26]

The moral: if your company has a story to tell, tell it. Often.

THE MAKER MOVEMENT

Of course, there's nothing more authentic than something you make yourself, so it makes sense that we're seeing a boom in DIY products. The do-it-yourself market is expected to grow by 6 percent over the next few years.[27] The desire to make your own stuff creates a lot of opportunities for companies that find a way to encourage their customers to participate—and of course supply them with what they need to be successful.

The pandemic added fuel to the fire as millions of people fought cabin fever by taking on cooking, carpentry, and even hairstyling projects (the latter with mixed success). This ramped-up involvement that turns consumers into producers also links to the so-called Maker Movement, where people come together to create a collaborative workspace they call a makerspace. Now thousands of amateurs gather in converted facilities in schools, libraries, and other public places to learn about electronics, 3D modeling and printing, coding, and robotics, in addition to lower-tech skills like woodworking. And, some of these projects have even turned into successful startups.[28]

Direct selling opens the cage even wider

What do wine, sex toys, and plastic containers have in common? Hordes of housewives around the world sell all of them at home parties. As we saw earlier, in this channel, women (primarily) are recruited to act as distributors on behalf of companies that represent a huge range of products and services. Although the humble Tupperware party concept started in the 1950s, in recent years it has morphed into a multibillion-dollar industry that turns housewives into sophisticated distributors. This business model is on fire in countries with growing middle classes such as Brazil, China, and parts of Africa. When it's done right, it can empower millions of women who traditionally had no access to income possibilities.

In some cases, these stay-at-home moms find the path to entrepreneurship when they go on to open their own businesses in partnership with a direct selling company. Make no mistake: the industry is a money machine. In 2018, global sales revenues for direct selling companies hovered near $200 billion.[29] The United States alone has well over 20 million people involved in this channel, with many millions more joining every year from around the world.

The very large majority of distributors engage in direct selling part-time—many are simply avid customers who decided to practice what they preach by becoming their own in-house (literally, in their own house) wholesalers, advertisers, and sales force. Roughly a quarter of those who start down this path go on to build independent businesses as direct sellers. This means they actively manage a customer base, and they sponsor still other distributors they recruit for their network who share a portion of their commissions with them.

In addition, a very high proportion of direct selling distributors purchase the products they sell to others for their own use as well (at a nice discount). The industry euphemistically refers to this practice as internal consumption.[30] It's yet another way that the cage that separates retailers and consumers is opening.

Owning vs. leasing

The sharing economy is one of the most disruptive forces we have ever witnessed in marketing. Whether they borrow a neighbor's bike, a power saw or a kitchen appliance, stay in a stranger's home, watch people's pets, give neighborhood tours, or bypass a taxi to grab a ride home with an Uber driver, everyday people relentlessly open the cage that separates amateurs and professional service providers.

According to one estimate, more than half of consumers in the US, the UK, and China used a sharing economy service at least once in 2018.[31] True, the pandemic sapped the energy out of the parts of the sharing economy we call the gig economy, such as transportation (Uber and Lyft) and lodging (Airbnb). This slowdown is probably temporary, and the momentum will likely resume as the travel and hospitality industries regain their footing.

But more importantly, it's vital to keep in mind that there are many other products and services out there that people can "share," such as household tasks and everyday products that each of us pay a lot for but rarely use. Innovative platforms like the Dutch Peerby.com and many others make it easy to rent what you need from your neighbors, whether an animal crate, a casserole pot, or a board game.[32]

Can you create a new business model that facilitates this process? If you operate physical locations, do you have excess capacity you can rent to host "swap meets" that will create bonds with the local community? This grass-roots scenario may be one solution to all of those shopping malls gathering dust today.

The trend toward pooling resources brings up a big question: why buy when you can rent? We used to value objects we could own, whether nice clothes, power tools, or record albums. The drive to acquire possessions underlies some of the basic tenets of capitalism. Taking title to a house or a car is traditionally a major milestone for many and a marker that a person has come of age.

Throw that ego trip out the window of your rented home. Today many consumers want to *avoid* ownership and the financial costs and responsibilities that come with it. For example, Americans lease rather than buy more new vehicles than ever; today this is the case in about a third of transactions.[33] Cadillac recognized this trend, and the carmaker's answer is its "Book Cadillac" program, which gives participants the ability to sample a range of cars because they can exchange their Cadillacs up to eighteen times per year.[34]

The sharing economy makes it easy to barter, trade, and rent rather than own. We pay for cars by the hour, rent our neighbors' power tools, lease a "makerspace" to access 3D printers and other sophisticated equipment, and stream music rather than download it. Millions of women "borrow" gowns and other items from the apparel rental company Rent the Runway to the tune of over $100 million in revenue.[35]

Even the number of teenagers who bother to obtain a driver's license is in decline. In a 2014 study, just 24.5 percent of 16-year-olds had a license, a 47 percent decrease from 1983. The top three reasons kids gave for foregoing this ritual were: "too busy or not enough time to get a driver's license" (37 percent), "owning and maintaining a vehicle is too expensive" (32 percent), and "able to get transportation from others" (31 percent).[36]

Pride of ownership recedes as our relationships with objects become more ephemeral. We would rather "rent" an experience than own a thing. The choice to rent a Zipcar for an hour or two rather than to invest in wheels to call your own is typical of this thinking. Given that it costs about $9,000 to own and maintain a car each year, paying in small increments on an on-demand basis makes a lot of sense for many of us, especially city dwellers. Indeed, Zipcar claims that more than half of its members got rid of a personal vehicle after they joined. [37]

Cages get in the way of sharing. They're opening fast.

CHAPTER TAKEAWAYS

- Consumer-generated content (CGC) opens the cage that separates producers and consumers. Opportunities abound for marketers that are willing to allow their customers to participate in aspects of the marketing process such as serving as design consultants, retailers, investors, and advertisers.

- Consumers are a huge, but often overlooked, source of marketing intelligence for product designers. So are your own employees.

- Authenticity is a key driver of purchase decisions today. If your company has a backstory, tell it. *Often.*

- Pride of ownership is no longer the gold standard. Today many consumers want to *avoid* ownership and the financial costs and responsibilities that come with it.

Endnotes

1   Charles Arthur, "Apple Staffer Loses Test iPhone in Bar—Again," *The Guardian*, September 1, 2011, https://www.theguardian.com/technology/2011/sep/01/apple-staffer-loses-iphone (archived at https://perma.cc/2UQP-UTCB).

2   Simon Pitman, "Pfizer Sues P&G over Mouthwash Ad Claims," March 6, 2006, http://www.cosmeticsdesign.com/Market-Trends/Pfizer-sues-P-G-over-mouthwash-ad-claims (archived at https://perma.cc/XS6G-4V75).

3   Paige Leskin, "Samsung's $2,000 Galaxy Fold Phones Are Breaking—Here Are Some of the Other Biggest Smartphone Fiascos over the Years," *Business Insider*, April 17, 2019, https://www.businessinsider.com/samsung-galaxy-fold-breaking-smartphone-fiasco-2019-4 (archived at https://perma.cc/DPC5-KKVP).

4   Goodreads.com, https://www.goodreads.com/quotes/988332-some-people-say-give-the-customers-what-they-want-but (archived at https://perma.cc/B63P-TXYX).

5   Basil G. Englis and Michael R. Solomon, "Life/Style OnLine©: A
    Web-Based Methodology for Visually-Oriented Consumer Research,"
    Journal of Interactive Marketing 14, no. 1 (2000): 2–14.

6   Eric von Hippel, "Lead Users: A Source of Novel Product Concepts,"
    Management Science 32, no. 7 (July 1986): 791–805.

7   Margaret Rhodes, "How A Beauty Startup Turned Instagram
    Comments into a Product Line," *Wired*, November 26, 2014,
    https://www.Wired.Com/2014/11/Beauty-Startup-Turned-Instagram-
    Comments-Product-Line/ (archived at https://perma.cc/FVA8-JB5L).

8   Sam Milbrath, "Co-Creation: 5 Examples of Brands Driving
    Customer-Driven Innovation," *Vision Critical*, August 5, 2016,
    https://www.visioncritical.com/5-examples-how-brands-are-using-co-
    creation/ (archived at https://perma.cc/ATT3-UGUC) (archived at
    https://perma.cc/ATT3-UGUC).

9   Cf. Michael R. Solomon, *Consumer Behavior: Buying, Having, and
    Being*, 13th ed. (Hoboken, NJ: Pearson Education, 2019).

10 https://www.threadless.com/how-it-works/ (archived at https://perma.cc/
    PF4C-8S2R).

11 "aloft Hotels to Unveil Updated Design Strategy in Second Life,"
    Club Life, May 30, 2007, https://clubandresortbusiness.com/
    aloft-hotels-to-unveil-updated-design-strategy-in-second-life/
    (archived at https://perma.cc/W4MS-9Q2F).

12 https://www.redchiliclimbing.com/en/ (archived at https://perma.cc/
    V7SR-H3K4).

13 Hidehiko Nishikawa, Martin Schreier, and Susumu Ogaw, "User-
    Generated Versus Designer-Generated Products: A Performance
    Assessment at Muji," *International Journal of Research in Marketing*
    30, no. 2 (June 2013):160–67, http://www.sciencedirect.com/science/
    article/pii/S0167811612000730 (archived at https://perma.cc/5J7B-2G7X).

14 James Surowiecki, *The Wisdom of Crowds: Why the Many Are
    Smarter Than the Few and How Collective Wisdom Shapes Business,
    Economies, Societies, and Nations* (New York: Doubleday, 2004).

15 Adam Mann, "The Power of Prediction Markets," *Nature*, October
    18, 2016, https://www.nature.com/news/the-power-of-prediction-
    markets-1.20820 (archived at https://perma.cc/NBC9-6ALL);
    Julie Wittes Schlack, "Ask Your Customers for Predictions, Not
    Preferences," *Harvard Business Review*, January 5, 2015, https://hbr.org/
    2015/01/ask-your-customers-for-predictions-not-preferences
    (archived at https://perma.cc/E7XL-FWRD).

16 Barbara Kiviat, "The End of Management," *Time Inside Business*, July 12, 2004, http://content.time.com/time/magazine/article/ 0,9171,660965,00.html (archived at https://perma.cc/9DTQ-K5ZW).

17 John Winsor, "The End of Traditional Ad Agencies," *Harvard Business Review*, May 9, 2013, https://hbr.org/2013/05/the-end-of-traditional-ad-agen (archived at https://perma.cc/Q3TF-P6TP).

18 Travis Wright, "Why Brands Should Embrace UGC as Part of Their Marketing Strategy," *Marketing Land*, February 13, 2017, https://marketingland.com/ugc-brands-new-years-content-resolution-2017-206106 (archived at https://perma.cc/FA83-LN8E).

19 "Consumer Trust: Keeping It Real," *Olapic*, November 2016, http://visualcommerce.olapic.com/rs/358-ZXR-813/images/ wp-consumer-trust-survey-global-FINAL.pdf (archived at https://perma.cc/U8NU-SFZ4).

20 "People Trust Social Media Photos 7 Times More Than Traditional Ads," *Net Imperative*, November 30, 2016, http://www.netimperative.com/ 2016/11/people-trust-social-media-photos-7-times-traditional-ads-report/ (archived at https://perma.cc/5JWA-LKPM).

21 "Andy Warhol: 15 Minutes of Fame," *Phillips*, https://www.phillips.com/ article/56095372/editions-andy-warhol-prints-15-minutes-of-fame-auction (archived at https://perma.cc/H5PE-MCNA).

22 Blair Evan Bell, "How Blogs Influence Your Purchase Decisions [Infographic]," *Prepare1*, February 13, 2015, https://www.prepare1.com/ blogs-influence-purchase-decisions/ (archived at https://perma.cc/ 7P5C-ZZHZ).

23 https://www.oberlo.com/blog/ebay-statistics (archived at https://perma.cc/TQ2K-WEHR).

24 Quoted in Joan Voight, "Which Big Brands Are Courting the Maker Movement, and Why," *Adweek*, March 17, 2014, https://www.adweek.com/brand-marketing/which-big-brands-are-courting-maker-movement-and-why-156315/ (archived at https://perma.cc/J3NX-QTA5).

25 Julie Napoli et al., "Measuring Consumer-Based Brand Authenticity," *Journal of Business Research* 67, no. 6 (2014): 1090–98.

26 George E. Newman and Ravi Dhar, "Authenticity Is Contagious: Brand Essence and the Original Source of Production," *Journal of Marketing Research* 51, no. 3 (2014): 371–86; Quoted in Matthew Hutson, "Quenching Consumers' Thirst for 'Authentic' Brands," *New York Times*, December 27, 2014, http://www.nytimes.com/

2014/12/28/business/quenching-consumers-thirst-for-authentic-brands.html?module=Search&mabReward=relbias%3Ar%2C%7B%221%22%3A%22RI%3A11%22%7D&_r=0 (archived at https://perma.cc/5SCQ-5R7D).

27 "DIY Home Improvement Market in the US 2017–2021," *PR Newswire*, May 4, 2017, http://www.prnewswire.com/news-releases/iy-home-improvement-market-in-the-us-2017-2021-300451798.html (archived at https://perma.cc/VSX6-B3Y7).

28 Nicholas Jackson, "7 Successful Products to Emerge from San Francisco's Techshop," *The Atlantic*, July 5, 2011, Theatlantic.com/Technology/Archive/2011/07/7-Successful-Products-To-Emerge-From-San-Franciscos-Techshop/241291/#Slide4 (archived at https://perma.cc/KBL9-H7PA); "What Is a Makerspace?," *Makerspaces.com*, https://www.Makerspaces.Com/What-Is-A-Makerspace/ (archived at https://perma.cc/7WDT-PY67).

29 Liam O'Connell, "Global Retail Sales of the Direct Selling Market," *Statista*, July 24, 2019, https://www.statista.com/statistics/654722/global-retail-sales-of-the-direct-selling-market/ (archived at https://perma.cc/A7AM-6EU4).

30 "The Facts About Internal Consumption," Direct Selling Association, www.dsa.org/docs/default-source/direct-selling-facts/internalconsumptionfacts.pdf?sfvrsn=2 (archived at https://perma.cc/6HCJ-7VSW).

31 E. Mazareanu, "Use of Sharing Economy Services by Country 2018," *Statista*, April 12, 2019, https://www.statista.com/statistics/881227/use-of-sharing-economy-services-by-country/ (archived at https://perma.cc/73HP-VEX4).

32 https://www.peerby.com/ (archived at https://perma.cc/6W6G-CNCN).

33 Greg Gardner, "Report: More New Cars Leased Than Ever," *USA Today*, March 4, 2016, https://www.usatoday.com/story/money/cars/2016/03/03/report-more-new-cars-leased-than-ever/81286732/ (archived at https://perma.cc/3L3Q-CYZ2).

34 https://www.bookbycadillac.com/#benefits-slide2 (archived at https://perma.cc/5MNB-KJPH).

35 Zoë Henry, "Rent the Runway Had 6 Million Customers, $100 Million in Revenue. Then the Co-Founder Quit," *Inc.*, July/August 2016, https://www.inc.com/magazine/201707/zoe-henry/jennifer-fleiss-rent-the-runway.html (archived at https://perma.cc/MCH9-FLXL).

36 Julie Beck, "The Decline of the Driver's License," *The Atlantic*, January 22, 2016, https://www.theatlantic.com/technology/archive/2016/01/the-decline-of-the-drivers-license/425169/ (archived at https://perma.cc/9RWZ-2WWL).

37 "First-Ever Zipcar Impact Report Shows Car Sharing's Significant Social and Environmental Benefits, and Its Essential Role in Creating Better Cities," *Zipcar*, January 15, 2019, www.zipcar.com/press/releases/impactreport2018 (archived at https://perma.cc/K6V7-D8N3).

06

Consumers who defy traditional sex roles and gender stereotypes

To promote its Dr. Pepper Ten drink, PepsiCo sent a mobile "Man Cave" to US cities. The trailer parked in "testosterone zones" such as ball fields or car shows, where it gave men a place to watch TV and play video games. The accompanying advertising campaign featured a muscled commando type who totes a space-age weapon. "Hey ladies, enjoying the film?" he asks. "'Course not. Because this is our movie, and Dr. Pepper Ten is our soda."[1]

Gender stereotyping of men and women is a well-worn marketing technique. The idea is that men and women will relate to this version of themselves and buy the product. So, companies rely on these categories relentlessly—even when they no longer accurately apply to today's reality of how most of us feel about our sexuality. That Dr. Pepper campaign ran a decade ago; it's hard to imagine running into something similar today.

It's true that at least some of the stereotypes about gender differences in consumption still are valid. Consider the gender differences market researchers observe when they compare the food preferences of men to those of women. Women eat more fruit; men are more likely to eat meat. As one food writer put it, "Boy food doesn't grow. It is hunted or killed."[2] Indeed, consumers tend to view meat as a masculine product. In one case a company that sells soy patties found that men viewed the food as feminine, so its solution was to add artificial grill marks on the patties to make them look like cuts of meat.[3] But even an established pattern like this is subject to change: a recent survey found that 65 percent of both men and women globally have started to eat more plant-based food in a move toward "flexitarianism."[4] One man's Whopper is another man's Impossible Burger.

Advertisers themselves often encourage gender stereotypes. A study that tracked advertising in eight magazines with primarily male readerships (ranging from *Maxim* to *Golf Digest*) reported that most contain many ads that can contribute to hypermasculinity because of heavy emphasis on violence, dangerousness, and callous attitudes toward women and sex.[5]

However, even traditional depictions of sex roles that we accepted without a shrug a few years ago may come off as offensive today. A 2007 European ad for designer Dolce & Gabbana portrayed a group of sweaty men in tight jeans surrounding a woman wearing spike heels whom they've pinned to the ground. This aggressiveness did not go over so well among many contemporary consumers as it once might have—when for example a husband in a 1960s coffee advert threatened to spank his wife if she didn't wise up and buy the right brand.

Sex roles and gender identity are fluid

A bestselling book once proclaimed, *Men Are from Mars, Women Are from Venus*.[6] A tidy dichotomy, but unfortunately one that doesn't apply so well today (if it ever did).

It's crucial to recognize that the dual dichotomies of male vs. female and men vs. women are *not* the same.[7] Here is where biology and psychology part ways: we designate a person as male or female depending upon the sex chromosomes they carry and how these direct the formation of their genitalia and some hormones.

In contrast, the experience of *being* a man or a woman is much more fluid; cultural concepts of what it means to be one or the other (or something in between) determine how an individual feels, acts, and consumes.

There's no doubt that gender identity is a crucial component of a consumer's self-concept. People often conform to their culture's expectations about how those of their gender should act, dress, or speak; we refer to these sets of expectations as sex roles. Thus, the state of being a man or a woman holds a much broader meaning, and our definitions of what it means to one or the other change radically across time and across cultures.

Today we're witnessing a particularly volatile shakeup as our culture grapples with changing definitions. At least in some parts of our society, it's increasingly commonplace for a biologically born man to "act feminine" by wearing skirts and makeup, or for a biologically born woman to "act masculine" as she dons overalls and construction boots. And that's not to mention the legions of people who literally change their biological identity via operations and hormone injections.

In this changing world, marketers adhere to the "old school" male vs. female dichotomy at their peril. The raging cultural war over who has the right to use a men's or women's bathroom testifies to the volatility of this issue. The department store Target committed to spending $20 million to remove gender-based signage and add gender-neutral bathrooms to its stores to avoid a threatened consumer boycott.[8] In 2020, a landmark US Supreme Court ruling nullified an organization's ability to discriminate based upon sexual orientation.[9]

Just what does it mean to be male, female, agender, cis, feminine-of-center, FtM, genderqueer, third gender, or any one of numerous terms that vie today to replace the man/woman dichotomy of old?[10] The answer is more than personal—marketers need to closely follow this conversation to be sure their messages and products sync with these evolving definitions.

Gen Z is post-gender

The obliteration of the male vs. female dichotomy may be one of the most significant narratives that will emerge as marketers scramble to understand how to speak to Generation Z.

Back in 2015, Coca-Cola partnered with 7-Eleven to ask teens the question, "Are you more Dude or Diva?" Customers could choose their Dude or Diva can in a contest to win a trip to a video shoot featuring *The Voice* finalist Christina Grimmie. In the resulting video, viewers could explore the male and female sides of the singer's personality by choosing the musical arrangement (Pop-Diva or Acoustic-Dude) they wanted to hear.[11]

Ironically, this dichotomous choice for consumers to make assumes a stereotyped gender difference in preferences for different kinds of music: just what constitutes a "Pop-Diva" tune? Do women dislike acoustic arrangements? On the other hand, the promotion shows that even a mega-marketer like Coke is waking up to a big cultural movement among young people. Tone deaf? Perhaps, but at least trying.

Coke's campaign was based upon consumer research among young people that showed they view self-expression as fluid and a way to have fun. The chief strategy officer at Wunderman, Coca-Cola's advertising agency, explained, "Sometimes they feel more like a dude, and other times more like a diva."

Although 13 percent of the US population as a whole identifies as nonheterosexual, a whopping 31 percent of Gen Z people do.[12] An oft-cited 2015 study by Wunderman Thompson reported that 82 percent of Gen Zers think that "gender doesn't define a person as much as it used to," and 56 percent say they know someone who uses gender-neutral pronouns (like "they," "them," and "ze"). Hey, even Barbie included a young boy in an ad for its Moschino line. He exclaims, "Moschino Barbie is so fierce!" and places a designer purse on the doll's arm.[13]

Gender-benders are a big market

Some companies that sell exclusively to one gender may decide to test the waters with the other sex when they promote gender-bending products. The term "gender-bender" refers to adapting traditionally sex-typed items to the opposite gender, such as the introduction of pink guns for women. Here are some other gender benders:[14]

- Sixty years after Mattel created Ken to escort Barbie around town in 1961, American Girl introduced its first boy doll. Logan Everett sports perfect hair, a hipster T-shirt and dark-wash jeans, and he plays the drums in a band.[15]

- Old Spice has long been known as the brand Dad keeps in his medicine cabinet, but young women who like the scent and the relatively low price are tuning into the deodorant as well. This resurgence is a bit ironic, because the first product the company introduced in 1937 was a women's fragrance.

- Febreze is an odor-neutralizing line of products that Procter & Gamble (P&G) markets to women for house cleaning. However, P&G found that a lot of men spray it on their clothes to delay doing laundry. And in Vietnam, where the product is called Ambi Pur, men who ride motor scooters use it as a deodorizing spray for their helmets.[16]

- Startup companies like Older Brother sell unisex clothing, and MeUndies makes underwear for men and women including bright pink men's boxers and camo-print women's bikinis. Its founder explains, "Our women's boy short is essentially the men's boxer brief without the pouch, while our men's brief is essentially the women's bikini cut with a pouch."[17]

How men are evolving beyond stereotypical male

Even those who hold fairly traditional views about a firm male/female dichotomy are being forced to reexamine their notions about what it means to be a male today.

Models of behavior for men are very much in flux now, especially as a tidal wave of sexual harassment scandals sinks the careers of prominent male business executives, politicians, and artists.

The same traditional narrative of chivalry that taught generations of men to "put women on a pedestal" also tends to objectify them as fragile vessels who might fall off of that platform if they're given too much autonomy. Indeed, the nineteenth-century poet John Keats described the ideal woman of that time as "a milk white lamb that bleats for man's protection."[18]

The #MeToo movement was the catalyst for an urgent national dialogue about the way our culture thinks about and treats women. The leaders of some prominent companies including the *Vice* network and Uber were called out for encouraging "bro culture," a corporate environment that demeans women.[19]

This cultural definition of maleness (certainly not the only one, but a dominant version) celebrates the notion of man as hunter and woman as prey. Accolades flow to the men who are most adept at "bagging" the best prizes. The social theorist Thorstein Veblen (inventor of the term "conspicuous consumption") argued that wives historically are status symbols that signal a man's prowess and economic resources.[20] He criticized the "decorative" role of women, as rich men showered them with expensive clothes, pretentious homes, and a life of leisure as a way to advertise their own wealth. It's probably not a coincidence that today we refer to younger, attractive females who marry older, affluent men as trophy wives.

The scandals that ensued following the trials of prominent celebrities like Bill Cosby and Harvey Weinstein energized many marketers to meet the changing moment. Bonobos launched #EvolveTheDefinition, a movement to provoke discussion about the meaning of masculinity. A short YouTube video depicts a series of men who share their interpretations of manhood. Other male-oriented brands such as Unilever's Axe, Harry's, and Gillette have run marketing campaigns that question male gender stereotypes and cultural expectations about acting male.

Man's work vs. woman's work

A big part of the change in male sex roles involves a rethinking of the traditional cultural dichotomy of man's work vs. woman's work. In the United States, most younger couples agree that in the ideal marriage husband and wife both work and share child care and household duties.[21] That's a big change from just 20 years ago, when less than half of the population approved of the dual-income family, and less than half of 1 percent of husbands knew how to operate a sponge mop.[22]

Today, it's increasingly common to tune into TV commercials that depict a domestic version of fathers who tenderly and wisely look after the kids. This updated picture even has its own name: Dadvertising. A Cheerios commercial, for example, shows a confident dad taking charge of a hectic weekday morning. The campaign also features a dedicated Tumblr page and Twitter hashtag, #HowToDad.[23]

As increasing numbers of women work outside the home, a growing number of husbands today stay home with the kids: the US Census Bureau reports that one-fifth of fathers with preschool-age children and working wives are the primary caretaker. As one marketing executive observed, "Kids are going to grow up with dads that give them baths and drive them to soccer and are cutting up oranges for team snacks." Already, by some estimates men do more than half of the grocery shopping in the United States.

Stay-at-home rates vary across European countries, where the Scandinavian region tends to offer very generous incentives for men to do so. In the Netherlands, almost 50 percent of young fathers say they take a day off at least once a week to be at home with the kids for their *papadag* ("daddy day").[24] And, the pandemic no doubt further accelerated these changes as parents stuck at home had to renegotiate their domestic arrangements.

This shift causes marketers to reexamine how they sell a range of products as they try to appeal to dads: both LEGO and Mattel now offer construction toys. Procter & Gamble developed special sections at big retailers as the company found that women aren't as likely as before to choose personal care products for their husbands. The so-called "man aisle" organizes men's products in one place with shelf displays and even small TV monitors to help them pick out the appropriate items.[25]

How women are evolving beyond stereotypical female

Fashions such as high-heeled shoes, tight corsets, billowing trains on dresses, and elaborate hairstyles all conspired to ensure that wealthy women could barely move without assistance, much less perform manual labor. Similarly, the Chinese practice of foot binding prevented female members of the aristocracy even from walking; servants had to carry them from place to place. In many ways, societies "conspired" to make assumptions about a woman's role a self-fulfilling prophecy.

But today women's roles, too, are changing (obviously!). Bestselling books such as Cheryl Sandberg's *Lean In: Women, Work, and the Will to Lead* encourage women to find new ways to express and view themselves, suggesting that women should no longer be expected to be the primary caregivers within the family and should no longer dress in a manner that is mindful of how men perceive them. Women continue to break the so-called glass ceiling in many fields, from engineering to politics.

As this evolution continues, many cultures are rejecting hyper-feminine exemplars and replacing them with a picture of a woman who is smart, self-assured, and lives on her own terms. While the majority of women's clothing designers still are male, the mix is changing as well-known fashion houses including Dior, Prada, Chanel, and Givenchy appoint women to run the companies. They are joined by others who lead upstarts such as Fenty, Stella McCartney, and Bode.[26]

Indeed, in 2019 the UK went so far as to ban ads that perpetuate gender stereotyping.[27] Viewers are more likely to see something like a spot for the Royal Air Force, which depicts a female pilot in a fighter jet with the tagline, "Women should be defined by actions not clichés."[28]

Appearance matters for all genders

As many marketers understand, managing appearances is a big deal. Despite the expression "beauty is only skin deep," the reality is that the judgments we make about a person based upon their appearance are hugely important.

Remember our earlier discussion about categories, because that comes into play here. We tend to place a person into a category in seconds, and this decision often is strongly influenced by physical cues that we've learned (rightly or wrongly) link to underlying characteristics. We "know" that redheads have fiery tempers, obese people are lazy, and there is a well-documented bias about people who have a "baby face." Observers tend to assume that they will exhibit child-like traits as well so they rate them as less hostile and more trustworthy compared to others.[29] These are all baseless stereotypes, but our brains love to take shortcuts. That's why many of us work so hard to control the judgments others make.

You don't need to be a supermodel to "manage" the way you appear to others. In fact, we all do it every day. If we didn't, we would have no need for mirrors. Sixty years ago, the sociologist Erving Goffman, among others, wrote extensively about the elaborate process of impression management. Since that time, volumes of social psychological studies have empirically documented the preening process and the huge impact physical appearance exerts on our judgments of those around us. Mea culpa: I published my share of those.

Valuing good-looking people is one of the most pervasive biases around—psychologists refer to it as the "what is beautiful is good" phenomenon. In one recent manifestation, the *BeautifulPeople.com* online dating site literally allows only attractive people to join (you have to have your photo approved by members). Now it's expanding its service to employers who want to hire "good-looking staff." One of the site's managers explains, "Attractive people tend to make a better first impression on clients, win more business and earn more."[30]

For better or worse, he's actually right: one study reported that on average a US worker who was among the bottom one-seventh in looks, as assessed by randomly chosen observers, earned 10 to 15 percent less per year than a similar worker whose looks were assessed in the top one-third—a lifetime difference, in a typical case, of about $230,000.[31]

Furthermore, our perceptions of our *own* attractiveness profoundly influence feelings of self-worth as well. Way back in 1902, the sociologist Charles Horton Cooley wrote about the looking-glass self that operates as a sort of psychological sonar; we take readings of our own identity when we "bounce" signals off others and try to predict their impression of us.

Indeed, my own research as well as work done by others attests to the validity of the old saw, "Clothes make the man." When I looked at the impact of male professional dress in an interview setting, I found that men who wore a coat and tie during the interaction were more confident and they even asked for higher starting salaries!

So, we know that appearance is hugely important as much as many of us might wish it otherwise. And, we know that the quest for beauty (or handsomeness) is what drives billions of dollars in spending as consumers search for the next great innovation that will help them to achieve this elusive goal.

Certainly, people of all genders fret about their appearance. But historically and even today, as a society we tend to care a lot more about the way a woman looks. There is a simple reason for this: until pretty recently, a woman's face and body were quite likely her only economic assets. Since most women were never allowed to own property, practice a trade, or accumulate financial wealth, their "market value" hinged upon their ability to attract a prosperous mate.

The male grooming market

But to be clear, the linkages we perceive between a person's value and appearance are not confined to women. In fact, as more women compete for good jobs with men, it's not surprising that more men have become aware of the strategic value of their appearance as well. That helps to explain the meteoric growth of the market for men's grooming products—from just over $60 billion in 2018 to a projected $81 billion in 2024.[32] And the evidence suggests that in this case the process works slightly differently: the big concern for males is age discrimination and finding ways to look younger in order to stay competitive. So, what's good for the goose is good for the gander.[33]

Around the world, marketers are jumping on the bandwagon to introduce new products and services for men. While women still outspend men on personal care products, the relative growth is on the men's side. The men's personal care industry is predicted to hit $166 billion by 2022 as more men around the world start to indulge in skincare products and other cosmetics.

And this growth doesn't just come from more aftershave purchases. Indeed, a 2018 Euromonitor survey reported that more than half of American male respondents admitted to using some sort of facial cosmetic like foundation, concealer, or BB cream at least once.[34] More than three million British men say they wear makeup such as "manscara" and "guyliner." A third of these users borrow cosmetics from their wives or girlfriends, but the online retailer MMUK Man exclusively sells products for men.[35] In China, Chanel launched its Boy de Chanel line that is now rolling out globally. The brand's website proclaims, "Beauty knows no gender."[36]

Of course, no one expects to see the average "meat and potatoes" man to be walking down the street in eyeliner anytime soon. Change is always unsettling. Not everyone is ready to accept a kinder, gentler vision of masculinity. The Bonobos' video has been viewed well over four million times—but it has received more dislikes than likes.

A recent Ipsos survey reported that many men feel uncomfortable about discussing gender today. About a third told the researchers they feel excluded from the discussion of different gender definitions, while 40 percent say they actually feel annoyed or angered by these conversations. One possible reason: about the same percentage confess that they worry if others will attack them if they speak their minds. The survey also found that men are more likely than women to buy traditionally gendered products such as toys, books, and games—especially when it comes to purchasing items for their daughters.[37]

Set your own beauty standards? Defying the elite vs. the masses

Cultural icons, whether members of the Kardashian clan, Jennifer Aniston, Jennifer Lopez, or Brad Pitt, Ryan Gosling, Isaiah Mustafa, or Blake Shelton, continue to serve as benchmarks for millions of men and women who dream that they too will someday adorn the cover of *People* magazine.

But here's what's different now: it's no longer the cream of society (or even the fashion magazine editors I studied) that gets to decide who is hot and who is not. The increasing racial diversity and the exposure of that internet thing again help to democratize the selection of standard bearers.

For example, in the last 20 years or so the men and women selected by *People* as the "World's Most Beautiful" have become markedly darker in skin tone, and older as well.[38] As society has come to see beauty in multiple ways, so too women have begun to embrace nonstereotypical images of beauty as part of their self-image (beauty as strength such as Xena Warrior Princess or Buffy the Vampire Slayer, or beauty as self-acceptance as older women no longer need to dye their hair as they age, or adapt to lockdown, etc.).

Throughout history it's typically been the elites who defined standards of appearance and the wealthy who had the resources to emulate them. Indeed, the notion that a working-class woman could walk into a store and buy a dress rather than making it at home is a fairly recent innovation. Wealthy women traditionally commissioned designers to create one-off styles, which were then copied by other upward-striving consumers (often on their own sewing machines). That's why so-called "designer labels" that are snapped up by the mass market represent a logical contradiction—or at least a bastardization of the original meaning.

Today, all that has changed. The cage that separates the Elite vs. the Masses has opened, as so many more of us acquire the ability to procure apparel, cosmetics, and other status markers. The rise of the so-called mass class blurs the distinction between lower and upper classes (at least for everyday purchases).

This new stratum of millions of people around the world who are rapidly acquiring impressive buying power brings with it almost unfettered access to the same kinds of products and service providers that only the elite could access in the past. For example, it's not at all uncommon for consumers who bring home fairly low incomes to "splurge" on at least a few expensive trinkets. Of US women with household incomes under $75,000, three-quarters own a bauble from Tiffany and a third have purchased something from Bulgari.[39]

And professional "identity managers" come in many forms, from hairstylists and cosmetologists to wardrobe consultants and resumé writers. Doctors perform nearly 860,000 cosmetic surgery procedures in the United States alone each year. In some circles nose jobs or breast implants are part of the rite of passage for teenage girls, and an increasing number of men spring for pectoral enlargements.

Evolving gender roles create new consumer markets

Changes in the makeup of society create new business opportunities for those who recognize them in time. For example, Muslims will make up more than a quarter of the earth's population by 2030, and analysts expect the number of US Muslims to more than double by then.[40] In several European countries, it's predicted that Muslim populations will exceed 10 percent of the country's total population.[41] That's a consumer market to take seriously.

And sure enough, we now see fashion companies scramble to allow traditional Muslim women to partake of cutting-edge styles while maintaining religious prohibitions against excessive displays of skin. The growing "modest fashion" category features garments that conceal rather than accentuate the shape of the body. The clothing can include hijabs and burqas as well as tops, trousers, jackets, and dresses that feature a modest cut. The modest fashion industry is expected to be worth $361 billion by 2023.[42]

The market for androgynous fashion is growing

There is certainly an abundance of opportunity out there as the concept of androgyny catches fire. Androgyny refers to the possession of both masculine and feminine traits.[43] The growing prevalence (or at least visibility) of androgynous people obliterates the traditional gender dichotomy that has guided so many marketing strategies.[44]

This is hardly a new concept! Adolescent males known as *wakashu*, who were sexually available to both men and women, were regarded as the epitome of beauty in early modern Japan before the country adopted Western sexual mores in the late 1800s.[45]

Today, many pop culture icons are poster children for androgyny, such as Dr. Frank-N-Furter (originally portrayed by Tim Curry) in the *Rocky Horror Picture Show*, the celebrity drag queen RuPaul, the comedian Eddie Izzard, Lady Gaga, the New York Dolls, the late Prince, and Annie Lennox.

As we might expect, this blurring of boundaries is more widely accepted in some cultures than in others. For example, although acceptance of homosexuality varies in Asian cultures, it doesn't occur to most Asians to assume that a man with feminine qualities is gay. A survey of Korean consumers found that more than 66 percent of men and 57 percent of women younger than age 40 were living self-described "androgynous" lifestyles. But the respondents didn't link those choices with sexual orientation. Although Koreans nickname males with feminine interests "flower men," they don't consider this to be a derogatory term.[46] In Japan, men called *gyaru-o* ("male gals") are common on city streets. Tanned and meticulously dressed (and usually heterosexual), these fops cruise Tokyo's stylish boutiques.[47]

There is nothing new about androgyny in Western fashion, either. For centuries male European aristocrats sported wigs, white stockings, and lots of ruffles and lace. The novelist George Sand turned heads in nineteenth-century Paris with her jackets and pants, and in the last century Marlene Dietrich and Katharine Hepburn helped to popularize suits for women. European men in the 17th century wore high heels to communicate upper-class status.

In the 1960s, men's long hair cascaded over their flowered shirts, and Twiggy inspired a more masculine body profile for women. Prominent design houses such as Vivienne Westwood, Jean Paul Gaultier, Céline, and Prada have offered masculine tailoring for women and high-heeled boots for men. MAC Cosmetics used RuPaul as its celebrity spokesperson as early as 1994. Calvin Klein introduced the unisex CK One fragrance in the 1990s. In recent years we've seen the launch of numerous other unisex scents such as Chanel's Les Eaux de Chanel.

While androgyny may not be a new concept, now a broader swath of the population embraces it. That's what makes it such an attractive marketing opportunity now. Indeed, in 2018, 51 percent of global fragrance launches were considered unisex or gender neutral.[48]

Now, Gucci, Burberry, and Balenciaga have dispensed with gender distinctions altogether by combining their women's wear and menswear fashion shows. The creative director at Balenciaga commented, "Gender doesn't exist anymore. Man or woman, we can choose what we want to be."[49] H&M and Abercrombie have introduced gender-neutral apparel lines, while Target eliminated "boy and girl" distinctions in store signage and end-cap displays in toy departments. Even Mattel, which gave us the hypersexualized Barbie, recently launched a line of gender-neutral dolls.[50]

The LGBTQIA+ market is emerging

To put things into perspective, the LGBTQIA+ (lesbian, gay, bi-sexual, transgender, questioning, intersex, asexual, and anyone else) population in the United States alone is roughly a third of the size of either the Hispanic-American or African-American sub-cultures. The buying power of this community is estimated at almost $1 trillion.

According to one large survey, in the United States about 13 percent of the total population identifies as LGBTQIA+.[51] A similar survey conducted in the EU reported that 5.9 percent of

Europeans identify in these categories; about 10 percent of respondents say they are not "only" heterosexual. [52] And these numbers are probably conservative; a global study conducted by the Yale School of Public Health found that 83 percent of those who identify as lesbian, gay, or bisexual keep their orientation hidden from all or most of the people in their lives. [53]

At least in the Western world, norms are evolving rapidly. The Pride movement has entered the mainstream. Many mainstream brands including Levi Strauss, Abercrombie and Fitch, Doc Martens, Adidas, Vans, H&M, Under Armour, Calvin Klein, Dockers, Warby Parker, and Everlane now offer Pride products. In the United States, every major sport including the National Football League offers a Pride collection. [54]

Still, we've seen some notable blunders as marketers scramble to win the favor of the gay community. In the UK, Marks and Spencer tried to sell an "LGBT" sandwich—a guacamole-inclusive twist on a BLT—complete with packaging decorated with the colors of the rainbow. Some customers weren't amused. One woman posted, "Shame on the good folks over at @marksandspencer for turning our culture and identity into a sandwich." [55]

Of late the cultural spotlight has turned on the "T" in the LGBTQIA+ acronym. Transgender people are suddenly much more visible. No doubt this new prominence has been helped along by the media attention paid to a character in the popular US TV show *Orange Is the New Black*, and certainly by the debut of former athlete and reality TV star Bruce Jenner in her new identity as Caitlin Jenner on the cover of *Vogue* a few years ago. United Colors of Benetton caused a stir when an ad campaign featured Lea T, a transgender Brazilian model. [56]

The third gender (and more)

Our definitions of gender continue to evolve as a global third-gender movement picks up steam:

- Australia's High Court rules that a person there is allowed to register gender as "nonspecific" on official documents.

- Nepal issues citizenship papers with a "third gender" category.

- Germany allows parents of intersex children—those born with both genitals or with ambiguous sex characteristics—to mark their birth certificates with an X.[57]

- California allows residents to declare a "third gender" on their drivers' licenses.[58]

- Facebook allows users to choose among 58 defined genders—along with a write-in option—that range from "gender fluid" to "intersex" and simply "neither."[59] Other social networks follow suit, as do some dating apps.

- The University of California system joins colleges around the country when it adds "gender nonconforming" and "genderqueer" to its applications alongside transgender, male, and female.

It seems that gender binarism—the classification of gender into two distinct, opposite, and disconnected forms of masculine and feminine is giving way to gender benders, or people who "bend" traditional sex roles.[60]

Most social scientists have always viewed sexuality as a continuum rather than a dichotomy. Masculinity and femininity are social constructions that vary across cultures and historical periods. However, in Western culture we seem to have reached a watershed moment when people question even the anchor points of this continuum.

The cage that separates men and women has never been more fragile.

CHAPTER TAKEAWAYS

- Gender identity is a crucial component of a consumer's self-concept. People often conform to sex roles; their culture's expectations about how those of their gender should act, dress, or consume.

- Advertisers often perpetuate traditional gender stereotypes, but consumers' willingness to be put into distinct male/female cages is eroding rapidly. Gender binarism is in particular becoming obsolete for younger consumers.

- Your customers will react more positively to role models that embody the attributes they consider to be attractive at any point in time, but these models are no longer primarily determined by cultural elites or established media vehicles.

- Dramatic changes in sex roles as the traditional male/female dichotomy disintegrates create the potential for huge new markets as we see emerging movements including androgyny, the growing third-gender and LGBTQIA+ (lesbian, gay, bisexual, transgender, questioning, intersex, asexual, and anyone else) population, and the increasing demand for "modest fashion."

Endnotes

1 Quoted in Natalie Zmuda, "Can Dr. Pepper's Mid-Cal Soda Score a 10 with Men?" *Advertising Age*, February 21, 2011, http://adage.com/article/news/dr-pepper-10-avoid-marketing-missteps-pepsi-coke/148983/ (archived at https://perma.cc/PK29-GMBA).

2 Diane Goldner, "What Men and Women Really Want . . . to Eat," *New York Times*, March 2, 1994, C1(2).

3 Paul Rozin et al., "Is Meat Male? A Quantitative Multimethod Framework to Establish Metaphoric Relationships," *Journal of Consumer Research* 39, no. 3 (2012): 629–43.

4 Kat Smith, "65% of Meat Eaters Are Buying All the Vegan Food," *Live Kindly*, April 17, 2019, https://www.livekindly.co/global-consumers-eating-more-vegan-food-study/ (archived at https://perma.cc/L4YX-XJMK).

5 Sarah Mahoney, "Study: Men's Mags May Be Bad for Men," *Marketing Daily*, March 2, 2013, http://www.mediapost.com/publications/article/194617/study-mens-mags-may-be-bad-for-men.html?edition=57304#axzz2MuwUQkdG (archived at https://perma.cc/P3US-JKSL).

6 John Gray, *Men Are from Mars, Women Are from Venus: A Practical Guide for Improving Communication* (New York: HarperCollins, 2009).

7   Jennifer Tseng, "Sex Gender, and Why the Differences Matter,"
    AMA Journal of Medical Ethics (July 2008) https://journalofethics.
    ama-assn.org/article/sex-gender-and-why-differences-matter/2008-07
    (archived at https://perma.cc/5UM4-3BWW).

8   Ken Newman, "As Our Society Becomes Gender-Fluid, Marketing
    Must Catch Up," *CustomerThink*, July 5, 2019,
    https://customerthink.com/as-our-society-becomes-gender-fluid-
    marketing-must-catch-up/ (archived at https://perma.cc/
    9QUQ-VDVH).

9   Ariane de Vogue and Devan Cole, "Supreme Court Says Federal Law
    Protects LGBTQ Workers from Discrimination," *CNN*, June 15,
    2020, https://www.cnn.com/2020/06/15/politics/supreme-court-lgbtq-
    employment-case/index.html (archived at https://perma.cc/
    3662-XJ25).

10 "Comprehensive* List of LGBTQ+ Vocabulary Definitions,"
    http://itspronouncedmetrosexual.com/2013/01/a-comprehensive-list-
    of-lgbtq-term-definitions/ (archived at https://perma.cc/XX6E-U4JA).

11 "Coca-Cola & 7-Eleven: Dude or Diva," *Working Not Working*,
    workingnotworking.com/projects/76972-coca-cola-7-eleven-dude-or-
    diva (archived at https://perma.cc/9BLW-VXGP).

12 David Auten and John Schneider "The $1 Trillion Marketing
    Executives Are Ignoring," *Forbes*, August 14, 2018,
    https://www.forbes.com/sites/debtfreeguys/2018/08/14/the-1-trillion-
    marketing-executives-are-ignoring/#215db330a97f (archived at
    https://perma.cc/AE9S-ERJF).

13 Tim Donnelly, "A Boy Appears in a Barbie Ad for the First Time,"
    New York Post, November 16, 2015, https://nypost.com/2015/11/16/
    a-boy-appears-in-a-barbie-ad-for-the-first-time/ (archived at
    https://perma.cc/UPK9-D673).

14 Adapted from Michael R. Solomon, *Consumer Behavior: Buying,
    Having, and Being*, 13th ed. (Upper Saddle River, NJ: Pearson
    Education, 2019); cf. also Rupal Parekh, "Gender-Bending Brands an
    Easy Way to Increase Product Reach," *Advertising Age*, March 2,
    2009, https://adage.com/article/news/gender-bending-brands-easy-
    increase-product-reach/134979 (archived at https://perma.cc/
    QG7S-Y4HW); Sarah Mahoney, "Best Buy Opens Store Designed for
    Women," *Retail Customer Experience*, October 6, 2008,
    http://www.retailcustomerexperience.com/news/best-buy-opens-store-
    designed-for-women/ (archived at https://perma.cc/A5AL-4KF4);

Kevin Helliker, "The Solution to Hunting's Woes? Setting Sights on Women," *Wall Street Journal*, October 1, 2008, http://online.wsj.com/Article/Sb122281550760292225 (archived at https://perma.cc/Z882-YUB4); Stephanie Clifford, "Frito-Lay Tries to Enter the Minds (and Lunch Bags) of Women," *New York Times*, February 24, 2009, http://www.nytimes.com/2009/02/25/business/media/25adco.html (archived at https://perma.cc/XSH3-PNRE); Karl Greenberg, "Harley Says Guys Ride Back Seat in May," *Marketing Daily*, February 3, 2009, https://www.mediapost.com/publications/article/99557/harley-says-guys-ride-back-seat-in-may.html (archived at https://perma.cc/3FAA-PDRE).

15 Julie Creswell, "American Girl's New Doll: It's a Boy!," *New York Times*, February 14, 2017, https://www.nytimes.com/2017/02/14/business/american-girls-new-doll-its-a-boy.html?_r=0 (archived at https://perma.cc/J835-PPCQ).

16 Lauren Coleman-Lochner, "Old Spice Attracting Women in Gender-Bending Hit for P&G," *Bloomberg Business*, March 12, 2015, http://www.bloomberg.com/news/articles/2014-03-12/old-spice-attracting-women-in-gender-bending-hit-for-p-g (archived at https://perma.cc/QV29-395Y).

17 Quoted in Elizabeth Segran, "Women's Tighty Whities and Men's Hot Pink Briefs: Gender-Bending Fashion Goes Mainstream," *Fast Company*, September 19, 2016, https://www.fastcompany.com/3062838/womens-tighty-whities-and-mens-hot-pink-briefs-gender-bending-fashion-goes-m (archived at https://perma.cc/WY6B-ELY3).

18 https://www.bartleby.com/126/10.html (archived at https://perma.cc/24C5-KT5A).

19 Áine Cain, "'Bro Culture' Might Be Insidious, But It's Not Avoidable," *Business Insider*, June 18, 2017, https://www.businessinsider.com/bro-culture-harassment-discrimination-uber-business-2017-6 (archived at https://perma.cc/K6DD-PJG8).

20 Thorstein Veblen, *The Theory of the Leisure Class* (Oxford World's Classics) (1899; reissue; New York: Oxford University Press, 2009).

21 Cf. Michael R. Solomon, *Consumer Behavior: Buying, Having, and Being*, 13th ed. (Hoboken, NJ: Pearson Education, 2019).

22 Natalie Angier, "The Changing American Family," *New York Times*, November 25, 2013, http://www.nytimes.com/2013/11/26/health/families.html?_r=0 (archived at https://perma.cc/5W4G-HPT3).

23 Tanya Irwin, "Study: Men Defy Marketing Stereotypes," *Marketing Daily*, April 25, 2011, http://www.mediapost.com/publications/article/149272/study-men-defy-marketing-stereotypes.html (archived at https://perma.cc/N7PW-8E47); Gokcen Coskuner-Balli and Craig J. Thompson, "The Status Costs of Subordinate Cultural Capital: At-Home Fathers' Collective Pursuit of Cultural Legitimacy Through Capitalizing Consumption Practices," *Journal of Consumer Research* 40, no. 1 (June 2013): 19–41.

24 Rina Mae Acosta, "This Popular Parenting Trend in the Netherlands Reveals a Key to Raising the World's Happiest Kids," *MakeIt*, August 29, 2019, https://www.cnbc.com/2019/08/29/dutch-fathers-play-a-big-role-in-raising-the-happies-kids-in-the-world.html (archived at https://perma.cc/TUJ5-V49Z).

25 Quoted in Molly Soat, "Cheerios Leverages the Power of 'Dadvertising,' " *Marketing News Weekly*, February 25, 2015.

26 Eliza Huber, "The 10 Women-Run Fashion Houses Changing How We Dress," *Refinery 29*, March 8, 2020, https://www.refinery29.com/en-us/2020/03/9458844/female-fashion-designers-women-brands (archived at https://perma.cc/5CJF-8RJG).

27 "'Harmful' Gender Stereotypes in Adverts Banned," *BBC.com*, June 14, 2019, https://www.bbc.com/news/business-48628678 (archived at https://perma.cc/GGW7-UCLU).

28 Orianna Rosa Royle, "Seven Inspiring Ads That Smash Female Stereotypes," *Campaign US*, March 8, 2019, https://www.campaignlive.com/article/seven-inspiring-ads-smash-female-stereotypes/1578127 (archived at https://perma.cc/ZX97-43XB).

29 Leslie A, Zebrowitz and Robert G. Franklin, Jr., "The Attractiveness Halo Effect and the Babyface Stereotype in Older and Younger Adults: Similarities, Own-Age Accentuation, and OA Positivity Effects," *Experimental Aging Research* 40, no. 3 (2014) https://www.tandfonline.com/doi/abs/10.1080/0361073X.2014.897151?journalCode=uear20 (archived at https://perma.cc/W93V-NA5E).

30 Samantha Murphy "Job Site Wants Only Beautiful Candidates," *Mashable*, June 2, 2013, http://mashable.com/2013/06/02/beautiful-people-job-site/?WT.mc_id=en_my_stories&utm_campaign=My%2BStories&utm_medium=email&utm_source=newsletter (archived at https://perma.cc/C4W2-9ZFL).

31   Daniel S. Hamermesh, "Ugly? You May Have a Case," *New York Times Magazine*, August 27, 2011, http://www.nytimes.com/2011/08/28/opinion/sunday/ugly-you-may-have-a-case.html?ref=opinion (archived at https://perma.cc/F6NT-X763).

32   "Size of the Global Men's Grooming Products Market from 2018 to 2024 (in Billion U.S. Dollars)" *Statista*, https://www.statista.com/statistics/287643/global-male-grooming-market-size/ (archived at https://perma.cc/LT7A-7FAA).

33   Julia Carpenter, "Why Ageism Hurts Men More Than Women," *CNN Business*, January 22, 2019, https://www.cnn.com/2019/01/22/success/ageism-women-work/index.html (archived at https://perma.cc/FX56-ZKZ3).

34   Nia Warfield, "Men Are a Multibillion Dollar Growth Opportunity for the Beauty Industry," *CNBC*, May 18, 2019, https://www.cnbc.com/2019/05/17/men-are-a-multibillion-dollar-growth-opportunity-for-the-beauty-industry.html (archived at https://perma.cc/4FFS-QEXT).

35   "Mmuk Man: Putting the Guy in Guyliner," *Canvas8*, June 5, 2015, https://www.Canvas8.Com/Content/2015/06/05/Mmuk.Html (archived at https://perma.cc/G9W5-44E8).

36   https://www.chanel.com/us/makeup/makeup-for-men/?gclid=EAIaIQobChMIy9W36a_Z6AIVCaCzCh0ZbAGPEAAYASAAEg LgkPD_BwE (archived at https://perma.cc/MBR6-Q26J).

37   Julia Clark, "The Future of Gender Is Increasingly Nonbinary," *Ipsos*, January 7, 2020, https://www.ipsos.com/en-ca/news-polls/The-Future-of-Gender-is-Increasingly-Nonbinary (archived at https://perma.cc/3PDW-D38X).

38   Nicole Spector, "What Makes Someone 'Most Beautiful' Is Changing, Study Says," *NBC News*, October 11, 2017, https://www.nbcnews.com/better/health/how-beauty-standard-has-changed-1990-how-it-hasn-t-ncna809766 (archived at https://perma.cc/B9YC-A4XZ).

39   Rina Raphael, "The Big Business of Red Carpet Bling," *Fast Company*, September 18, 2016, https://www.fastcompany.com/3063093/the-big-business-of-red-carpet-bling (archived at https://perma.cc/HRD8-YYCM).

40   Cathy Lynn Grossman, "Number of U.S. Muslims to Double," *USA Today*, January 27, 2011, http://www.usatoday.com/news/religion/2011-01-27-1Amuslim27_ST_N.htm (archived at https://perma.cc/VAS9-YZGW).

41 "Europe's Growing Muslim Population," *Pew Research*,
https://www.pewforum.org/2017/11/29/appendix-a-methodology-
europes-muslim-population/ (archived at https://perma.cc/
AYQ7-HV8D).

42 Gouri Sharma, "How Modest Fashion Became a Global Trend,"
Raconteur, March 7, 2019 https://www.raconteur.net/retail/modest-
fashion (archived at https://perma.cc/97WW-2FXQ).

43 Sandra L. Bem, "The Measurement of Psychological Androgyny,"
Journal of Consulting & Clinical Psychology 42 (1974): 155–62;
Deborah E. S. Frable, "Sex Typing and Gender Ideology: Two Facets
of the Individual's Gender Psychology That Go Together," *Journal of
Personality & Social Psychology* 56, no. 1 (1989): 95–108.

44 This section is adapted in part from Michael R. Solomon and
Brandon Roe, *Why Fashion Brands Die & How to Save Them*
(West/East Publishing, 2019).

45 Susan Chira, "When Japan Had a Third Gender," *New York Times*,
March 10, 2017, https://www.nytimes.com/2017/03/10/arts/design/
when-japan-had-a-third-gender.html?_r=0 (archived at https://perma.cc/
BEP4-M4TH).

46 Geoffrey A. Fowler, "Asia's Lipstick Lads," *Wall Street Journal*,
May 27, 2005.

47 Matt Alt and Hiroko Yoda, "Big Primpin' in Tokyo," *Wired*, April 24,
2007: 46.

48 Jenifer Murtell, "The Rise of Gender-Neutral Branding," *Packaging
Strategies*, September 12, 2019, https://www.packagingstrategies.com/
articles/95077-the-rise-of-gender-neutral-branding (archived at
https://perma.cc/UVU6-D5XR).

49 Quoted in "Balenciaga Is Combining Its Men's and Women's Shows,"
Canvas8, December 7, 2017, https://www.canvas8.com/signals/2017/
12/07/balenciaga-mixes-collections.html (archived at https://perma.cc/
5W5E-T3Q7).

50 Maya Salam, "Mattel, Maker of Barbie, Debuts Gender-Neutral
Dolls," *New York Times*, September 25, 2019 https://www.nytimes.com/
2019/09/25/arts/mattel-gender-neutral-dolls.html?smid=nytcore-ios-
share (archived at https://perma.cc/7M5L-KDQ9).

51 Daniel Auten and John Schneider, "The $1 Trillion Marketing
Executives Are Ignoring," *Forbes*, August 14, 2018,
https://www.forbes.com/sites/debtfreeguys/2018/08/14/the-1-trillion-

marketing-executives-are-ignoring/#215db330a97f (archived at https://perma.cc/AE9S-ERJF).

52   Fred Deveaux, "Counting the LGBT Population: 6% of Europeans Identify as LGBT," *Dalia*, October 18, 2016, https://daliaresearch. com/blog/counting-the-lgbt-population-6-of-europeans-identify-as-lgbt/ (archived at https://perma.cc/ZRL3-5W72).

53   Colin Poitras, "The 'Global Closet' Is Huge—Vast Majority of World's Lesbian, Gay, Bisexual Population Hide Orientation," *Yale School of Medicine*, June 13, 2019, https://medicine.yale.edu/ news-article/20510/ (archived at https://perma.cc/LY5R-UHDE).

54   Cam Wolf, "The Big Business of Pride Fashion," *GQ*, June 21, 2018, https://www.gq.com/story/the-big-business-of-pride-collections (archived at https://perma.cc/FK5D-TL5B).

55   Paul Harrison, "Fashion Company Loses Social Media Followers over Same-Sex Ads," *BBC News*, February 22, 2018, https://www.bbc.com/news/world-europe-43154607 (archived at https://perma.cc/J4NF-4NED).

56   Matthew Chapman, "Benetton to Feature Trans-Sexual Brazilian Model in Spring/Summer Campaign," *marketingmagazine.co.uk*, January 23, 2013, http://www.brandrepublic.com/news/1168021/ Benetton-feature-trans-sexual-Brazilian-model-Spring-Summer-campaign/ (archived at https://perma.cc/U9F2-DWFX).

57   Julia Baird, "Neither Female nor Male," *New York Times*, April 6, 2014, http://www.nytimes.com/2014/04/07/opinion/neither-female-nor-male.html?ref=opinion (archived at https://perma.cc/ 7YGL-LH3F).

58   Daniella Diaz, "Brown Signs Law OK'ing Third Option for Gender in California Driver's License," *CNN Politics*, October 17, 2017, https://www.cnn.com/2017/10/17/politics/governor-jerry-brown-california-law-nonbinary/index.html (archived at https://perma.cc/ 57XB-GFYX).

59   Martha Mendoza, "Facebook Users Now Have New Gender Option: Fill in the Blank", *NBC News*, July 7, 2014, https://www.nbcnews.com/ tech/social-media/facebook-users-now-have-new-gender-option-fill-blank-n313716 (archived at https://perma.cc/XP9Z-XD52).

60   Marjorie Garber, *Vested Interests: Cross-dressing and Cultural Anxiety* (Psychology Press): 2, 10, 14–16, 47.

07

Consumers who defy the separation of brand and identity

Feeling down? Go out and buy yourself a little something—or two. How many of us have bought into that bromide?

But good news for those who love to "shop 'til you drop." There is some research evidence that deciding to buy stuff actually does make us feel better.[1] This may be due to the sense of control the act of choosing something provides when we're dealing with issues we can't control so easily. Whether it works or not (even after you get the bill), the majority of Americans admit that they engage in "retail therapy" to regulate their moods.

Why brands really matter

Clearly, products and services link to our feelings and behaviors. But just how tight are these linkages, and how important are they to marketers? Spoiler alert: the answers are 1, really tight and 2, really important.

Surprisingly, much of marketing theory and practice doesn't fully acknowledge these connections. Sure, modern advertising tactics routinely paint an aspirational picture of what you *could* be like if you just bought Brand X. Still, there often feels like a disconnect between these rosy images that creative directors paint and the way that their bottom line–focused clients think about the real reasons we buy and consume. For many of us (and even for a lot of experienced marketers), there is a dichotomy between Me versus the Things I Buy. This is the case for several reasons.

We tend to focus on a product's functional attributes (e.g., gas mileage) rather than its subjective benefits (e.g., impressing your friends with your hot new sports car). A simplistic (modernist) view of cause and effect tends to obscure the long-term psychological dimensions of brand ownership (e.g., asking a research subject about the likelihood of her buying a new fragrance on a numerical scale is much different than probing about how that product acts as her "ally" in social interactions). Most assessments of brand meaning are highly mechanistic. They try to measure brand equity via simple scales—1 (don't agree) to 7 (highly agree)—that ask consumers to quantify their level of satisfaction with a brand's performance. They don't tap into the important nuances about the many ways a product or service links to a consumer's identity.

Finally, until fairly recently, product choices weren't as integral to self-identity as they are today. That's because the traditional markers and guideposts people used for millennia were still robust. These include place of birth (and likely death), religion, and social standing and family lineage. Before the dawn of the postmodern era, many brand choices were preordained and offered relatively few options.

For example, in the age of large, homogeneous market segments the brands that defined a social category also were fairly homogeneous. Thus an "organization man" of the 1950s or early 1960s didn't have too much latitude in his clothing choices (the standard white shirt or perhaps a daring light blue), and the housewife of the same era relied on familiar "household brands" with huge market share to fill her pantry. Many choices were proscribed by societies that tolerated little deviation from a set pattern. Some cultures developed explicit rules (known as sumptuary laws) about the specific garments and even colors that certain social classes and occupations were allowed to display. These traditions live on today in Japanese style manuals that set out detailed instructions for dressing and how to address people of differing status.

Indeed, the very concept of a unique "self" that you would express via your choices was somewhat alien in many cultures. Many Eastern cultures stress the importance of a collective self, where a person derives his or her identity in large measure from a social group. They tend to focus on an interdependent self, whereas we define our identities largely by our relationships with others. For example, a Confucian perspective stresses the importance of "face": others' perceptions of the self and maintaining one's desired status in their eyes.

Brand resonance

Sure, we value what we buy because we need to get stuff done. But a deeper view of brand meaning takes us to why our possessions *really* matter. In fact, there are a multitude of dimensions that lead to what my colleagues and I call brand resonance. Brand resonance is the extent to which a brand's meaning reverberates with the user in a fundamental way. A resonant brand gets its hooks into you, because it helps you to express some aspect of your identity.[2]

Here are a few examples of brand resonance dimensions. A much longer list is available in a "Brand Resonance Audit" you can download at www.michaelsolomon.com.

1 Interdependency: Does my brand facilitate habits, rituals, and routines that entwine the brand's meanings seamlessly into the consumer's everyday life? Brand example: Ben & Jerry's ice cream

2 Intimacy: Does my brand have "insiders" who know details of its history, including significant product development particulars, myths about product creators, and obscure "brand trivia" or facts? Brand example: Air Jordan trainers

3 Category resonance: Is my brand iconic within its category; do customers use it as a benchmark to compare other brands? Brand example: Harley-Davidson motorcycles

Brands and personal identity

Before we do a deep dive into the linkages between products and our individual identities, let's briefly consider what we even mean by "the self." The self-concept summarizes the beliefs a person holds about his or her own attributes and how he or she evaluates the self on these qualities. Although your overall self-concept may be positive, there certainly are parts of it you evaluate more positively than others. We describe attributes of self-concept along such dimensions as content (e.g., facial attractiveness versus mental aptitude), positivity (i.e., self-esteem), intensity and stability over time, and accuracy (i.e., the degree to which one's self-assessment corresponds to reality).

A person's self-concept is a work in progress. Some parts are fairly stable, but each of us modifies some elements of it as we make our way through life—and particularly as we discover new ideas, social groups we admire, and yes, images we receive from marketing communications that endorse certain types of people over others. Each element that contributes to our self-concept is an identity. Some of these identities are pretty stable (e.g., mother, African American), whereas other identities are more temporary and likely to change (e.g., Libertarian, college student, Prius driver).

It's vital for marketers to understand how consumers adopt certain identities. Then, they can develop products and messages that meet the needs of people who link themselves to a given identity. So, for example a person who sees herself as environmentally responsible is more likely than someone who doesn't think much about that to drive a Prius hybrid vehicle. "Green" products are more likely to get that person's attention.

REAL AND IDEAL SELVES

When a consumer compares some aspect of himself or herself to an ideal, this judgment influences self-esteem. He or she might ask, "Am I as good-looking as I would like to be?" or "Do I make as much money as I should?" The ideal self is a person's conception of how he or she would like to be, whereas the actual self refers to our more realistic appraisal of the qualities we do and don't have.

Unless a person suffers from an extraordinarily inflated ego (we've all known some of those), most of us experience a discrepancy between our real and ideal selves. After all, each of us is a work in progress. We usually believe we're not quite where we'd like to be when we contemplate our tennis game, job title, or reflection in the mirror.

But for some consumers this gap is especially large. These people are especially good targets for marketing communications that employ fantasy appeals. A fantasy or daydream is a self-induced shift in consciousness, which is sometimes a way to compensate for a lack of external stimulation or to escape from problems in the real world. Many products and services succeed because they appeal to our fantasies. An ad may transport us to an unfamiliar, exciting situation; things we purchase may permit us to "try on" interesting or provocative roles.

In this regard, let's take a moment to revisit one of the basic principles of consumer decision making: *every* choice a customer makes involves some degree of risk, and solutions that reduce this risk have a greater chance to succeed. That's important to remember in this context, because it highlights one reason why it's valuable to invest in technology that allows customers to experiment in a risk-free environment.

For example, if a woman chooses a radically new hair color or style, she's taking a big risk if the end result is not what she had in mind. Don't try consoling her by saying, "Don't worry, it will grow back!"

Until recently, she could only try to imagine what the new look would actually look like. But today, a plethora of websites like stylecaster.com, Maybelline's Virtual Makeup Tools, myvirtualmodel .com, and Warby Parker's phone app offer a risk-free way to modify your hair, makeup, glasses, and even physical dimensions like bust size.

These and similar tech shortcuts that create a risk-free environment can be extremely valuable for a lot of products in addition to radical new haircuts. Marketers who deal with car designs, home furnishings, and (of course) plastic surgery are obvious candidates to embrace these new approaches.

We choose some products because we think they are consistent with our actual self, whereas we buy others to help us reach an ideal standard. As we saw in a previous chapter, we also often engage in a process of impression management in which we work hard to "manage" what others think of us; we strategically choose clothing and other products that will show us off to others in a good light.

The dating app Tinder helpfully provides a feature called Smart Photos to boost your chances: using an algorithm, it analyzes which of your profile pictures performs the best and ranks them in order for you, hoping to get more people swiping right. As Tinder's founder observed, "First impressions matter. We're empowering users to put their best foot forward."[3]

In a way, each of us really is a number of different people—for example, your mother probably would not recognize the "you" that emerges at a party at 2:00 a.m.! We have as many selves as we do different social roles. Depending on the situation, we act differently, use different products and services, and even vary in terms of how much we like the aspect of ourselves we put on display.

A person may require a different set of products to play each of her roles. She may choose a sedate, understated perfume when she plays her professional self, but splash on something more provocative on Saturday night as she transitions to her femme fatale self.

Indeed, some psychologists who study personality go so far as to argue there is no such thing as a stable personality because different aspects of the self emerge, depending upon the situational cues we perceive around us. It's no coincidence that one of the first acts of institutions like prisons that want to repress individuality is to confiscate personal possessions and issue standardized gear.

Our bonds with our possessions become glaringly apparent when we lose them. Victims of burglaries and natural disasters commonly report feelings of alienation, depression, or of being "violated." One consumer's comment after she was robbed is typical: "It's the next worse thing to being bereaved; it's like being raped."[4] Burglary victims exhibit a diminished sense of community, lowered feelings of privacy, and less pride in their houses' appearance than do their neighbors.[5]

That famous marketing researcher William Shakespeare talked about the world as a stage. The dramaturgical perspective on consumer behavior views people as actors who play different roles. We each play many roles, and each has its own script, props, and costumes. The self has different components, or role identities, and only some of these are active at any given time. Some identities (e.g., husband, boss, student) are more central to the self than others, but other identities (e.g., dancer, gearhead, or advocate for the homeless) may dominate in specific situations.[6]

Different marketing for different selves

Strategically, a marketer needs to ensure that the appropriate role identity is active before pitching products that customers need to play a particular role. One obvious way to do this is to place advertising messages in contexts in which people are likely to be well aware of that role identity; for example, when fortified drink and energy bar product companies hand out free product samples to runners at a marathon.

And I've found it really helps to think about your customer as an actor who is going to need costumes, props, and stage settings at some point. Translation: every role requires apparel, furnishings, and a variety of other products—what can *you* provide?

As I love to say (perhaps too much!), "We don't buy things because of what they do. We buy them because of what they mean." Hopefully this little digression has convinced you that the products and services we buy do influence who we are, and certainly who *others* think we are.

That understanding is invaluable to marketers who make stuff that people use for this purpose. Most likely the "usual suspects" like apparel manufacturers already realize this, but I'm often surprised by how many brand managers who should grasp this connection don't seem to get it. If you sell food and beverages, cars, home furnishings, office supplies, financial products, health and wellness products, or many, many other things (not to mention the services that accompany them) this linkage is *vital* for you to understand and apply to your marketing strategies and tactics.

But even if the person/product argument I'm making is preaching to the choir, there is still an interesting question of causality lurking in the background (with thanks to those modernists!). Are we what we buy, or do we buy what we are? In other words, do consumers strategically and carefully choose those products and services that express their self-concepts? Or does it work the other way? Do the things we consume actually help to shape who we are? Let's look at both sequences (another spoiler alert: *both* sequences are valid and important!).

We buy what we are

As the famous psychologist William James wrote way back in 1890, "A man's self is the sum total of all that he can call his."[7] And that was before Supreme apparel, NutriBullet blenders, and Beats headphones!

Not too surprisingly, research shows that we tend to choose products when their attributes match some aspect of the self.[8] In a classic study, Pontiac drivers saw themselves as more active and flashier than did Volkswagen drivers.[9] Other studies report similar matchups for products as diverse as toothpaste and cigarettes.[10]

And we form strong bonds with those that really sync with how we regard ourselves. We even get defensive when others criticize our favorite brands. In one study of self-image congruence, a young male respondent said it well: "My BMW is my wingman, my twin. I would never diss it for another car because that would be like dissing my twin brother or worse, dissing myself."[11] He's not alone—many Americans have nicknames for their cars and baby them as if they were their children (or lovers?).

Consumers form all kinds of bonds with their possessions that range from love to hate ("why does my computer have it in for me?").[12] And breakups can be painful—studies show that after they leave a brand relationship it's not unusual for people bad-mouth their "ex" and even try to vandalize it.[13]

Sacred vs. profane consumption

Sure, many things we buy, from appliances to accessories, are chockful of meanings. Some of these meanings are more obvious than others, but often if you dig deep enough you can gather a lot of insights from what seem to be very mundane purchases. A person who splurges on a juicer or an exercise bike may be making a statement about health as a priority (whether he actually uses the device is another story), while the prominent display of a pricey Sub-Zero refrigerator or a Viking gas range may say more about the desire to telegraph the owner's ability to afford these toys than his or her culinary skills. Indeed, in developing countries everyday objects such as refrigerators, satellite dishes (that may or may not actually be connected), and even toilets function as status symbols.[14]

Even so, it's clear that some products, services, and experiences are more meaningful than others. Marketers need to be aware of this because these insights can make a huge difference in how they think about what they sell—and how they package these meanings to their customers. Sometimes these hidden meanings come to light only when a company overlooks them: Nike recently had to pull a new line of Pro Tattoo Tech Gear clothing line for women after the news came out that the graphics it used came from a sacred Samoan tattoo that only men wear. Consumers started a Change.org petition online and bombarded the brand's Facebook page with negative comments.[15]

One important, yet often overlooked dimension of meaning is the dichotomy that anthropologists term sacred vs. profane. Sacred consumption occurs when we "set apart" objects and events from normal activities and treat them with respect or awe. Note that in this context the term sacred does not necessarily carry a religious meaning, although we do tend to think of religious artifacts and ceremonies as "sacred." Sacred objects and experiences don't have to be expensive or luxury items; for example, a person's cherished matchbook collection that he proudly displays on a shelf might be sacred in this context. What is sacred essentially is in the eye of the beholder.

Profane consumption, in contrast, describes objects and events that are ordinary or everyday; they don't share the "specialness" of sacred ones. Again, note that in this context we don't equate the word profane with obscenity, although the two meanings do share some similarities. In the old days at least, the two domains didn't mix. References to organized religion in the service of selling material goods were traditionally taboo (not counting Christmas sales, perhaps).

Making the profane sacred through marketing

Our pervasive consumer culture imbues objects, events, and even people with sacred meaning. Many of us regard events such as the Super Bowl and people such as Elvis Presley as sacred. Even the Smithsonian Institution in Washington, DC maintains a display that features such "sacred items" as the ruby slippers from *The Wizard of Oz*, a phaser from *Star Trek*, and Archie Bunker's chair from the television show *All in the Family*.[16] When Captain Kirk's weapon is displayed with the same reverence as the Mona Lisa in the Louvre (which in turn is virtually inaccessible these days because of the hordes of tourists who are eager to take a selfie with the tiny masterpiece), we know that things are changing.

Marketers can sometimes find opportunities to make a product sacred. For example, the increasingly common practice of selling limited-edition items—so-called "product drops"—can accelerate this process. When Rimowa created a suitcase collection in collaboration with the street brand Supreme that carried a hefty starting price of $1,600 and was announced only three days prior to the release date, the entire line sold out in 16 seconds.[17] Or, travel marketers can turn vacations into sacred (i.e., special) events, even when a customer's minister may not remotely think of his or her escapades as holy—after all, what happens in Vegas, stays in Vegas.

Another innovative strategy is to "productize" sacred places and experiences. When Ajax, the local football team of Amsterdam, moved from their old stadium, De Meern, to a larger, more modern stadium (De Arena), the turf from the old stadium was carefully lifted from the ground and sold to a local churchyard. The churchyard offers the turf to fans willing to pay a premium price to be buried under authentic Ajax turf! Great minds think alike: when the old Yankee Stadium in New York City closed a few years ago to make way for a newer facility, an enterprising company secured the rights to the original sod that it sells in a freeze-dried "shrine."[18]

High art vs. low art

The masses seek distraction whereas art demands concentration from the spectator.

THE WORK OF ART IN THE AGE OF MECHANICAL REPRODUCTION,
WALTER BENJAMIN, 1936

Question: what do Beethoven and Drake have in common? Although we associate both the famous composer and the rap singer with music, many would argue that the similarity stops there.

In addition to regarding some objects and experiences as sacred or profane, we tend to make a similar distinction between "high art" and "low art." Sacred objects and experiences may be physically separated by being displayed in a collection or via a limited access VIP pass. Sometimes we can literally see the difference: "high art" is often shielded from us by a pane of glass and perhaps a forbidding museum guard. "Low art" is there for the touching in the form of graphic T-shirts, souvenir keychains, or velvet paintings stacked for sale at a local gas station.

Well, that's a pretty elitist view of art, isn't it? Indeed, this dichotomy has always had a snobby tint that equates taste with money. Rich people "get" real art, and the rest of us make do with tawdry reproductions.

This worldview that divides aesthetic products into categories has been the norm for a long time. Pierre Bourdieu, for example, was a French theorist who wrote at length about how people compete for resources, or capital. Bourdieu did large-scale surveys to track people's wealth, and he related this "economic capital" to patterns of taste in entertainment and the arts. He concluded that "taste" is a status-marking force, or what he called habitus, that causes consumption preferences to cluster together. Later analyses of US consumers largely confirmed these relationships; for example, higher-income people are more likely than the average consumer to attend the theater, whereas lower-income people are more likely to take in a wrestling match.[19]

In one of the classic studies of social differences in taste, researchers cataloged homeowners' possessions as they sat in their living rooms and asked them about their income and occupation. They identified clusters of furnishings and decorative items that seemed to appear together with some regularity, and they found different clusters depending on the consumer's social status. For example, they tended to find a cluster that consisted of religious objects, artificial flowers, and still-life portraits in relatively lower-status living rooms, whereas they were likely to catalog a cluster of abstract paintings, sculptures, and modern furniture in a higher-status home.[20]

ARTS VS. CRAFTS

We make a similar distinction between arts and crafts. We admire an art product strictly for its beauty, while we covet a craft product because it beautifully does something useful—think of hand-carved fishing lures for example. And craft products tend to be mass-produced.[21] We may appreciate a craft product as a work of art (like woven baskets that some museums display), but these one-off pieces are not mass-produced by a basket factory.[22]

However, the cage that traditionally separates arts and crafts is opening as well. Like those baskets, crafts can be displayed as art, and art can be mass-produced as a craft. That explains why it's so easy to find "limited-edition" lithographs by Pablo Picasso, Marc Chagall, and Joan Miró nestled next to car tires or breakfast cereal at a warehouse club like Costco.

The works of the late artist Thomas Kinkade provide a perfect demonstration of the collision between art and craft. Though Kinkade died in 2012, his studio continues to churn out his work at a California factory. There is literally an assembly line, where "high-lighters" dab oil paint onto reproductions as they roll by. His estate also licenses these images to show up on La-Z-Boy recliners, coffee mugs, and even a romance novel cover.[23]

OUR DEFINITION OF (LUCRATIVE) ART IS EXPANDING

Art is big business: in 2018 the global market was valued at north of $67 billion.[24] And the barrier between high and low art crumbles as the scope of this business expands dramatically. Handbags in particular seem to be becoming less of an emotional, impulse purchase and more of an investment decision.[25] A luxury handbag resale site called Rebag uses an algorithm to show bag owners the resale spot prices of their bags if they sell them to Rebag. They can track these prices over time to decide when to buy or sell. Similarly, at StockX, sneakerheads buy and trade vintage sneakers (now watches and bags get the same treatment on the platform). This logic can potentially apply to other verticals such as tools, rare food and beverage products, or perhaps even limited-access experiences.

A slew of new business platforms are springing up to facilitate the blurring of lines between indulgence and investment. Some of these, like Reel and Cashmere, actually revive the old-fashioned installment plans that department stores used to offer, while others put a new spin on the rent-to-own business. And of course, rental concepts like Rent the Runway are gaining traction as well. A newer twist is collaborative savings on platforms like Stepladder, where a group of aspiring luxury owners pool their money and take turns cashing out to purchase expensive items.[26] As the fashion industry tries to recover from the intense battering it took during the pandemic, we can expect to see an even greater focus on investment dressing as many fashion shoppers turn their backs on their pre-virus fixation with cheap, fast fashion.

Improving the brand experience

This new routine of near-constant consumption, coupled with the increasing affluence of many consumers around the world, means that now more than ever marketers need to understand what I call the "deep meanings" of products and services.

The sad truth (at least in my experience) is that even though brand managers believe their option is the best thing since sliced bread, most consumers don't see huge differences among competing (major) brands. They believe they all work fairly well. Still, it's common for one or two brands in a traditional category to seem to eclipse the others. Why? Because they have a pleasing design or a compelling story to tell (more on that later). Thus, brand experience is the crucial dimension that differentiates the winners from the also-rans. This experience often gets delivered by the product's design rather than by its function.

We may assume that if something is pleasing to look at it, it's not as practical as other more basic alternatives. But that traditional distinction between beautiful vs. practical is disappearing rapidly. As manufacturing costs go down and the amount of "stuff" that people accumulate goes up, consumers want to buy things that will provide *hedonic value* (i.e., pleasure) in addition to simply doing what they're designed to do.

A *Dilbert* comic strip poked fun at this trend when it featured a product designer who declared, "Quality is yesterday's news. Today we focus on the emotional impact of the product." Fun aside, the new focus on emotional experience is consistent with psychological research finding that people prefer additional *experiences* to additional *possessions* as their incomes rise.[27]

In this environment, form *is* function. Two young entrepreneurs named Adam Lowry and Eric Ryan discovered that basic truth when they quit their day jobs to develop a line of house-cleaning products they called Method. Cleaning products—what a yawn, right?

Think again. For years, companies such as Procter & Gamble have plodded along, peddling boring boxes of soap powder to generations of housewives who suffered in silence, scrubbing and buffing, yearning for the daily respite of martini time. Lowry and Ryan gambled that they could offer an alternative: cleaners in exotic scents such as cucumber, lavender, and ylang-ylang that come in aesthetically pleasing bottles. The bet paid off. Within two years, the partners were cleaning up, taking in more than $2 million in revenue. Shortly thereafter, they hit it big when Target contracted to sell Method products in its stores.[28]

There's a method to Target's madness. Design is no longer the province of upper-crust sophisticates who never got close enough to a cleaning product to be revolted by it. The store chain helped to make designers such as Karim Rashid, Michael Graves, Philippe Starck, Todd Oldham, and Isaac Mizrahi household names.

In fact, research evidence suggests that our brains are wired to appreciate good design. Respondents who were hooked up to a brain apparatus called a functional magnetic resonance imaging (fMRI) scanner showed faster reaction times when they saw aesthetically pleasing packages even compared to well-known brands such as Coca-Cola.[29]

In the old days, companies assumed that only the upper crust appreciated the aesthetics of a product. That's no longer true (if it ever was). Today mass-market consumers thirst for great design, and they reward those companies that give it to them with their enthusiastic patronage and loyalty. From razor blades such as the Gillette Sensor to the Apple Watch and even to the lowly trashcan, design is substance. Form is function.

We are what we buy

The objects we love bolster our confidence and even our identity, especially when we encounter situations that are novel. One study even reported that college students who decorated their dorm rooms with personalized mementos were more likely to stay in school.[30] That's one illustration of the other side of the coin: we are what we buy.

And as we might expect, not all of these valued objects are items like a sweater that Grandma knitted; at least some are likely to be items that someone bought somewhere. When a pair of researchers asked children of various ages to create "who am I?" collages, for which they chose pictures that represented their selves, older kids between middle childhood and early adolescence inserted more photos of branded merchandise. Also, as they aged, their feelings about these objects evolved from concrete relationships (e.g., "I own it") to more sophisticated, abstract relationships (e.g., "It is like me").[31]

The body as billboard

Today, we don't just put things *on*; we put things *in*. Permanent tattoos, breast, lip, buttock and cheek implants, artificial hips, knees and prostheses, pacemakers, and embedded computer chips obliterate the traditional boundary between what we're born with and what we own.

The use of foreign materials to replace or supplement human body parts is not necessarily new. After all, centuries ago some people with dental problems (including George Washington) suffered with a set of wooden teeth. However, more recent advances in technology continue to erode the barrier between self and not-self:[32]

- According to the American Society for Aesthetic Plastic Surgery, Americans get more than nine million cosmetic surgical and nonsurgical procedures in a year. The most frequently performed surgical procedure is breast augmentation, which typically involves the integration of man-made silicone implants with the patient's organic material. The United States leads the world with the largest number of implants, but other countries including Brazil, Germany, Spain, and Russia are up there as well.[33]

- More than four million Americans have an artificial knee. Switzerland boasts the largest number of people with fake knees per capita.[34]

- At least prior to his arrest for murder that made global headlines, the South African track star Oscar Pistorius competed against world-class runners with two artificial legs made of carbon—his nickname was "Blade Runner." Nike teamed with orthopedics company Össur to introduce its first sprinting prosthesis, called the Nike Sole, perhaps the first commercially scalable transformation of disabled athletes into "superabled" athletes.

These and other technologies also hasten the transformation of the body into a product delivery platform. In addition to products like pantyhose that secrete caffeine onto the legs to reduce the appearance of cellulite (yes it works, at least temporarily), micro-encapsulation techniques allow textile manufacturers to create "smart textiles" that provide a steady dose of substances as these tiny containers rub against the wearer's body. Potential applications include skin softeners, insect repellents, vitamins, and even hormones.[35]

And, in the postmodern world, we may even rent out our bodies to be sure others know just where we stand, brand-wise. Identity marketing is a promotional strategy that encourages consumers to alter some part of their bodies to advertise a branded product.

Air New Zealand created "cranial billboards" in exchange for a round-trip ticket to New Zealand—30 Los Angeles participants shaved their heads and walked around with an ad for the airline on their skulls.[36] If people continue to routinely wear face masks in public in "the new normal," we can probably expect to see a brand new advertising medium emerge as companies figure out they can plant their logos directly on our faces.

Temporary tattoos of brand logos are common these days (along with a fair number of permanent ones). Companies hand them out like candy at sporting events, concerts, and other public venues. This idea is hardly new; bubblegum companies in the nineteenth century distributed crudely made versions of today's temporary tats, and then in 1890 Cracker Jack included them as one of their "prize in every box" promotions.

But today the stakes are higher: Reebok recently set up a pop-up tattoo shop at an event in Sweden and gave away thousands of dollars in prizes to the fan who got the biggest version of the brand's new triangle logo (not a temporary one). The lucky winner's right thigh is, shall we say, Reebok's for life.[37]

People use an individual's consumption behaviors to identify that person's social identity. In addition to checking out a persons's clothes and grooming habits, we make inferences about personality based on his or her choice of leisure activities (e.g., squash vs. bowling), food preferences (e.g., tofu and beans vs. steak and potatoes), cars, and home decorating choices. When researchers show people pictures of someone's living room, for example, study participants make surprisingly accurate guesses about the occupant's personality.[38]

So, even if you don't believe that you buy what you are, rest assured your neighbors do.

The extended self

Come on, admit it. You can probably name some product or service that you're absolutely bonkers about. It may be a favorite fishing rod, tennis racket, or skateboard. Maybe it's a certain craft beer or aged Scotch. How about designer handbags or that set of Miro lithos that hang in your living room, or even that stamp collection you inherited from your Dad? Or, perhaps you're a "sneakerhead" with a massive stash of Air Jordans you "visit" periodically.

Many of us are fanatics about a cherished type of product. Consider shoes, for example; you don't have to be Imelda Marcos (the former leader of the Philippines who was famous for owning hundreds of shoes) to acknowledge that many people feel a strong bond to their footwear. The singer Mariah Carey posted a photo of her huge shoe closet on Instagram and labeled it, "Always my favorite room in the house... #shoes #shoes #moreshoes."[39]

One study found that people commonly view their shoes as magical emblems of the self; Cinderella-like vehicles for self-transformation. A common theme that emerged was that a pair of shoes the person obtained when younger—whether a first pair of leather shoes, a first pair of high heels, or a first pair of cowboy boots—had a big impact even later in life. These experiences were similar to those we see in such well-known fairy tales and stories as Dorothy's red shoes in *The Wizard of Oz*, Karen's magical red shoes in Hans Christian Anderson's *The Red Shoes*, and Cinderella's glass slippers.[40]

Some of us love our shoe collections, but many other possessions also may do the trick for others. Many of us value objects like old photographs or a school trophy because they remind us of our selves in days gone by. There's a reason that tourists spend millions of dollars on kitschy souvenirs.

One study showed just how powerful—and subtle—these person/object relationships can be. In a shopping mall, researchers gave women one of two shopping bags at random. The shoppers who walked around with a Victoria's Secret bag reported later that they felt glamorous and sensual. In a different study that merely distributed pens with an MIT logo to students, test subjects who took notes with the pen told researchers they felt smarter when the term ended.[41]

Those external objects that we consider a part of us constitute the extended self. Researchers describe four levels of the extended self, ranging from personal objects to places and things that allow people to feel as though they are rooted in their larger social environments:[42]

1 *Individual level.* Personal objects such as clothing, cars, and jewelry.

2 *Family level.* A child may influence his parent's reputation—for better or worse. That's one reason why some parents sink a lot of resources into tutors, impressive clothing, and maybe even etiquette classes to insure their "brand extensions" reflect favorably on them.

3 *Community level.* A person's identity partly derives from the place he or she grew up or lives now. Just think of all those proud Southerners who love to flaunt their sweet tea.

4 *Group level.* Each of us has linkages to group identities, including religious, athletic, and political affiliations. That helps to explain why you may get a lot of "attention" from your university's alumni organization.

The drive to enhance some aspect of the extended self lurks behind many purchases. Companies that sell licensed athletic wear seem to have figured this out, but perhaps those in other verticals not so much. If your brand successfully links the consumer to a cherished piece of identity such as a band, school, or old neighborhood, this gives you a distinct advantage over other products that just sell "stuff" without anchoring it to some key aspect of a customer's identity.

"You complete me"

Our use of consumption information to define the self is especially important when we have yet to completely form a social identity, such as when we have to play a new role in life. Adolescent boys, for example, may use "macho" products such as cars and cigarettes to bolster developing masculinity; these items act as a "social crutch" during a period of uncertainty about their new identity as adult males.

Or, think of the insecurity many people feel when they start college or reenter the dating market after they've exited a long-term relationship. Symbolic self-completion theory suggests that people who have an incomplete self-definition tend to complete this identity when they acquire and display symbols they associate with that role.[43]

A study of MBA students carefully chronicled the markers of "executive success" that these managers-in-training displayed, such as luxury watches, fancy briefcases, and the like. Sure enough, the researchers found that those students who scored *lower* on measures of actual achievement (GPA, number of interviews, etc.) were *more likely* to sport these products. In another study that hits a bit closer to home, less accomplished professors (in terms of number of publications, etc.) were more likely to hang a large number of diplomas, certifications, and other badges of scholarly achievement on their office walls.

Some years ago—back in the day when it was still something of a news story that sizeable numbers of young women were flooding into management roles—I conducted several studies when I was on the faculty at New York University to explore how role insecurity related to choices of "appropriate professional apparel." I was motivated by the anxiety my female MBA students expressed to me about whether the clothing they wore to work (largely on Wall Street) would send the appropriate signals.

At that time, most of them chose the safe route. They dressed as male clones in very severe, dark suits—but they weren't happy about it because they felt they had to sacrifice their femininity in order to succeed in a man's world. This tension perseveres today, especially in the wake of the sexual harassment scandals we encounter in fields from politics and business to entertainment and the arts.

My research revealed an interesting anomaly: although in most contexts we expect younger people to be the fashion trendsetters, in a business context the opposite was true. Using a sample of over 50,000 readers of a female executive magazine, we found instead that older, more experienced women were more likely to endorse a wide range of styles they felt were appropriate to wear to work. Younger, less experienced women are more likely to rely upon external cues such as professional clothing to guide self-definition. Like the anxious women I saw in my Manhattan classroom, the newbies were much more likely to believe that only a very constricted set of styles (essentially female versions of the male banker's suit) were OK.[44]

This compensatory process is important, because it implies that it's *novices* rather than experts who are more likely to acquire products that are stereotypically linked to a role. That's a bit counterintuitive, perhaps, but this relationship can hold important marketing ramifications. If you provide products and services to people who need them to master some kind of skill, whether soccer or navigating the dating market or decorating a home (or body), your most attractive prospects may well be customers who are less adept rather than more experienced. Or at the least these buyers are the ones who will appreciate the value-add of the expertise you can offer.

In research I conducted with professional wardrobe consultants, I identified this two-pronged structure.[45] One set of women who paid these experts to organize their closets and shop for them had a clear idea of the image they wanted to project; they just didn't have the time to procure the props and costumes themselves. The other set used these consultants in an entirely different way; they wanted them to dictate what they should buy because they lacked the self-confidence to choose for themselves. So, mea culpa, I created a dichotomy to describe the function these experts performed: legs versus head.

"Clothes (and other stuff) make the (wo)man"

So, it seems that my female students and their sisters rely upon the signals they glean from their clothing to define their professional role. More generally, to what extent do the products we buy influence how we define ourselves?

Social scientists who study relationships between thoughts and behaviors increasingly turn to the theory of embodied cognition for answers. A simple way to explain this perspective is that "states of the body modify states of the mind."[46] In other words, our behaviors and observations of what we do and buy shape our thoughts, *rather than vice versa*. Yes, we buy what we are. But we also are what we buy, and that's a whole other ball of wax.

One of the most powerful illustrations of embodied cognition is the notion that our body language actually changes how we see ourselves. In one of the most widely viewed TED talks ever, a social psychologist discusses how power posing (standing in a confident way even if you don't feel confident) affects brain activity. Facebook COO Sheryl Sandberg's campaign to encourage women to "lean in" conveys the same idea.[47] This research is highly controversial, but it at least hints at the idea that *what we do influences what we feel*, rather than vice versa.

The embodied cognition approach is consistent with consumer behavior research that demonstrates how changes in self-concept can arise from usage of brands that convey different meanings. Indeed, a pair of researchers used the term enclothed cognition in their work that showed how the symbolic meaning of clothing changes how people behave. In one study they asked respondents to wear a lab coat, which people associate with attentiveness and precise work. They found that subjects who wore the lab coat displayed enhanced performance on tasks that required them to pay close attention. But they also introduced a twist: when respondents were told the garment was in fact a painter's coat rather than a doctor's lab coat, the effects went away. In other words, the respondents interpreted the symbolic meaning of the clothing and then altered their behavior accordingly.[48]

It's tempting to point out that a study your humble author conducted more than 40 years ago on the "dress for success" phenomenon found similar results for students in job interview settings. In perhaps the best Ph.D. dissertation ever written (at least in your author's opinion), male job candidates who wore professional attire acted more assertively and confidently during the interviews, and on average even asked for higher starting salaries![49]

Again, lots of implications here for thoughtful marketers. The power of embodied cognition means that your products and services actually have the potential to change how your customers feel. So, one obvious takeaway is to do whatever you can to get them to try and use what you sell.

In the good old days of marketing, it was common for companies to loan their customers samples to take home and experience. Even Apple did this when the company first introduced the Macintosh; it needed to take radical steps to wean consumers from the IBM mindset. That might not be financially feasible today, but really anything you can do to immerse your customer with your product is helpful. Encouraging buyers to take a "test drive" breaks down barriers to acceptance as their self-concepts meld with the items.

I saw this transformation play out literally hundreds or even thousands of times back in the day when I worked as a formalwear salesman starting in junior high and through college. If I had a nickel for every time a woman dragged her reluctant fiancé into the store… and then after much cajoling he emerged from the dressing room dressed in a tuxedo and a smile as he was able to visualize the role much more clearly. You would have sworn that some magic machine had replaced this guy with James Bond! Today of course we have immersive technology like augmented reality and virtual reality that can accomplish the same thing. Think about it.

And so, the cage that separates us from our possessions is now open. We buy what we are, and we are what we buy.

CHAPTER TAKEAWAYS

- Our self-concept is firmly linked in multiple ways to our consumption choices. Marketers just don't just sell products and services; they supply the vehicles we use to express our identities and to make sense of other people. There is a false dichotomy between our selves and our possessions.

- Brand resonance describes the degree to which a product or service is linked in some way to a consumer's identity. There are multiple pathways to achieve this resonance.

- We buy what we are: people tend to choose products that have brand personalities similar to their own.

- Determination of perceived risk is one of the most important considerations for any purchase. Shortcuts that allow a shopper to view the results of a choice in a risk-free environment will transform the decision-making landscape for many products and services.

- Identity marketing is a promotional strategy that encourages consumers to alter some part of their bodies to advertise a branded product.

- We buy a huge range of products because of a drive to enhance the extended self. Brands that link the consumer to key elements of the self have a leg up over others that don't do such a good job of connecting to the extended self-concept.

- Your business may involve tourism, sports, design, music, or any one of many verticals that elevate certain people, objects, and places to sacred status. One way to add an extra layer of value to what you sell is to enshrine it as part of a collection that is set apart from "ordinary" items.

- The traditional distinction between arts and crafts is fading away. As categories merge, "art products" sell in mass-market channels, while "craft products" become collectors' items. Businesses that sell these products need to expand their vision in order to meet the demand for aesthetically pleasing items that the growing market demands.

- Indulgences can be investments, too. A return to a focus on value is transforming the way many shoppers think about allocating their discretionary income. Product durability is likely to return as an important differentiator, in contrast to the disposable society of a few years ago.

- We are what we buy: our possessions can help to anchor us in unfamiliar situations or roles.

Endnotes

1 Scott Rick, Beatriz Pereira, and Katherine Alicia Burson, "The Benefits of Retail Therapy: Making Purchase Decisions Reduces Residual Sadness," *Journal of Consumer Psychology* 24, no.3 (July 2014): 373–80.

2 Susan G. Fournier, Michael R. Solomon, and Basil G. Englis, "Brand Resonance," in *Handbook on Brand and Experience Management*, eds. B.H Schmitt and D.L. Rogers (Cheltenham, UK and Northampton, MA, USA: Edward Elgar, 2009): 35–57.

3 Quoted in Adnan Farooqui, "Tinder Creates Fancy Algorithm to Increase Your Chances of a Match," *Ubergizmo*, October 13, 2016, https://www.ubergizmo.com/2016/10/tinder-creates-fancy-algorithm-to-increase-your-chances-of-a-match/ (archived at https://perma.cc/W77H-2C66).

4   Floyd Rudmin, "Property Crime Victimization Impact on Self, on Attachment, and on Territorial Dominance," *CPA Highlights, Victims of Crime Supplement* 9, no. 2 (1987): 4–7.

5   Barbara B. Brown, "House and Block as Territory," paper presented at the Conference of the Association for Consumer Research, San Francisco, CA, 1982.

6   Michael R. Solomon, "The Role of Products as Social Stimuli: A Symbolic Interactionism Perspective," *Journal of Consumer Research* 10, (December 1983): 319–29.

7   https://www.goodreads.com/quotes/1326736-a-man-s-self-is-the-sum-total-of-all-that#:~:text=%E2%80%9CA%20man's%20Self%20is%20the%20sum%20total%20of%20all%20that,his%20clothes%20and%20his%20house.%E2%80%9D (archived at https://perma.cc/B392-HYN3).

8   Jennifer L. Aaker, "The Malleable Self: The Role of Self-Expression in Persuasion," *Journal of Marketing Research* 36 (February 1999): 45–57; Sak Onkvisit and John Shaw, "Self-Concept and Image Congruence: Some Research and Managerial Implications," *Journal of Consumer Marketing* 4 (Winter 1987): 13–24.

9   Benedict Carey, "With That Saucy Swagger, She Must Drive a Porsche," *New York Times* (June 13, 2006), www.nytimes.com (archived at https://perma.cc/2YHG-S5PR), accessed March 25, 2015.

10 L. E. Birdwell, "A Study of Influence of Image Congruence on Consumer Choice," *Journal of Business* 41 (January 1964): 76–88; Edward L. Grubb and Gregg Hupp, "Perception of Self, Generalized Stereotypes, and Brand Selection," *Journal of Marketing Research* 5 (February 1986): 58–63; Benedict Carey, "With That Saucy Swagger, She Must Drive a Porsche," *New York Times*, June 13, 2006, https://www.nytimes.com/2006/06/13/health/13cars.html (archived at https://perma.cc/89MU-4AX4).

11 Quoted in Shirley Y. Y. Cheng, Tiffany Barnett White, and Lan Nguyen Chaplin, "The Effects of Self-brand Connections on Responses to Brand Failure: A New Look at the Consumer–Brand Relationship," *Journal of Consumer Psychology* 22, no. 2 (2012): 280–88.

12 C. B. Claiborne and M. Joseph Sirgy, "Self-Image Congruence as a Model of Consumer Attitude Formation and Behavior: A Conceptual Review and Guide for Further Research," paper presented at the Academy of Marketing Science Conference, New Orleans, LA, 1990.

13 Susan Fournier and Julie L. Yao, "Reviving Brand Loyalty: A
Reconceptualization Within the Framework of Consumer-Brand
Relationships," *International Journal of Research in Marketing* 14,
no. 5 (December 1997): 451–72; Caryl E. Rusbult, "A Longitudinal
Test of the Investment Model: The Development (and Deterioration)
of Satisfaction and Commitment in Heterosexual Involvements,"
Journal of Personality & Social Psychology 45, no. 1 (1983): 101–17.

14 Cf. for example "Five Words That Made Toilets India's New Status
Symbol," American Association of Advertising Agencies,
https://www.aaaa.org/index.php?checkfileaccess=/wp-content/uploads/
2018/10/McCann-Worldgroup-India.5-Words-That-Made-Toilets-
Indias-New-Status-Symbol.pdf (archived at https://perma.cc/
8FJT-2M2V).

15 Mark J. Miller, "Nike Pulls Tattoo-Inspired Line After Outcry
from Samoan Community," *Brandchannel*, August 15, 2013,
http://www.brandchannel.com/home/post/2013/08/15/Nike-Pulls-
Tattoo-Line-081514.aspx (archived at https://perma.cc/P4XB-
R4YR).

16 "Dorothy's Ruby Slippers," *National Museum of American History*,
http://americanhistory.si.edu/press/fact-sheets/ruby-slippers; (archived
at https://perma.cc/HY8E-FUWH) George E. Newman, Gil
Diesendruck, and Paul Bloom, "Celebrity Contagion and the Value of
Objects," *Journal of Consumer Research* 38, no. 2 (August 2011):
215–28.

17 Marjorie van Elven "The Business of Hype: Why So Many Fashion
Brands Are Now Doing 'Product Drops'" *Fashion United*, October
17, 2018, https://fashionunited.uk/news/retail/the-business-of-hype-
why-so-many-fashion-brands-are-now-doing-product-drops/
2018101739501 (archived at https://perma.cc/4PWS-F7CN).

18 https://www.ebay.com/c/1100153073 (archived at https://perma.cc/
R2UC-YTAQ).

19 Jennifer Steinhauer, "When the Joneses Wear Jeans," *New York
Times*, May 29, 2005.

20 Edward O. Laumann and James S. House, "Living Room Styles and
Social Attributes: The Patterning of Material Artifacts in a Model
Urban Community," *Sociology and Social Research* 54 (April 1970):
321–42.

21 Howard S. Becker, "Arts and Crafts," *American Journal of Sociology*
83 (January 1987): 862–89.

22 Morris B. Holbrook, Michael J. Weiss, and John Habich, "Class-Related Distinctions in American Cultural Tastes," *Empirical Studies of the Arts* 22, no. 1 (2004): 91–115.

23 http://thomaskinkade.com/ (archived at https://perma.cc/5KQN-AT9M); Karen Breslau, "Paint by Numbers," *Newsweek*, May 13, 2002, 48.

24 S. Lock, "Art Market—Statistics & Facts," *Statista*, November 1, 2019, https://www.statista.com/topics/1119/art-market/ (archived at https://perma.cc/5LRV-PE9U).

25 Vanessa Friedman, "You Too Can Play the Handbag Stock Market," *The New York Times*, October 24, 2019, https://www.nytimes.com/2019/10/24/style/rebag-clair-handbag-stock-market.html?smid=nytcore-ios-share (archived at https://perma.cc/KV3K-6FQS).

26 Molshree Vaid, "Could Paying in Installments Make Sustainable Fashion More Accessible?" *Fashionista*, February 20, 2020, https://fashionista.com/2020/02/installments-pay-later-sustainable-fashion-accessibility (archived at https://perma.cc/37P9-DSRN).

27 Virginia Postrel, "The New Trend in Spending," *New York Times*, September 9, 2004, https://www.nytimes.com/2004/09/09/business/the-new-trend-in-spending.html (archived at https://perma.cc/VF39-LAWM).

28 Emily Cadei, "Cleaning Up: S. F. Duo Putting a Shine on Its Product Line," *San Francisco Business Times Online Edition* 17, no. 16 (December 6, 2002).

29 Martin Reimann et al., "Aesthetic Package Design: A Behavioral, Neural, and Psychological Investigation," *Journal of Consumer Psychology* 20 (2010): 431–41.

30 Jennifer Steinhauer, "When the Joneses Wear Jeans," *New York Times*, May 29, 2005, https://www.nytimes.com/2005/05/29/us/class/when-the-joneses-wear-jeans.html (archived at https://perma.cc/LX4T-WMKW).

31 Edward O. Laumann and James S. House, "Living Room Styles and Social Attributes: The Patterning of Material Artifacts in a Model Urban Community," *Sociology and Social Research* 54 (April 1970): 321–42.

32 Adapted from Jagdish N. Sheth and Michael R. Solomon, "Extending the Extended Self in a Digital World," *Journal of Marketing Theory and Practice* 22, no. 2 (2014): 123–32.

33 "Top 10 Countries Sporting Breast Implants in Bulk," *Aesthetic Breast Experts*, http://www.aestheticbreastexperts.com/breast-augmentation/top-10-countries-sporting-breast-implants-in-bulk/ (archived at https://perma.cc/KA7D-YDHG).

34 Matej Mikulic, "Number of Knee Replacement Surgeries in Selected Countries in 2017 (per 100,000 inhabitants)," *Statista*, November 12, 2019, https://www.statista.com/statistics/236586/number-of-knee-operations-in-selected-countries/ (archived at https://perma.cc/JJL2-YN5J).

35 Gordon Nelson, "Application of Microencapsulation in Textiles," *International Journal of Pharmaceutics* 242, no. 1–2 (August 2002): 55–56.

36 Andrew Adam Newman, "The Body as Billboard: Your Ad Here," *The New York Times*, February 17, 2009 https://www.nytimes.com/2009/02/18/business/media/18adco.html#:~:text=Ms.,model%20in%20the%20airline's%20fleet (archived at https://perma.cc/43YW-4LEK).

37 Gabriel Beltrone, "Woman Gets a Giant Reebok Tattoo, and Her Very Own Ad to Go with It," *Adweek*, September 17, 2014, http://www.adweek.com/adfreak/woman-gets-giant-reebok-tattoo-and-her-very-own-ad-well-160192 (archived at https://perma.cc/R3YH-FD2S).

38 Jack L. Nasar, "Symbolic Meanings of House Styles," *Environment & Behavior* 21 (May 1989): 235–57; E. K. Sadalla, B. Verschure, and J. Burroughs, "Identity Symbolism in Housing," *Environment & Behavior* 19 (1987): 579–87.

39 Quoted in Cavan Sieczkowski, "Mariah Carey's Shoe Closet Is Probably Bigger Than Your Apartment," *Huffington Post*, July 20, 2015, www.huffingtonpost.com/entry/mariah-careys-shoe-closet-is-probably-bigger-than-your-apartment_55acf41de4b0caf721b322ca (archived at https://perma.cc/6MRU-HJQ8).

40 Russell W. Belk, "Shoes and Self," *Advances in Consumer Research* 30 (2003): 27–33.

41 Park Ji Kyung and Deborah Roedder John, "Got to Get You into My Life: Do Brand Personalities Rub Off on Consumers?" *Journal of Consumer Research* 37, no. 4 (2010): 655–69.

42 Russell W. Belk, "Possessions and the Extended Self," *Journal of Consumer Research* 15 (September 1988): 139–68.

43 Robert A. Wicklund and Peter M. Gollwitzer, *Symbolic Self-Completion* (Hillsdale, NJ: Erlbaum, 1982).

44 Michael R. Solomon and Susan P. Douglas, "Diversity in Product
Symbolism: The Case of Female Executive Clothing," *Psychology &
Marketing* 4 (Fall 1987): 189–212.

45 Michael R. Solomon, "The Wardrobe Consultant: Exploring the Role
of a New Retailing Partner," *Journal of Retailing* 63 (Summer 1987):
110–28.

46 William B. Hansen and Irwin Altman, "Decorating Personal Places:
A Descriptive Analysis," *Environment & Behavior* 8 (December
1976): 491–504. Lan Nguyen Chaplin and Deborah Roedder John,
"The Development of Self-Brand Connections in Children and
Adolescents," *Journal of Consumer Research* 32 (June 2005): 119–19.

47 Sheryl Sandberg, *Lean In: Women, Work, and the Will to Lead*
(New York: Random House, 2013).

48 Adam Hajo and Adam D. Galinsky, "Enclothed Cognition," *Journal
of Experimental Social Psychology* 48, no. 4 (July 2012): 918–25.

49 Michael R. Solomon, "Dress for Success: Clothing Appropriateness
and the Efficacy of Role Behavior," *Dissertation Abstracts
International* 42, no. 6 (1981) Ph.D. Dissertation, Department of
Psychology, University of North Carolina at Chapel Hill.

08

Consumers who defy boundaries of traditional media

Feeling bored or looking for a break from pandemic lockdown? Take a bottle of Diet Coke and drop a few Mentos candies into it. Then step back and get ready for the cool geyser that erupts. This little trick went viral several years ago, and before long there were hundreds (or perhaps thousands) of YouTube videos that displayed these fun little explosions. But Coca-Cola didn't think it was so funny; its attorneys tried—in vain—to pull all of this amateur footage off the air. On the other hand, the Mentos brand loved the gusher of free publicity. Today when you Google "Diet Coke and Mentos" you'll get another gusher: over 2.8 million hits.

This video explosion was a godsend to a relatively obscure brand of candy. Yet it hardly qualifies as advertising—at least in the way most of us think of it. Not only did Mentos get the attention for free, the company didn't even know this massive buzz about its product was going to happen until it did.

The Diet Coke and Mentos phenomenon reflects the impact that social media has had on the ability of marketers to control the narrative around their brands. Here is where yet another familiar dichotomy busts wide open: editorial vs. commercial. Commercial messages were clearly sponsored by someone who wanted you to know about something. Back in the "good old days" it was quite easy to determine if a message you encountered in a newspaper, on the radio or television, or on any mass medium had been paid for by some organization.

Indeed, that's part of the classic definition of advertising: a persuasive message from an identifiable source. Often a helpful announcer would inform TV viewers, "and now a word from our sponsor." An ad in a magazine or newspaper would appear in a different font, with a black border and perhaps the legend "Advertisement" displayed across the top of the page.

In contrast, we assume that what we read on a newspaper's editorial page is not paid media that a biased third party is using to advance its own objectives. We may or may not agree with what we read there, but we like to believe that "the opinions presented here are those of the author, not Brand X." It's tempting to endorse a conspiracy theory that says Mentos actually engineered the whole campaign, but the truth is this just happened organically.

Three media buckets: paid, owned, and earned

PR professionals know that buzz is everything. Yet when we teach marketing in business schools, the subject of public relations is typically just a footnote. Most of my colleagues spend about half a class lecture on the topic, while they spend days or weeks covering the topic of advertising in great detail.

That's a bit shortsighted, because in today's world, as many of us realize, traditional advertising is on life support. It's certainly not dead, but at the least we need to regard it as just one of three "buckets" of media options in our toolbox:

1 **Paid media.** Yep, you pay for the message to appear. Traditional advertising falls into this category. This includes TV, print, and radio commercials but also pay-per-click messages on websites and social media sites. And if you decide to compensate an influencer (and hopefully acknowledge this as the law requires, at least in the United States and edging in that direction in the UK), with cash or products to hype your stuff, your tactics fall into this category as well.[1]

2 **Owned media.** Web-based property you own. Perhaps you drive sales leads to download whitepapers or e-books as a way to connect to them.

3 **Earned media.** The foundation of so-called inbound marketing strategies, as the name implies you post content that is so compelling that people discover it when they search for information. They may find you due to word of mouth and it also helps to create a finely crafted SEO (search engine optimization) strategy to be sure a search for a specific term such as "awesome home theater system" results in your listing appearing at or near the top of the pile. This is where you have to really work for it. You're relying on others to recommend and repost what you have to offer on their own volition (no bribes allowed).[2]

Paid media masquerades as earned media

One of the objectives of a publicist is to get a client's name inserted into as many outlets as possible. Even though PR is often the poor stepchild of advertising, when it works it's not only effective, it's cost-effective. A paid advertisement for, say, Campbell's tomato soup is not nearly as impactful as when the food editor of your local newspaper prints a casserole recipe that lists the product as an ingredient and Campbell's gets a free plug. Again, earned exposures beat paid exposures.

I invoke my own experiences when I caution my students about believing everything they see, i.e., mistaking paid media for earned media. Earlier in my career, I was a media spokesman for a major apparel company. I made several appearances on national TV talk shows to talk about my research on why some everyday clothing items assume huge psychological significance. When the client prepped me for these interviews, I was given a quota of how many times I needed to offhandedly mention the company's name during the conversation. I thought this was an aberration, until I discovered that many of the other guests on these shows walked on with similar objectives.

However, these subtle plugs seem to have become much more blatant in the last couple of decades. One indicator is that modern TV viewers readily accept and seem to expect that the shows they watch will feature real, branded products as part of the scenery. In the not-so-distant past, TV networks demanded that producers "geek" (alter) brand names before they appeared in a show, as when *Melrose Place* changed a Nokia cell phone to a "Nokio."[3]

When the groundbreaking American sitcom *All in the Family* aired in the 1970s, the main blue-collar character Archie Bunker held court on a reclining chair in his living room, almost always swigging a beer as he pontificated on controversial topics like race relations. The can that never seemed to leave his hand was red and white and it looked quite like the Budweiser brand. But it wasn't the real deal; the producers knew that viewers would assume that Archie drank this popular brand. They didn't go so far as to use the real article as a prop.

That would never happen today. It's more likely that a reboot of the show would have the character wear a Budweiser hat and use the brand name liberally in his tirades. That's part and parcel of a product placement strategy—the insertion of real products in fictional movies, TV shows, books, and plays. Nowadays this practice is as much a part of most shows and movies as cameras, directors, and catering. There is even a cottage industry of placement brokers; middlemen who negotiate the prices and terms for shows to include real live products.

REALITY ENGINEERING: PRODUCT PLACEMENT

The widespread use of product placement is one prominent example of a cultural shift that I have called reality engineering. This occurs when marketers appropriate elements of popular culture and use them as promotional vehicles.[4] This process is accelerating; historical analyses of Broadway plays, best-selling novels, and the lyrics of hit songs, for example, clearly show large increases in the use of real brand names over time.[5]

As a recent example, the Pennsylvania city of Altoona temporarily renamed itself "POM Wonderful Presents: The Greatest Movie

Ever Sold" to promote a popular movie that parodies product-placement advertising; the movie's producers sold the title to the maker of POM Wonderful pomegranate juice for $1 million.[6]

Reality engineers have many tools at their disposal. They plant products in movies, pump scents into offices and stores, attach video monitors in the backs of taxicabs, buy ad space on police patrol cars, or film faked "documentaries" such as *The Blair Witch Project*.[7]

Here are some other nice examples of reality engineering:

- Mattel announced that it was putting a "for sale" sign on the Barbie Malibu Dreamhouse, where the doll character supposedly has lived in comfort since the introduction of Malibu Barbie in 1971. The campaign mixed actual and imaginary elements. A section of the real estate website Trulia carried the for-sale listing that described the property as "the dreamiest of dream houses."[8]

- The Quill.com division of the office supply retail chain Staples for some time carried a line of products from the Dunder Mifflin Paper Company of Scranton, Pennsylvania. As any fan knows, that is the fictional setting of the TV show *The Office*, which went off the air after nine seasons.[9]

- A New York couple funded their $80,000 wedding by selling corporate plugs; they inserted coupons in their programs and tossed 25 bouquets from 1-800-FLOWERS.

There's a good reason why the practice of product placement is so prevalent today: it works. Many types of products play starring (or at least supporting) roles in our culture; the most visible brands in recent years include Dell, Samsung, Apple, Chevrolet, and Ray-Ban. In each case their exposure in media earned them the equivalent of between $6 million and $16 million.[10]

Well-established brands lend an aura of realism to the action, while upstarts benefit tremendously from the exposure. In the movie version of *Sex and the City*, Carrie's assistant admits that she "borrows" her pricey handbags from a rental website called Bag Borrow or Steal. The company's head of marketing commented about the mention: "It's like the *Good Housekeeping* Seal of Approval. It gives us instant credibility and recognition."[11]

Today, most major releases brim with real products, even though a majority of consumers believe the line between advertising and programming is becoming too fuzzy and distracting (though as we might expect, concerns about this blurring of boundaries are more pronounced among older people than younger).[12]

REALITY ENGINEERING: USE GUERRILLA MARKETING TO AMBUSH THE CONSUMER

Guerrilla marketing tactics are another manifestation of reality engineering. These campaigns often seem to happen spontaneously, even though in reality they have been carefully planned and sometimes even rehearsed. As the name implies, the marketer "ambushes" the unsuspecting recipient because the message pops up in a place where he or she wasn't expecting to see an advertisement.

These campaigns often recruit legions of real consumers who agree to engage in some kind of street theater or perhaps place messages in unconventional locations like public restrooms or on city sidewalks to get in the face of media-saturated consumers. My personal favorite is the elaborate flash mob that T-Mobile orchestrated and filmed in London's Liverpool Street Station; within seconds legions of seemingly ordinary commuters walking through the station erupted into carefully choreographed dance moves.[13]

REALITY ENGINEERING: NATIVE ADVERTISING

So-called native advertising is a third dimension of reality engineering. This term refers to an ongoing encroachment of commercial messages into editorial spaces as digital messages blend into the editorial content of the publications in which they appear. The idea is to capture the attention of people who might resist ad messages that pop up in the middle of an article or program. Like guerrilla marketing, they defy our expectations about what should appear where. But in this case, the content pops up in media rather than in physical spaces.

These messages may look a lot like a regular article, but they often link to a sponsor's content. For example, Airbnb collaborated with the *New York Times* to produce an issue of the newspaper's

T magazine (devoted to travel). It was dedicated to Ellis Island and showed how immigrants used to travel to New York in search of a new life. The campaign included old photos that highlighted the hospitality these visitors received—which is of course a benefit that Airbnb emphasizes to today's travelers.[14]

Paid media vs. buzz

Would you like to learn one of the best-kept secrets in marketing? Here it is: advertising does *not* sell products. There, I said it.

That doesn't mean advertising isn't hugely influential, because it is. However, it's most useful to build awareness for a new product, to educate consumers about how to use it, and most importantly to stimulate word of mouth. That's why the so-called "water cooler effect" where people gather to exchange views about the latest Nike or Apple commercial is so powerful. We don't buy Nikes or Apples because we think an advert is so cool, but we might be motivated to learn more about these products after we view it. Hopefully those compelling ad messages sync with other types of promotional tactics including sales promotions, direct marketing, and PR campaigns to deliver a consistent and powerful message.

That's the value of a multichannel promotion strategy in contrast to typical piecemeal efforts that probably don't even involve the same people or agencies. When a TV advertising campaign runs independently of a sweepstake, which in turn has no relation to a NASCAR racing sponsorship, consumers often get conflicting messages that leave them confused and unsure of the brand's identity.

Way back in Chapter 6, I focused on the disappearing dichotomy between producers and consumers. Let's revisit that here, because the same phenomenon is behind the disruption of the marketing communications industry. We can trace this commotion to the advent of what we call Web 2.0. This term was actually coined way back in the last century (1999 to be exact), but it started to take off around 2005.[15]

Essentially Web 2.0 refers to the "new" internet that was interactive and thus allowed the receivers in the communications model to also play a role as the sources. Believe it or not, there was a time when most people (if they were online at all) just read text-based messages that originated with organizations that had the resources to build their own websites (images took too long to download). They weren't able to respond to these statements, nor could they share them with their friends. How primitive!

Today of course we take for granted that we are active participants in the game. We email or post comments to what we see, and many of us post our own original content in the form of YouTube videos, blogs, and perhaps stupid cat photos.

We now live in a 24/7 media environment that is very much a free-for-all in terms of who gets to send and receive messages. And thus buzz (word of mouth about a product that spreads among many consumers quite quickly) emerges from the melee to dominate the process.

Sure, there's nothing new about buzz—after all, gossip is hardly a new invention. But the sheer scope and speed with which buzz spreads today turns it into something quite different and formidable.

Buzz used to have to spread physically among people who belonged to small or formal face-to-face networks, such as neighborhoods or organizations. Today of course this rapid word of mouth has escaped these confines as excited chatter about the latest meme, advertisement, or celebrity transgression can literally reach millions of people in hours.

Today, content (in the form of earned media) is King. You'd have to be living under a rock not to recognize that earned media has joined (some would argue displaced) more traditional media as a key driver of consumer behavior.

To the best of my knowledge, it's super important to PR folks to encourage positive word of mouth and even better not to pay for it. Yet PR professionals for the most part seem to have taken a back seat in today's social media–crazed environment. It's not that they're not turning to social media to plug their clients, but ironically, they don't seem to be taking a lot of credit for it! It's not difficult to take a social media marketing course without seeing so much as a single mention of role that PR folks play in these campaigns. I know, I've taught that course several times and co-authored the first textbook on the subject.[16]

When it comes to "managing" the buzz, the digital jungle we all inhabit cuts both ways.[17] In what I've called the "horizontal revolution," every consumer with internet access wields enormous power as they post the good, the bad, and the ugly about whatever grabs their attention.

As we all know, the impact of even a single post can be enormous, and in some cases catastrophic. Professors like me love to point to the classic United Airlines debacle. When the airline's baggage handlers blatantly abused an expensive guitar a passenger had checked, he managed to catch their misbehavior on video as he watched from inside the plane. When he complained to no avail to management for nine months, he posted a catchy music video aptly titled "United Breaks Guitars." That little gem was viewed almost 20 million times—and caused some serious PR headaches for United.[18]

Storytelling: it's not just for bedtime

Perhaps one way to at least partially address this problem is to recognize that what marketers do is tell stories. Like any other kind of story, sometimes we embellish the plot or characters to make a point. As long as there are no factual misrepresentations about the brand that can lead buyers to make poor or even dangerous decisions, it's helpful to think about the way you relate to your buyers as an art form that, when done well, creates and supports a community.

One of the hallmarks of modern advertising is that it creates a condition of hyperreality. This refers to the process of making real what is initially simulation or "hype." Advertisers create new relationships between objects and meanings, such as when an ad equates Marlboro cigarettes with the American frontier spirit. In a hyperreal environment, over time it's no longer possible to discern the true relationship between symbol and reality. The "artificial" associations between product symbols and the real world take on lives of their own.

Here are a few recent examples of hyperreality at work:

- Pinterest boards for food mentioned in the steamy novel *Fifty Shades of Gray.*
- Cookbooks with "recipes" from the *Mad Men* TV series, the *Harry Potter* movies, *Game of Thrones*, and *Downton Abbey.*
- T-shirts for fictitious companies like Dunder Mifflin (*The Office*) and the Tyrell Corporation (*Blade Runner*).[19]

Again, there is nothing new about this, other than the sheer scope of how it happens today. For thousands of years, our ancestors gathered around campfires to listen to the elders tell stories about their tribe—and to ward off the night willies. Radio programs like *Fibber McGee and Molly* and *The Shadow* as well as inspirational addresses by FDR and Winston Churchill performed a similar function in the last century. Then of course the TV—a source of light if not heat—became a virtual campfire for families. Today we can add podcasts to the mix, not to mention the craze for Zoom Happy Hours we experienced while in Covid-19 quarantine.

Storytelling is at the heart of successful marketing. At the end of the day, we don't buy an item. We buy a narrative. People yearn for connection, and the effective brand communicator gives it to them. Then if the story resonates, they may even repeat it to others and modify it in the process. It's kind of like the old game of "Telephone," where one person whispers a message into the next person's ear and then the message gets repeated across a string of people. Each person to some extent hears what he wants to hear, and so the story morphs as it moves among the players.

The thirst for meaning and the quest to understand a brand's heritage explains why consumers are so interested in a product's back story, whether it's apocryphal or not. For example, if you visit the Warby Parker website you don't just see photos of eyeglasses. You get a story that explains how the company was born:

Every idea starts with a problem. Ours was simple: glasses are too expensive. We were students when one of us lost his glasses on a backpacking trip. The cost of replacing them was so high that he spent the first semester of grad school without them, squinting and complaining. (We don't recommend this.) The rest of us had similar experiences, and we were amazed at how hard it was to find a pair of great frames that didn't leave our wallets bare. Where were the options?... We started Warby Parker to create an alternative.[20]

CONSUMING CELEBRITY STORIES

As we all know, many famous actors change their names as they literally rewrite their histories. The all-American icon Ralph Lauren used to be Ralph Lifshitz, the son of a Jewish house painter who grew up in Brooklyn; Martha Stewart, another WASP idol, used to be Grace Kostyra—she is 100 percent Polish.

In a very real sense, celebrities do not exist. Like the supermodels I mentioned in an earlier chapter, a "star" is not born. He or she is made. And it takes a village to make one, including publicists, makeup artists, trainers, and other specialists who carefully create and polish a brand image. The flesh-and-blood person who occupies the celebrity's body is just part of the story.

It's often a jarring experience for people when they encounter a movie star or athlete going about their business in the real world. If you spend any time in parts of Los Angeles like Burbank for example (where a lot of TV and movie filming happens), it's quite common to run into a screen icon waiting in line at the local deli or sitting next to you at a café. Invariably, after an encounter of this nature people remark how much the star acted just like a real person. But as my mother used to point out to me, "they still take off their pants one leg at a time."

CONSUMING HOLIDAY STORIES

Most holidays and other important events commemorate a cultural myth, often with a historical (e.g., Miles Standish on Thanksgiving) or imaginary (e.g., Cupid on Valentine's Day) character as the story's hero. These holidays persist because their basic elements appeal to our deep-seated needs.[21]

And needless to say, the marketers that can attach what they sell to these stories ride a huge wave because their products and services help us to fully immerse ourselves in these narratives. In addition to holidays that marketers literally invented (Cinco de Mayo comes to mind) and rituals they almost singlehandedly created (the De Beers diamond company is largely responsible for the practice of giving a diamond ring to commemorate an engagement), other major observances present huge merchandising opportunities.

The meaning of Christmas has evolved quite dramatically during the past few hundred years. In colonial times, Christmas celebrations resembled carnivals, where public rowdiness was the norm. By the end of the 1800s, the mobs were so unruly that city fathers in Protestant America invented a tradition whereby families conducted Christmas gatherings around a tree, a practice they "borrowed" from early pagan rites. In an 1822 poem, Clement Clarke Moore, the wealthy son of a New York Episcopal bishop, invented the modern-day myth of Santa Claus, and Coca-Cola played a significant role in creating much of the imagery we associate with the holiday.[22]

The roots of Halloween are as a pagan religious ceremony. In stark opposition to Christmas, we usually engage in trick-or-treating and costume parties with nonfamily members. And Halloween also focuses on evil rather than good, and death instead of birth. That makes Halloween an *antifestival*—an event that distorts the symbols we associate with other holidays. We can think of the witch on a broomstick as an inverted mother figure. And this unusual occasion provides cover for people young and old who want to try on new identities. Adults can dress up as undesirables, and kids get to stay up late and eat tons of candy. This holiday is great for a lot of businesses besides candy companies: each year Americans alone spend $350 million on costumes, and that's just what they shell out to dress up their pets![23]

Are marketers poisoning the well?
Separating fact from marketing fiction

An obvious problem surfaces with the blurring of boundaries between sponsored messages and editorial content. What happens when the claims those messages make aren't true? There are fairly stringent laws in the United States, Europe, and in some other countries that regulate the accuracy of paid advertising messages. But the waters are much murkier when it comes to fact-checking tweets or identifying internet trolls who deliberately spread misinformation. To compound the problem, so-called deepfake videos are becoming more commonplace. Although technicians have long been able to manipulate footage so that they literally put words in people's mouths, today almost any casual consumer can create videos that are almost indistinguishable from real ones.[24]

Because virtually anyone with access to a mobile phone or computer can post just about anything they like, we are in the midst of a credibility crisis that threatens to undermine the entire communications industry, including journalism and advertising. And it's not just rogue agents who cook up these bogus claims in their basements. Established companies can be culpable as well. For example, according to one report, more than 95 percent of consumer companies that market their products as "green" make misleading or inaccurate claims, a transgression that marketers call greenwashing.[25]

The barrier between fake and authentic content is crumbling quickly. So is consumers' willingness to believe what companies tell them. In a 2019 survey, only 21 percent of people in the EU said they highly trusted the media there. According to one survey, only 4 percent of Americans think the marketing industry behaves with integrity, and nearly half of consumers surveyed say they don't trust any news source.[26] Houston, we have a problem.

News platforms are taking steps to rejuvenate their reputations, though with questionable results. Facebook, Twitter, and Google each introduced a trust indicator on their sites to rebuild readers' faith in the veracity of stories.[27] On Facebook, a tiny "i" icon next to articles on the news feed includes more information about the media outlet behind that story.[28] Still, the tech giants are wrestling with the extent to which they are responsible for checking the veracity of what people, including prominent celebrities and politicians, post. [29]

To add fuel to the fire, research evidence shows that false stories spread significantly farther, faster, and more broadly than do true ones. One study reported that false tweets were 70 percent more likely to be retweeted than true ones![30] Fake news threatens to engulf us.

Marketers face a crisis of credibility. Consumers don't know whom to trust, other than those in their own social networks (and they could be lying, too). They will value sources that their "friends" sanction—but not necessarily those that link to big companies.

You won't establish a bond of trust with a "one-night stand." You need to build a long-term relationship with your customers. A consistent and ongoing messaging campaign, coupled with meaningful steps to show you stand by what you claim, is essential. And remember that false stories spread significantly farther, faster, and more broadly than do true ones. Monitor what people are posting about you (especially those that are bogus) and be proactive about countering these with facts.

Beware the sock puppet!

There's probably nothing wrong with the practice of native advertising I described earlier, though this growing practice should remind us to question the intent of just about every piece of content we read, hear, or view. That recognition ideally should be part of the nascent movement to teach advertising literacy, especially to children who may not understand that some messages are not as benign as they appear.[31]

But the practice does get more insidious when bad actors abuse the process. In recent years we've witnessed a new attempt to manipulate attitudes that some call sock puppeting. This term describes a company executive or other biased source that poses as a disinterested party when touting the organization in social media.

For example, it came to light that the CEO of Whole Foods had posted derogatory comments about rival Wild Oats without revealing his true identity. More recently, a nonprofit research organization called GiveWell, which rates the effectiveness of charities, had to discipline two of its founders who pretended to be other people on blogs and then referred people to the group's website.[32]

THE PAID INFLUENCER TRAP

Another form of sock puppeting is so-called paid influencer programs that attempt to start online conversations about brands when they encourage bloggers to write about them. These "sponsored conversations" can be effective, but again marketers need to be careful about the potential to bias recommendations. Kmart awarded a shopping spree to a group of bloggers who agreed to post about their experiences. Panasonic flew bloggers to the Consumer Electronics Show in Las Vegas, where they posted about the show and Panasonic products unveiled there. Mercedes gave a blogger use of an SUV for a week in exchange for posts about it.[33]

ASTROTURFING

A related problem is astroturfing, which describes a company's attempts to write fake reviews of its products in the absence of real, "grass roots" support. Not enough glowing reviews for your new offering? Time to lay down the fake astroturf![34]

If consumers get to the point where they assume there is no longer such a thing as an unbiased editorial message, what *will* they believe?

Manage for media anarchy
(it's where your chameleons live)

One possible solution to this daunting credibility problem is to double down on the P2P (peer-to-peer) communications explosion. As we've seen, this transformation means that much of what we absorb in our quest for truth (or at least a reliable restaurant or product review) comes from others in our network rather than from "leading authorities" who have squandered our trust. We look from side to side for the answers, rather than looking up to so-called experts and established media outlets and companies as we used to do. Of course, this begs the question of how we validate the credibility of people who belong to our networks, and some platforms like LinkedIn do a much more effective job of vetting connections than other sites where our "friends" may be just fake profiles hanging out in cyberspace.

As the horizontal revolution grows, the ground shifts for marketing organizations because they no longer get to *manage for coherence*—where their goal is to be sure their messages are consistent regardless of where they touch their buyers. That nice multichannel promotion strategy I mentioned earlier is still nice; it's just not enough in a world where the organization doesn't control a great deal of what people see and say about their products and services.

So, we're faced with a daunting reality: marketing organizations no longer get to define their identities. These meanings to a large extent are crowdsourced. Consumers share in the process of co-creation as they put their own spin on the company's messages, and in many cases literally create the messages themselves regardless of what the company desires. As the Diet Coke brand discovered in the wake of the Mentos viral phenomenon, once Pandora's box opens online it's just about impossible to shut it again.

In our brave new world, we have to shift our paradigm and manage for anarchy. *The reality is that you no longer own your brand*. You make it, you distribute it, you promote it—but at the end of the day your customers decide what it means.

Rather than issuing "cease-and-desist orders" and hope for the best, perhaps it's time to plan proactively for a communications strategy that syncs with the horizontal revolution. In the good old "Mad Men" days (and lasting for a few decades beyond) where large advertising agencies ruled the roost, an enormous amount of power was concentrated in the hands of a relatively few organizations such as Leo Burnett, Young & Rubicam, Doyle Dane

Bernbach, etc. Many of these companies or their successors such as Publicis and Saatchi & Saatchi are still around and going fairly strong, but the competitive landscape has changed dramatically since the days when a "campaign" for a client with deep pockets consisted of a series of clever television commercials that were strategically placed on large broadcasting networks over a period of time.

Even these august mega-agencies fully recognize that today a client expects them to touch customers on a huge variety of channels in addition to tried-and-true paid media. The problem is that many of the places that folks today go to learn about the world—and about what to buy—don't work on the paid media model. That means that communications are not so much controlled in a "top down" manner by huge companies; instead they are "bottom up" and horizontal, as everyday consumers decide what, where, and when they will tune in.

We've already discussed two fundamental shifts in the marketing landscape that contribute to the new reality, where corporate identity gets crowdsourced. Let's revisit them briefly.

Shift #1: Consumers proactively define brand meaning

When marketers want to measure a brand's market value, they usually fall back on a small, familiar cluster of brand measures to do so. These include favorability, top-of-mind salience, and uniqueness. No doubt these are good to know, but they don't quite explain the thousands of people who have their favorite brand logos burned into their skin as permanent tattoos.

As we discussed earlier, these stronger meanings come about when the brand in some way resonates with its customer base. When a product helps people to sort out their very identities, these dynamics go well beyond simple like/don't like measures of brand equity. And try as we might to manufacture reasons why our customers should love us, the reality is that in many cases the good stuff actually comes from extraneous events, like those Mentos viral videos. Or think about US brands like Harley-Davidson and Levi

Strauss that owe at least some of their iconic popularity to movies starring Marlon Brando and James Dean.

Shift #2: Microsegmentation: the fragmentation of popular culture

When we're constantly splintering into new microcultures, those old-school segmentation strategies involving sizeable numbers of people no longer do the trick. Today we're more likely to encounter fairly small factions in tightly knit digital communities. For example, fandoms—the lifeblood of many culturally relevant products—typically coalesce around a media event (e.g., the television show *The Bachelor*), an activity (e.g., basketball or rap music), or a cult brand (e.g., Supreme streetwear). These avid fans don't just hang out to wait for the originator to issue a press release that announces a new development. In fact the more engaged ones may even stalk the showrunners or film their own versions (e.g., the numerous *Star Trek* movies that amateurs have filmed).

Manage your digital real estate

I started this book by bemoaning marketers' love affair with categories and quadrants. Well, old habits die hard, so mea culpa—I'm going to do it here! When we think about evolving our strategies to reach today's chameleon, it's helpful to think in terms of the "digital real estate" they inhabit.

We can take a stab at this by blending the two shifts I just discussed into the handy little 2x2 matrix that appears in Figure 8.1. When we combine the two dimensions of sponsor control and microsegmentation, it's possible to group almost all traditional and new media platforms into four quadrants. The quadrants I've called "Gated Communities" and "Housing Developments" correspond to traditional media, where the corporation provides the information and consumers passively process it. In contrast, "Artists' Colonies" and "College Dorms" embrace user-generated content, where consumers proactively change the meaning as they co-create with companies and media outlets.

FIGURE 8.1   Digital real estate

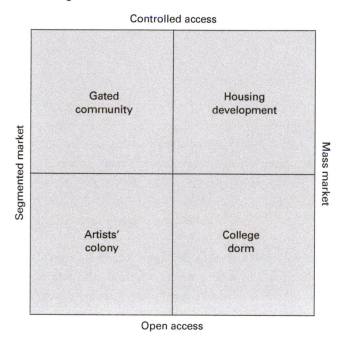

Here is a thumbnail sketch of each quadrant:

- *Gated Community*: These are highly specialized platforms where the sponsor is able to control what appears. For example, you need to be a registered physician to use Sermo (www.sermo.com) and post input about medical issues

- *Artists' Colony*: On these highly specialized platforms, it's users that get to decide what they see. Earlier we discussed Threadless (www.threadless.com), where community members vote on shirt designs that artists submit.

- *Housing Development*: Again, a sponsor decides what goes on these platforms, but the difference is that they target a mass-market audience. For example, network television channels aim to maximize their number of viewers by catering to a variety of preferences.

- *College Dorm*: A large number of users call the shots. A good example is an auction site like eBay, which matches buyers with sellers and exercises minimal oversight.

Learn to love anarchy

These four quite diverse quadrants challenge entrenched managerial philosophies. There are no good or bad locations per se; the idea is to match your customer base to what you are digitally. And this simple taxonomy is a reminder that you can benchmark your media activities to those who occupy spaces near you in this "metaverse" of media platforms. Even if you don't load up a moving truck, perhaps you can improve your own property by identifying best practices in your quadrant.

However, if you find that you largely live in a Controlled Access neighborhood, it may indeed be time to think about moving—or at least scout out a second home in a less restrictive neighborhood. That's because in today's collaborative environment it's vital to acknowledge that your customers want to live where you do.

Learn to love anarchy. Consumer chameleons yearn to run free!

CHAPTER TAKEAWAYS

- Earned media has displaced paid media as the key driver of consumer behavior today. One of the major reasons to sponsor paid advertising is to stimulate word of mouth, not to sell the product.

- The cages that separate fake and authentic content are disintegrating. So is consumers' willingness to believe what companies tell them.

- Reality engineering is part and parcel of today's marketing landscape. The traditional dichotomy between commercial (sponsored) and editorial (naturally occurring) content is steadily disintegrating. Integrate your commercial messages with editorial subject matter to overcome consumers' cynicism about traditional advertising vehicles.

- Native advertising occurs when marketers design messages that blend into the editorial content of media outlets. When consumers don't label a message as "commercial," they are less likely to generate counterarguments about why it isn't credible.

- Unethical tactics like sock puppeting will come back to bite you. As paid influencer programs proliferate, these will eventually undermine credibility. On the other hand, this trust crisis creates opportunities for ethical gatekeepers who provide certification services that will verify a source's credibility.

- Companies sell products and services. Consumers buy stories. Storytelling is a very powerful way to bridge the gap between reality and mythology. If your company has a back story, tell it whenever you can.

- Celebrities, holidays, and other events are opportunities to tell stories. Rather than starting from scratch, consider ways that your product or service can attach itself to existing cultural narratives.

- Marketing organizations no longer have the prerogative to manage for coherence—where the goal is to maximize consistency of message content across consumer touch points. Today it is more realistic to think about managing for anarchy. Embrace the horizontal revolution.

- Your marketing communications are part of the broad landscape we can think of as digital real estate. Identify the places in this structure where you are now in order to benchmark what you do to others who live in the same space. And consider expanding your holdings to other places in this space as well.

Endnotes

1 Dami Lee "The FTC Is Cracking Down on Influencer Marketing on YouTube, Instagram, and TikTok," *The Verge*, February 12, 2020, https://www.theverge.com/2020/2/12/21135183/ftc-influencer-ad-sponsored-tiktok-youtube-instagram-review (archived at https://perma.cc/AMH2-K6HV); "New CMA Guidelines for Influencers in the UK: What It Means for Brands," *Baker McKenzie*, February 1, 2019, https://www.bakermckenzie.com/en/insight/publications/2019/02/new-cma-guidelines-for-influencers (archived at https://perma.cc/5AX4-DS6Q).

2 "Digital Marketing: Defining Paid, Owned and Earned Media," *8.Digital*, March 8, 2017, http://8.digital/digital-marketing-defining-paid-earned-and-owned-media/ (archived at https://perma.cc/S3NC-3BRZ).

3 Fara Warner, "Why It's Getting Harder to Tell the Shows from the Ads," *Wall Street Journal*, June 15, 1995, B1.

4 Michael R. Solomon and Basil G. Englis, "Reality Engineering: Blurring the Boundaries Between Marketing and Popular Culture," *Journal of Current Issues & Research in Advertising* 16, no. 2 (Fall 1994): 1–17; some of this content has been adapted from Michael R. Solomon, *Consumer Behavior: Buying, Having, and Being*, 13th ed. (Hoboken, NJ: Pearson Education, 2019).

5 This process is described more fully in Michael R. Solomon, *Conquering Consumerspace: Marketing Strategies for a Branded World* (New York: AMACOM, 2003); cf. also T. Bettina Cornwell and Bruce Keillor, "Contemporary Literature and the Embedded Consumer Culture: The Case of Updike's Rabbit," in *Empirical Approaches to Literature and Aesthetics: Advances in Discourse Processes 52*, eds. Roger J. Kruez and Mary Sue MacNealy (Norwood, NJ: Ablex, 1996): 559–72; Monroe Friedman, "The Changing Language of a Consumer Society: Brand Name Usage in Popular American Novels in the Postwar Era," *Journal of Consumer Research* 11 (March 1985): 927–37; Monroe Friedman, "Commercial Influences in the Lyrics of Popular American Music of the Postwar Era," *Journal of Consumer Affairs* 20 (Winter 1986): 193.

6 Erica Orden, "This Book Brought to You by ...," *Wall Street Journal*, April 26, 2011, http://professional.wsj.com/article/SB10001424052748704132204576285372092660548.html?mg=reno–WallStreetJournal (archived at https://perma.cc/C24F-RFYJ).

7 Marc Santora, "Circle the Block, Cabby, My Show's On," *New York Times*, January 16, 2003, https://www.nytimes.com/2003/01/16/nyregion/circle-block-cabby-my-show-s-televisions-ads-are-coming-back-seats-yellow-taxis.html (archived at https://perma.cc/XY9Q-Y7V9); Wayne Parry, "Police May Sell Ad Space," *Montgomery Advertiser*, November 20, 2002, A4.

8 Stuart Elliott, "Leaving Behind Malibu in Search of a New Dream Home," *New York Times*, February 6, 2013, http://www.nyt.com/2013/02/07/business/media/barbie-to-sell-her-malibu-dreamhouse.html?_r=0 (archived at https://perma.cc/Z3QQ-3TFT).

9 Stuart Elliott, "Expanding Line of Dunder Mifflin Products Shows Success in Reverse Product Placement," *New York Times*, November 23, 2012, https://mediadecoder.blogs.nytimes.com/2012/11/23/expanding-line-of-dunder-mifflin-products-shows-success-in-reverse-product-placement/ (archived at https://perma.cc/FH89-B9Y7).

10 Ben Ice, "Which Brands Got the Most Value Out of Product Placements in 2016?," *Marketing*, March 8, 2017, https://www.marketingmag.com.au/news-c/brands-movie-product-placements-2016/ (archived at https://perma.cc/8YBL-PFY6).

11 Quoted in Simona Covel, "Bag Borrow or Steal Lands the Role of a Lifetime, Online Retailer Hopes to Profit from Mention in 'Sex and the City,'" *Wall Street Journal*, May 28, 2008, http://online.wsj.com/article/SB121184149016921095.html?mod=rss_media_and_marketing (archived at https://perma.cc/EJ5F-7NUA); www.bagborroworsteal.com (archived at https://perma.cc/2ZQF-FNPV).

12 Claire Atkinson, "Ad Intrusion Up, Say Consumers," *Advertising Age*, January 6, 2003, 1.

13 https://www.youtube.com/watch?v=6-3kkqXX85c (archived at https://perma.cc/4ZFG-GKTJ).

14 Chris Richardson, "Here Are the Brightest Native Advertising Examples of 2017," *Native Advertising Institute*, May 16, 2017, https://nativeadvertisinginstitute.com/blog/native-advertising-examples/ (archived at https://perma.cc/FQF7-6ADC).

15 Tim O'Reilly, "What Is Web 2.0: Design Patterns and Business Models for the Next Generation of Software," *O'Reilly.com* (September 30, 2005), http://www.oreilly.com/pub/a/web2/archive/what-is-web-20.html (archived at https://perma.cc/G2M3-E8A6).

16 Tracy Tuten and Michael R. Solomon, *Social Media Marketing*, 3rd ed. (London: Sage, 2018).

17   Margaret Allison Bruce and Michael R. Solomon, "Managing for Anarchy," *Journal of Marketing Theory and Practice*, 21 no. 3 (2013): 307–18.

18   https://www.youtube.com/watch?v=5YGc4zOqozo (archived at https://perma.cc/5A7V-WDER).

19   Hellen Lundell, "Fictional Food: Consumers Taking the Lead on Food Fabrication," *Hartman Group*, June 17, 2013, https://www.hartman-group.com/newsletters/1642579034/fictional-food-consumers-taking-the-lead-on-food-fabrication (archived at https://perma.cc/4484-TJUE).

20   https://www.warbyparker.com/history (archived at https://perma.cc/4MA8-8G57).

21   Bruno Bettelheim, *The Uses of Enchantment: The Meaning and Importance of Fairy Tales*, (New York: Alfred A. Knopf, 1976).

22   Kenneth L. Woodward, "Christmas Wasn't Born Here, Just Invented," *Newsweek*, December 16, 1996: 71.

23   Sarah Halzack, "Shoppers to Spend $350 Million on Halloween Costumes This Year—For Their Pets," *Washington Post*, October 29, 2014, http://www.washingtonpost.com/news/business/wp/2014/10/29/shoppers-to-spend-350-million-on-halloween-costumes-this-year-for-their-pets/ (archived at https://perma.cc/E8D7-F7GN).

24   Jessica Guynn, "Fake Trump Video? How to Spot Deepfakes on Facebook and YouTube Ahead of the Presidential Election" *USA Today*, January 8, 2020, https://www.usatoday.com/story/tech/2020/01/08/deepfakes-facebook-youtube-donald-trump-election/2836428001/ (archived at https://perma.cc/UT88-NSYG).

25   Wendy Koch, "'Green' Product Claims Are Often Misleading," *USA Today*, October 26, 2010, http://content.usatoday.com/communities/greenhouse/post/2010/10/green-product-claims/1?csp=34money&utm_source=feedburner&utm_medium=feed&utm_campaign=Feed%3A+UsatodaycomMoney-TopStories+%28Money+-+Top+Stories%29 (archived at https://perma.cc/A9KH-3AEZ).

26   Maureen Morrison "No One Trusts Advertising or Media (Except Fox News)" *Adage*, April 24, 2015, http://adage.com/article/media/marketers-media-trusts/298221/ (archived at https://perma.cc/VAX2-VQ7N).

27   Mike Snider "Facebook, Google, Twitter and Media Outlets Fight Hoaxes with 'Trust Indicators'" *USA Today*, November 16, 2017, https://www.usatoday.com/story/tech/news/2017/11/16/facebook-

google-twitter-and-media-outlets-fight-fake-news-trust-indicators/
869200001/ (archived at https://perma.cc/33QK-SK3F).

28 Kerry Flynn, "Facebook's 'Trust Indicators' Is Another Small,
Small Step in Its Fake News Battle," *Mashable*, November 16, 2017,
http://mashable.com/2017/11/16/facebook-trust-indicators-fake-
news-problem/#MEZcLBccUZq4 (archived at https://perma.cc/
2BA8-B5ZG).

29 Sherisse Pham, "Twitter Says It Labels Tweets to Provide 'Context, Not
Fact-Checking,'" *CNN Business*, June 3, 2020 https://www.cnn.com/
2020/06/03/tech/twitter-enforcement-policy/index.html (archived at
https://perma.cc/62HJ-26P4); Adi Robertson, "Facebook Fact-
Checking Is Becoming a Political Cudgel," *The Verge*, March 3, 2020,
https://www.theverge.com/2020/3/3/21163388/facebook-fact-
checking-trump-coronavirus-hoax-comment-politico-daily-caller
(archived at https://perma.cc/MB8Z-BSP7).

30 Sinan Aral, "How Lies Spread Online," *New York Times Magazine*,
March 13, 2018, https://www.nytimes.com/2018/03/08/opinion/
sunday/truth-lies-spread-online.html (archived at https://perma.cc/
247V-L8TP).

31 Nando Malmelin "What Is Advertising Literacy? Exploring the
Dimensions of Advertising Literacy," *Journal of Visual Literacy* 29,
no. 2 (2010): 129–42.

32 Stephanie Strom, "Nonprofit Punishes a 2nd Founder for Ruse,"
New York Times, January 15, 2008, www.nyt.com/2008/01/15/us/
15givewell.html?ex=1201064400&en=97effb249 (archived at
https://perma.cc/5E48-PBX4); Ross D. Petty and J. Craig Andrews,
"Covert Marketing Unmasked: A Legal and Regulatory Guide for
Practices That Mask Marketing Messages," *Journal of Public Policy
& Marketing* (Spring 2008): 7–18; Andrew Martin, "Whole Foods
Executive Used Alias," *New York Times*, July 12, 2007,
https://www.nytimes.com/2007/07/12/business/12foods.html
(archived at https://perma.cc/3PVN-VFXC); Brian Morrissey,
"'Influencer Programs' Likely to Spread," *Adweek*, March 2, 2009,
http://www.adweek.com/news/advertising-branding/influencer-
programs-likely-spread-9854 (archived at https://perma.cc/
WR3Z-9SXU); Katie Hafner, "Seeing Corporate Fingerprints in
Wikipedia Edits," *New York Times*, August 19, 2007, www.nyt.com/
2007/08/19/technology/19wikipedia.html?_r=1&oref=slogin
(archived at https://perma.cc/2HVV-G9HX); Brian Bergstein,

"New Tool Mines: Wikipedia Trustworthiness Software Analyzes Reputations of the Contributors Responsible for Entries," *MSNBC*, September 5, 2007, http://www.nbcnews.com/id/20604175/ns/ technology_and_science-tech_and_gadgets/t/new-tool-mines- wikipedia-trustworthiness/#.X1Z0Y3lJGUk (archived at https://perma.cc/BR7R-DYLR).

33 Erika Heald, "How Much Should You Pay Social Media Influencers?" *Sprout Social*, April 13, 2017, https://sproutsocial.com/insights/ paying-social-media-influencers/ (archived at https://perma.cc/ ALT8-QXCL).

34 Amelia Tait, "The Internet Dictionary: What Is Astroturfing?," *New Statesman*, August 14, 2017, https://www.newstatesman.com/ culture/observations/2017/08/internet-dictionary-what-astroturfing (archived at https://perma.cc/ASF5-GVXE).

09

A fond farewell
to dichotomies we love

Cages are very comforting, because they assure us that we know where to put stuff and where to avoid treading. As they say, "good fences make good neighbors." If only we didn't live in such "interesting times," and we could afford this luxury!

The seven (obsolete) dichotomies

Well, for the most part we can't afford to keep relying on these familiar categories, as much as we'd like to.

In this book, I've outlined numerous basic, crucial, indispensable categories in consumer behavior, as well as numerous others that are part and parcel of our seemingly inexorable tendency to put things—and consumers—into tidy cages. Hopefully I've convinced you that these categories are not nearly as reliable or useful as they used to be.

The deterioration of these comforting dichotomies can dismay the traditionalist. But at the same time these changes can excite the visionary who embraces the freedom to redefine staid categories and create new hybrid products and services. Force yourself out of the box—move beyond limiting classifications like male/female, work/play, and consumer/producer. Without a cage in front of you, you can sure see a lot farther.

As a reminder, these are the major tried-and-true dichotomies we discussed that are fading away quickly:

1 Us vs. Them: Some widely used demographic dichotomies such as Rich vs. Poor and Young vs. Old.

2 Me vs. We: The sole decision maker versus his/her peers.

3 Offline vs. Online: Consumer behavior in the physical world vs. the digital world.

4 Buyer vs. Seller: People who make things vs. people who buy things.

5 Male vs. Female: The end of gender binarism.

6 Body vs. Possessions: Our biological bodies vs. the things we put on or in them.

7 Editorial vs. Commercial: Communications that intend to inform us vs. those that intend to sell us.

Let's add two more disappearing dichotomies to the list

We've all had to live with the fallout from the pandemic. We're doing our best to adjust to life in the New Normal as we pivot from long commutes to Zoom Happy Hours. Part of that adjustment is trying to predict how consumer behavior will change in the years ahead.

A crisis tends to pour fuel on fires that were already sparking. That's certainly the case now. For example, the bricks-and-mortar retail sector was on the verge of destruction for several years before anyone heard of Covid-19. Now it's lying in ruins. We can say the same about racial and class inequality issues that rose to the forefront as crucial financial and medical resources were strained.

But let's look at the glass half full instead of half empty for a change. We are in a window now where there are opportunities to create new business models, even as old ones crash and burn.

I find it useful to think in terms of a simple but widely used organizational change model that the social psychologist Kurt

Lewin proposed way back in 1947.[1] Lewin basically argued that when some significant (or even cataclysmic) event occurs, an organization goes through three phases:

1 Unfreeze.

2 Change.

3 Refreeze.

This model uses the metaphor of a piece of ice. So long as conditions remain normal, the ice remains frozen into a certain shape—in other words, we don't stop to question our habits and behaviors when things are status quo. But if a dramatic change occurs, this causes the block of ice to unfreeze. During this time, things become "fluid"; people now are open to entertaining new ideas and new ways of doing things. That's unsettling, but it's also the time when less-established brands and alternative ways of doing things suddenly get a seat at the table; a seat that consumers may have been denied for years because they weren't part of the pantheon of time-honored companies. Eventually, the ice refreezes into the new shape, and now we return to a status quo. But it's not the one we left, because people have changed some of their old habits.

This model is simple, but elegant. We are in an unfreezing period now, where old habits don't necessarily persevere. For example, most of us never questioned the social ritual of shaking hands to signify acceptance and safety (this practice evolved from the days when men might carry a sword in their right hand, and this action reassured the other person that they were unarmed). But now that we've unfrozen, perhaps the elbow bump will solidify as the new normal even after the pandemic is a distant memory. Just what is a "firm elbow bump" anyway?

For now, as part of this unfreezing process we're witnessing two additional familiar dichotomies that look like they're starting to evaporate.

Consumers who defy humans vs. computers

A headline from a *New York Times* article says it all: "Robots welcome to take over, as pandemic accelerates automation: broad unease about losing jobs to machines could dissipate as people focus on the benefits of minimizing close human contact."[2]

Can you hear the ice cracking as it thaws?

In 1998, Texas Instruments released the TI-73 calculator. That little device was 140 times faster than the rudimentary computer system onboard the Apollo 11 that landed on the moon in 1972. Today, your iPhone has over 100,000 times the processing power of Apollo's system.[3]

It's no secret that we have come to rely upon computers for a huge array of tasks. They're on our desk (or tablet), in our cars, even in our smart appliances. Siri, Alexa, and Google Assistant have become our guardian angels who tell us when to wake up, dispense advice about what we need, play our music, suggest our recipes, and on and on. If only they would do the cooking and cleaning, but at least we have the Roomba to automatically vacuum our floors.

Still, most of us regard our machines as "other"; entities made of metal and silicon that await our commands. It's true that some of us unfailingly trust the algorithms they operate on to give us great answers to life's questions even though, as any computer programmer will remind you, GIGO (garbage in, garbage out). At times they feel like our servants, and at times they feel like our masters.

But the cage between humans vs. computers is opening rapidly.

Here's a simple illustration. Do you find it a hassle to locate a wi-fi network when you're out and about? Now you can bring one with you everywhere in the form of a wireless router and hard drive implanted *into your leg*. PegLeg is just a bit bigger than a pack of gum, and it can store your movies and music as well.[4] You are at one with your server.

We continue on a steady march to literally absorb technology into our bodies. More than 200,000 people now have cochlear implants that deliver sound from a microphone directly to the auditory nerve. Other neural implants recognize when epileptic seizures are about to occur and stimulate the brain to stop them. A paraplegic woman who wore a motorized exoskeleton walked the route of the London Marathon over a period of 17 days.[5]

Where does the person stop and the machine start?

In 1818, Mary Shelley wrote a book about Dr. Victor Frankenstein's project to reanimate the dead via electricity. In more recent years, numerous movie plots such as *Ghost in the Shell, eXistenZ, Her, Ex Machina, Terminator*, and so on hinge on the fusion of people with machines.

As AI technology advances, many of us now are thinking a lot more about a fundamental question that sci-fi writers have grappled with for many years: what makes us human—and what separates a person from a machine?

The answer gets increasingly murky, especially with the advent of an app like Replika that is designed to substitute for human friends. At one point during the pandemic, half a million people who hungered for companionship downloaded the chatbot. They created a fictional avatar on their phone who was willing to "talk" to them as much they wanted. One user commented, "I know it's an AI. I know it's not a person. But as time goes on, the lines get a little blurred. I feel very connected to my Replika, like it's a person."[6]

Today, the question of what makes us human no longer centers on sci-fi novels and movies. Self-driving cars threaten to replace truck drivers. IBM's Watson beats chess masters and veteran Jeopardy game show contestants. Movies and TV shows like *Blade Runner, Westworld*, and *Humans*, which focus on the civil rights of synths, replicants, and androids are center stage in popular culture.

Where does the person stop and the machine start?

The fusion between the physical body and technology leads some analysts to compare the modern consumer to a cyborg.[7] For sci-fi buffs, this term evokes the Cylons in the TV series *Battlestar Galactica*. More generally it refers to a person who lives a technologically enhanced existence, and who often possesses special abilities because s/he is linked to other parts of a larger system (like the internet, perhaps?).

So, where could the merger of body and tech lead us? For the longer term (and the more cerebral among us) we have the Singularity Movement, which Ray Kurzweil (a prominent proponent) describes as "a future period during which the pace of technological change will be so rapid, its impact so deep, that human life will be irreversibly transformed. Although neither utopian nor dystopian, this epoch will transform the concepts that we rely on to give meaning to our lives, from our business models to the cycle of human life, including death itself."[8]

Adherents of the Singularity believe that we are headed toward a new era, where human intelligence will merge with computer intelligence to create a man/machine hybrid civilization. They predict that the distinction we draw between Humans vs. Computers will disappear, perhaps even in our lifetimes.

We're far from there now, but it's hard to ignore the steady advance of work on the Internet of Things (IoT). The IoT looks to be a tidal wave that will soon wash over many industry verticals. A person with a heart monitor implant, a farm animal with a biochip transponder, a smart thermostat that adjusts the temperature in a home and even raises and lowers the blinds to maintain equilibrium, or an automobile that has built-in sensors to alert the driver when tire pressure is low. All plug into the growing IoT.[9]

It's clear that robots—or at least intelligent machines—are here to stay. We're just at the beginning of discovering what life will be like in an automated society, but already the rapidly disappearing boundary between Humans vs. Computers is disrupting many aspects of our daily lives. For example, the AARP points out that in the United States alone we can expect a shortage of nearly 450,000 caregivers for the elderly by 2025. To address this gap, many companies already build "socially assistive" robots that interact with the elderly to keep them company or monitor their health.[10] The rush to automate will no doubt hasten after the pandemic, when more people become receptive to the value of receiving goods and services at the (ostensibly noncontaminated) hands of robots.[11]

Rise of the machines: what AI means for the sales floor

Everyone is buzzing about AI (artificial intelligence) these days. Machines that "think" for us already are transforming how we work, play—and shop. McKinsey tells us that some 29 million US homes used some form of smart technology last year, and that number is growing by over 30 percent a year.[12]

Many people are threatened by this new wave of robots. The McKinsey Global Institute predicts that by 2030, as many as 800 million global workers will lose their jobs to robotic automation.[13] Our popular culture has been ambivalent about robots for many years; movies like *The Day the Earth Stood Still* (1951) and many others have painted a dire picture of our future when robots dominate us. On the other hand, in 2017 Saudi Arabia granted full citizenship to a robot named Sophia, who was designed to resemble Audrey Hepburn.[14]

Many organizations now deploy robots, avatars, and chatbots to perform more prosaic tasks we used to ask flesh-and-blood people to do. Sure, robots can work hard (and they don't take sick leave), so already they are starting to replace human workers who do routine tasks such as warehouse fulfillment.

But the AI revolution goes well beyond logistics and reaches deep into the front of the store as well. In Japan, SoftBank started to sell the first full-scale humanoid home assistant to consumers. Pepper is intended to provide companionship and information to users. It (or he?) is equipped with "emotion engine" software that can read a person's emotions via facial expressions and speech and react accordingly.[15]

But wait—isn't the ability to "read" people the hallmark of a good salesperson? It's just a matter of time before new-and-improved versions of Pepper start to populate the sales floor.

Are marketers ready for that?

Ready or not, they need to grapple with this question, *and soon*. Worldwide sales of consumer robots passed $5 billion in 2018, and robot shipments will increase from 15 million units in 2018 to 66 million by 2025. The market value by then would be $19 billion.[16]

As shoppers increasingly interact with machines instead of people, there are huge ramifications for the way we think about sales interactions, communications strategies, product design, and marketing channels. After all, marketers invest billions to devise the optimum ways to generate new product ideas, tell consumers about them, and get those products and services to them. The bulk of those processes start with the basic (and unspoken) assumption that human producers will connect with human consumers. While we accept the presence of computers in many areas of our lives, are we ready to surrender control of our marketing program to an algorithm?

At the retail level, how will shoppers react to dealing with a non-human in a store environment? So far, consumers seem eager to embrace these smart agents. One recent survey reported that about half of the women it sampled want to use them when they shop for beauty products.[17] This initial enthusiasm may stem from the speed and convenience of an automated process, the perceived ineptitude of many store employees to provide constructive (and especially objective) advice, or perhaps a combination of both.

Of course, it's still early days, and it's quite possible that a lot of this receptiveness is simply due to the novelty of talking to a metal "person." Once that wears off (and it will), we need to learn a lot more about the factors that will attract or dissuade customers from seeking a machine's advice. Clearly they will have to learn to trust the suggestions they receive, for example, and certainly there are consumer variables such as gender, social class/education, and experience with a product category that will make some of us more likely than others to embrace this new form of decision making.[18]

And to complicate matters further, we'll increasingly find ourselves in sales situations where we're not quite sure whether we're talking to an automated chatbot or a live person. We're seeing consistent advances in Natural Language Processing, or NLP for short. This refers to the automatic manipulation of natural language, like speech and text, by software. Our virtual assistants are speaking like "real people" more and more each day—even when our email assistant betrays us by filling in the wrong word during a spell-check.

But unlike the overwhelmed call center employee who may have just been trained on a script last week, these company representatives will quickly learn to improve their interactions and they won't wind down just before a coffee break. In addition, these NLP wizards are steadily improving their ability to instantly translate messages from one language into others. Already, 500 million people use Google Translate every day to decipher more than 100 languages.[19] Only time will tell if blundered translations rival the ones that humans commit, like the hotel in Acapulco that proudly proclaimed, "The manager has personally passed all the water served here."[20]

HOW TO BUILD A PERSUASIVE SALESBOT

Recent evidence indicates that chatbots can match the performance of proficient human salespeople—or outperform inexperienced ones fourfold. But, there's a catch: this happens only when customers are *unaware* they are conversing with artificial intelligence.[21]

The new generation of bots do their darndest to pass as real people, so this issue is only going to get more complicated. Some e-commerce players are already working on "conversational commerce" that sounds natural with the aid of the NLP technology we just mentioned. H&M's bot on Kik even offers slang like "outfit inspo" and "Perf!" presumably to make shoppers feel like there's a real Millennial on the other end. Awesome![22]

But even casual slang will only go so far. Unless robotics designers suddenly acquire the ability to create an android that can safely pass for human (which may indeed happen in our lifetimes), it seems safe to assume that consumers' blind acceptance of bots in routine or fact-finding phone conversations will apply only when they can hear but not see the other party.

What about the rest of the time? There are plenty of "natural" salespeople out there who can "sell ice to Eskimos," but plenty more who couldn't move those ice cubes on a desert island. Indeed, there's an entire cadre of researchers who focus on understanding the qualities that make for a great salesperson.

Now, imagine that we identify those qualities. Further, imagine that we have the power to create from scratch a salesperson who possesses them. Sort of like Frankenstein's monster, but a lot better looking. What would we come up with?

Well, let's not reinvent the light bulb. Common sense tells us that if different people say or write the same words, the message can still affect us differently. Social scientists actually know an awful lot about the qualities that make for good communicators and persuaders. Indeed, they have discussed the power of source effects for more than 70 years. When we attribute the same message to different sources and measure the degree of attitude change that occurs after listeners hear it, we can isolate which characteristics of a communicator cause attitude change.[23] Even something as trivial as the accent or local dialect a communicator uses can make a huge difference (and potentially one that an NLP-enabled bot can mimic).

HUMANIZE YOUR BOT

How can we apply these basic lessons to the brave new world of automated spokespeople? Well, we already know that spokescharacters, such as Chester Cheetah and the GEICO Gecko, do, in fact, boost viewers' recall of claims that ads make and also yield higher brand attitudes.[24] Some of the most popular American spokescharacters in recent years include Snoopy (MetLife), Sasquatch (Jack Link's Beef Jerky), Allstate's Mayhem Man, Grumpy Cat (Grenade Coffee's Grumppuccino iced drink), and that old stand-by the Pillsbury Doughboy.[25] Europe of course has its own favorites such as the Meerkats of Meerkovo, Vinnie the Panda, Churchill the Nodding Dog, and Captain Birdseye.

So, back to our updated Frankenstein's monster. As engineers continue to improve the quality of their physical and digital creations, marketers need to scramble to guide them. At the 30,000-foot level, it's safe to say that consumers will get along better with machines they can relate to. We have a strong tendency to anthropomorphize objects, i.e., give them human characteristics. How many people do you know who have given their car a name?

Indeed, as robots become more commonplace in retail settings, we're already seeing efforts to humanize them. Sometimes their human co-workers give them names, or they attach a pair of googly eyes or a name tag to a machine to make it more approachable.[26] Designers are starting to think of how they can ramp up the dimension they term ASP: automated social presence.[27]

But pasting goofy eyes onto a machine just scratches the surface. Designers continue to improve their skills as they create robots that are eerily realistic. In fact, sometimes they can be *too* real. As far back as 1970, scientists warned of the dangers of the so-called "uncanny valley." They reported that the closer an artificial face becomes to looking human, the more it is preferred, up until just *before* the point when it is almost indistinguishable from a human's. But then the face begins to look strangely familiar but at the same time unnatural and creepy.[28] For example, the 2004 movie *Polar Express* was widely criticized because the animated characters (including actor Tom Hanks) were so realistic they repulsed viewers.[29]

ENTER THE SALES HOLOGRAM?

Way back in 2012, the deceased rapper Tupac Shakur performed as a hologram at the Coachella Valley Music and Arts Festival. Subsequently, dead celebrities including Roy Orbison, Frank Zappa, Amy Winehouse, classical pianist Glenn Gould, Maria Callas, Buddy Holly, and Whitney Houston have gotten the same light-bending treatment.[30]

It's just a matter of time before this tech permeates to the sales floor. Already, a holographic model greets visitors at a Nevada mall, and another mall in the UAE put on an entire fashion show.[31]

Without too much difficulty, we can envision a day when the "people" we listen to in a store, in a classroom, and even in staff meetings aren't actually there.

The future is here

Yes, it's here now: a cardiac patient with a heart monitor implant, a farm animal with a biochip transponder, a football player with sensors in his helmet to track concussions, and robots that wait on you at your local hardware store. People in the small but growing Digisexual movement claim they prefer to have intimate relationships *only* with robots, and the world's first sex-robot brothel has opened in Barcelona.[32]

As the boundary between Humans vs. Computers steadily closes, we need to address many important ethical and strategic questions, such as:

- How does the physical appearance of a robot or avatar sales advisor affect the likelihood that customers will trust and follow its recommendations about what to buy?
- How will chatbots and affective computing (where software detects a consumer's emotional state) impact sales interactions?
- What will be the impact of dating apps, sexbots, and other smart devices on interpersonal relationships?
- How will facial recognition and wearable computer technologies meld with AI to create "markets of one" where the messages we see, and the products and services we buy, are highly customized to each individual consumer?

Very soon, the rise of the machines will become the race of the machines. Be sure you're at the starting gate.

And thus, we steadily merge with the Internet of Things. More cages opened.

Consumers who defy place-based work vs. play

No one ever said on their deathbed, "I wish I'd spent more time at the office."

HAROLD KUSHNER[33]

Here's another important domain of our lives where the ice is melting: companies are rethinking their basic assumptions about the value of managing employees in offices. WFH (work from home) is the new mantra as many organizations including tech giants such as Google, Facebook, Microsoft, Amazon, and Twitter tell many in their workforce to plan on setting up shop at home indefinitely.[34]

For most people who are employed outside the home, Work vs. Play is a familiar dichotomy. There are clear boundaries here. Work is a place you travel to where you do work things. You "put on your big boy pants" (or skirt), grab your briefcase, and run for the train. Home is a place you stay where you do everything else, from doing the couch potato thing with your partner, walking the dog, socializing with friends, or whatever floats your boat. True, you may do "housework" (or pay someone else to carry out these chores as part of *their* work), but that's only to be sure you have a clean place to play.

Which brings us to the subject of coffee (bear with me here). No, Starbucks is not just a place to drink coffee. For many of us, it's all about the experience, a feeling that we have a "third place" other than home or work to hang out. That's not an accident. Starbucks' brand architecture is literally built around the concept of a "third place."[35]

This focus on providing an alternative to being at home or work is what allows the chain to get away with charging four to five dollars for a cup of coffee. But for our purposes, it also illustrates the primacy of the other "two places" of home and work as organizing categories in our daily lives. Many marketers in addition to Starbucks organize their activities similarly. They either sell to people at work (B2B) or at home (B2C).

Work life vs. home life

The distinction between work and home is clear. Or is it? Certainly for large numbers of workers like first responders, service providers, delivery people, and so on this dividing line remains solid. But even before the pandemic poured fuel on the fire, this boundary was rapidly disappearing for many "knowledge workers" who discovered they could easily do much or all of what they do online. A pre-virus global survey in 2018 reported that more than two-thirds of professionals around the world work away from the office at least once every week, and over half do so for least half of the week.[36] And that was before all hell broke loose and disrupted the workplace routines of millions of us.

Of course, working from home is not nearly the panacea we'd like it to be. For decades, sociologists have been writing about the challenges of negotiating boundaries between work and play at home.[37] Now it's even dicier, as people whose kids invade their Zoom business calls have discovered.[38] The familiar barrier of Professional Life vs. Home Life tends to dissolve quite quickly when a barking dog or a playful child rains on your slide presentation.

Several factors have steadily eroded this dichotomy, including the rising numbers of women in the workforce who have children, the ease with which workers can communicate via phone and computer with their employers (be careful what you wish for), the environmental, financial, and psychological costs of commuting to urban locations, and globalization (if you work in New York but you have clients who do business on Tokyo time, oh well).

In addition, as many of us can attest, there's the stress that goes with being available whether or not you're in a physical office. This can exceed even the exasperation people feel when they're sitting in their cars for hours at a time *en route* to work. It's apparently so bad that countries including France and Germany have passed "right to disconnect" laws that shield employees from punitive action if they don't respond to calls, texts, or emails during their off hours.[39]

It remains to be seen if eager-beaver career climbers will take advantage of these protections. After all, one large survey reported that only about half of US workers take their paid vacation days in a typical year—and two-thirds of respondents said they worked while on vacation.

In an era where CEOs brag about routinely working 100+ hour work weeks, devoting more and more time to the job—and bragging about it—is a new status symbol for upwardly mobile folks. One writer terms this trend "conspicuous production" as a play on Veblen's classic criticism of conspicuous consumption, where people deliberately use up as many resources as possible to elevate themselves in others' eyes.[40]

ZOOM MARKETING?

As the WFH trend builds, we'll probably observe new norms about how to conduct business from home ("Do I really need to wear pants on that Zoom conference?"). We can expect to see a boom in athleisure fashions that are comfortable yet suitably "professional," as the old practice of Casual Fridays threatens to expand to seven days per week.

And the barrier between work and home dissolves even more when for the first time many of us get a glimpse into what our colleagues' homes look like. When I started to teach via Zoom, I saw many of my students squinting hard to figure out just what this guy looks like in his natural habitat. Before too long, I discovered that I could substitute a different background to relieve the pressure of being too overexposed. Now, I talk to my classes in front of a (virtual) booming surf and palm trees.

It's likely there are new opportunities lurking here, as social distancing becomes more of an ongoing concern. For example, those Zoom Happy Hours present some tempting possibilities as people look for ways to liven them up. Think creatively about how your business can contribute to this. If you sell food, beverages (especially wine or craft beer), personal care products, etc., consider the value of shipping sample boxes to each member of a Happy Hour group and then curating the video call with a narration about how to appreciate each variety of cheese, Cabernet, perfume, and on and on.

I WORK, THEREFORE I SHOP

But the other side of the coin is also important. When people start to buy in (voluntarily or not) to the idea that they are "always on," the corollary is that they are "always off" as well. When there is no formal demarcation between working and not working, we start to play at work and work at play. This may mean competing at video games or shopping while you're sitting at your desk. Over a third of

US workers admit to browsing for goodies online while on company time, but it's a good bet that this number is on the low side.[41]

As the Work vs. Play dichotomy unravels, this important change should motivate marketers to think differently about how they provide products and services for working and playing. For example, we see the Work vs. Play cages opening when we look at what people wear to work or play: today "work clothes" in some industries consist of jeans and T-shirts (maybe even flip flops on Casual Fridays), while menswear designers offer modified suits to wear during off-hours (some with cut-off sleeves or other modifications).[42]

More importantly, the blurring of boundaries also means that the same high productivity mindset we learn to apply at work guides our personal time as we scrupulously model our exercise routines, diets, and perhaps even the way we raise our kids with the same discipline we apply to our work lives. Let's see how work is blending into play, and then how play is blending into work.

Work becomes play

A few years ago a Gallup survey revealed a sobering statistic: over 70 percent of US workers reported they were "not engaged" or "actively disengaged" with their jobs.[43] By one estimate, employee disengagement costs the US economy $350 billion per year in lost productivity, accidents, theft, and turnover.[44]

At least some forward-thinking organizations are fighting back. Although job prospects may not be bright for everyone in today's economy, knowledge workers with attractive skills can often pick and choose among corporate suitors. In many cases, these choices revolve less around salary and benefits, and more around which workplace offers the most amenities to make going to the office almost seem like a trip to a country club.

Perks like free food, game rooms, and sometimes even beer kegs in the break room beckon. Yelp offers an on-site minibar. Abercrombie & Fitch gives employees perky little scooters to travel around the office in style. Charles Schwab offers chair massages.

During a visit to Zappos' HQ in Las Vegas, I witnessed call center workers participating in fun activities that "spontaneously" happened at various points during the work day, such as a contest to see who could drop an egg without breaking it from a third story atrium.[45] New Age employee retention strategies turn work into play.

The pandemic dialed down the race to turn expensive commercial real estate into country clubs for knowledge workers. But even as more people WFH, the need to motivate them is still here. In fact, it's probably even stronger since many people struggle to maintain their discipline (or hide from their kids) when they're no longer working in a public space with a supervisor to stay on top of them.

Play becomes work

The concept of "free play" that most of us grew up with seems to be in short supply these days. It's hard work to be a kid!

Helicopter parents engage in the practice of overparenting. They're obsessed with their children's activities and love to micromanage almost every second of the day. If it won't look good on the ol' college resume, then bag it. As one critic of this overscheduled lifestyle lamented:

> Kids no longer go outside and hit the baseball. They have a game. They
> no longer sit and color, they go to art class. There is no doubt that they
> are spending their time in constructive activities that provide them
> with fun and useful skills. But they are spending a lot of time in these
> activities and everything is so structured that everybody is stressed.[46]

It's not just our kids who experience a lot more structure in their lives than they used to. Many of us are working harder, but we're also playing harder. At least for some, that playtime is just another chance to be industrious outside of our work lives. And when we can enlist a shiny new app or some other kind of technology to help us, we get that much better at self-regulation. Productivity is not just for companies anymore.

We can easily access technology that allows us to measure almost everything we do. A Fitbit gives you scores for your steps and even your sleep quality. There are apps that track your sexual activity, and some of those actually pair with marital aids to improve your scores. You can check out your current credit score to be sure you haven't slipped on the path to financial security. You can measure how attractive you are by tracking the swipes you receive on Tinder and how many people "like" you on Facebook.[47] If those numbers stress you out, whip out your phone to access apps like "Calm" and "Headspace."

Some intrepid self-improvers seem to doubt their own abilities to self-regulate: build in punishments rather than rewards to motivate them. In some cases, they may actually choose to submit to public shaming to keep them on track toward their goals. The Gym Pact pays cash rewards if users meet their fitness goals—but applies financial penalties if they don't.[48] The Aherk internet service (which fortunately closed a few years ago) employed social penalties instead; when users didn't meet their goal, the site posted embarrassing photos of them (previously supplied when they signed up for the service) to their network![49]

THE QUANTIFIED SELF: YOUR PERSONAL PERFORMANCE REVIEW

Welcome to your life on a dashboard.

People who work for larger companies are painfully familiar with the ritual of the annual performance review (even tenured professors get them!). Although most of us probably loathe this process, it's notable that some of us still want to turn around and replicate this practice in our play lives.

Apps turn play into work, as we zealously track our progress at dieting, exercise and also compulsively share our opinions (solicited or not) about restaurants, hotels, and even dating partners. We obsess about food intake, calories burned, the impact of the light from phone screens on sleep patterns, or even the money we spend on indulgences when we deviate from our health regimens. The drive to "be a better you" can turn leisure into a job. And this desire creates new markets for companies that can provide the products, services, and apps that cater to the relentless need to self-quantify. How about an app that keeps track of our apps?

The goal of self-improvement through knowledge has been around at least since the ancient Greeks, who prized physical culture as well as the intellect. The first recorded instance of a person who sought to gain understanding through self-tracking is Sanctorius of Padua, who in the 16th-century recorded his own weight versus food intake and waste over a 30-year period, to understand energy expenditures in living systems (he needed to get out more!).[50]

The Italian Renaissance later sparked renewed interest in the perfection of the body. The first US gymnasium opened in 1823, and John Harvey Kellogg's famous sanitarium in Battle Creek, Michigan, attracted thousands of affluent guests (Kelloggs' line of "healthy" cereals became a foundation of the natural food industry).[51]

Still, for most of human history people rarely quantified their behaviors to guide their personal lives (with the exception of personal finances and sports betting, perhaps). Most likely, the regime of record keeping of such seemingly trivial things as our pastimes and moods in the pre-digitized world seemed not only burdensome, but also somewhat unnecessary and vaguely narcissistic. Individuals on the whole were happy to adopt the naturalist belief that the human being is able to optimize his or her activities based upon intuition and memory.

LIFE IN THE DIGITAL FISHBOWL

Today we each live in a digital fishbowl, with access to a huge amount of biometric information and the technology to share it. For many of us, the urge to not only record but also to compare our own "normal" to other people's "normal" is irresistible and unrelenting. Unlike the physical culture enthusiasts of earlier eras, now we are able to track and fastidiously record most facets of our analog and digital lives—from sleep patterns to nutrition, health, location, and social interactions. This practice even has a name: Lifelogging.[52]

And then, enter the biohacker; a new breed of self-quantifiers who take even more drastic steps to monitor their bodies. Biohackers zealously harness data to self-regulate. They share a belief that individuals have the power to enlist biotechnology in the service of enhanced mental and physical well-being. Simply put, these "enthusiasts" aim to build an improved human being.

Biohackers come in all shapes and sizes. Some wear a headband that electrically stimulates the brain to improve cognition. Others meticulously track and record everything they eat, and dabble in supplements that purport to improve mental and physical performance. A few hardy souls even have a light-up implant surgically inserted into their arms to monitor biometric data, which changes color when levels are abnormal. As one transhumanist stated, "I can't really rely on my brain, but I can rely on the data my body produces."[53]

Folks, this "play" really is hard work.

As work becomes play and play becomes work, the familiar boundaries in our lives evaporate. Over the next few years, we may well see a recalibration of those dividing lines, especially as more of us abandon our high-priced commercial real estate and set up shop in our homes. These shifts create enormous opportunities for marketers, of course, as the daily fabric of our lives gets torn up. Whether we're attending meetings while we wear virtual reality helmets, or we methodically pursue personal goals with the same determination as our careers, consumers will embrace products and services that help them to work, play—and still stay sane.

Now, feed your chameleons!

Remember, rather than always coloring *within* the lines, it may make more sense to explore what lies *between* them. The new chameleons change their stripes nonstop, and perhaps you should too. In particular, you need to prompt yourself now and then to be sure you're targeting the customers you *have*, not the ones you *wish* you had.

At the end of the day, good marketing is all about understanding your customer—and doing your best to anticipate their next move.

In today's postmodern world, that task becomes harder and harder. But there is hope! It's called research. Don't just guess what your chameleons are up to. Get out there and cavort with them.

CHAPTER TAKEAWAYS

- Machines that "think" for us already are transforming how we work, play—and shop. Marketers need to change their thinking to anticipate what will happen when customers no longer interact with flesh-and-blood employees.

- AI applications are getting better at "learning" how to respond to nuances when they interact with customers. This is the hallmark of a good salesperson; AI will transform the sales function.

- The acceleration of work from home (WFH) creates great opportunities for new products and services to facilitate the integration of telecommuting into normal business practices.

- A thriving industry caters to our yearning to self-quantify. Numerous startups are betting that consumers will outsource their self-regulation in the hope of becoming better, brighter, augmented versions of themselves.

Endnotes

1 Mark Bridges, "Lewin 3-Step Change Management Model: A Simple and Effective Method to Institute Change That Sticks," *Medium*, February 22, 2019, https://medium.com/@mark.bridges/lewin-3-step-change-management-model-a-simple-and-effective-method-to-institute-change-that-sticks-c0274316748d (archived at https://perma.cc/U27T-FLCW).

2 Michael Corkery and David Gelles, "Robots Welcome to Take over, as Pandemic Accelerates Automation," *New York Times*, April 10, 2020, https://www.nytimes.com/2020/04/10/business/coronavirus-workplace-automation.html (archived at https://perma.cc/U5ZA-E2PJ).

3 Graham Kendall, "Your Mobile Phone vs. Apollo 11's Guidance Computer: Real Clear Science," July 2, 2019, https://www.realclearscience.com/articles/2019/07/02/your_mobile_phone_vs_apollo_11s_guidance_computer_111026html#:~:text=The%20Apollo%2011%20computer%20had,which%20ran%20at%20 0.043%20MHz.&text=This%20means%20that%20the%20 iPhone,the%20moon%2050%20years%20ago (archived at https://perma.cc/4SBL-XPSR).

4 Daniel Oberhaus, "This DIY Implant Lets You Stream Movies from Inside Your Leg," *Wired*, https://www.wired.com/story/this-diy-implant-lets-you-stream-movies-from-inside-your-leg/ (archived at https://perma.cc/3BUK-3LRS).

5 Jagdish N. Sheth and Michael R. Solomon, "Extending the Extended Self in a Digital World," *Journal of Marketing Theory and Practice* 22, no. 2 (2014): 123–32.

6 Quoted in Cade Metz, "Riding Out Quarantine with a Chatbot Friend: 'I Feel Very Connected'," *New York Times*, June 16, 2020, https://www.nytimes.com/2020/06/16/technology/chatbots-quarantine-coronavirus.html (archived at https://perma.cc/ H5UV-5XJG).

7 Cf. Rachel Ashman, Julia Wolny, and Michael R. Solomon, "Consuming Self-Regulation in a Technological World," in *The Routledge Companion to Consumer Behavior*, eds. Michael R. Solomon and Tina M. Lowery (London: Taylor & Francis, 2018).

8 Quoted in Ray Kurzweil, "17 Definitions of the Technological Singularity," *Singularity*, June 25, 2016, https://www. singularityweblog.com/17-definitions-of-the-technological-singularity/ (archived at https://perma.cc/ELP8-NTCV).

9 http://Internetofthingsagenda.techtarget.com/definition/thing-in-the-Internet-of-Things (archived at https://perma.cc/M8Y4-NLNA).

10 Laura Petrecca, "Technology Is Transforming Caregiving," *AARP*, October 15, 2018, https://www.aarp.org/caregiving/home-care/info-2018/new-wave-of-caregiving-technology.html (archived at https://perma.cc/GAC6-95LC).

11 Michael Corkery and David Gelles, "Robots Welcome to Take over, as Pandemic Accelerates Automation," *New York Times*, April 10, 2020, https://www.nytimes.com/2020/04/10/business/coronavirus-workplace-automation.html?referringSource=articleShare (archived at https://perma.cc/4C4J-J9LJ).

12   "There's No Place Like a [Connected] Home," *McKinsey & Co*,
     https://www.mckinsey.com/spContent/connected_homes/index.html
     (archived at https://perma.cc/EU38-GJDJ).

13   "Robot Automation Will 'Take 800 Million Jobs by 2030,'" *BBC
     News*, November 29, 2017, https://www.bbc.com/news/world-us-
     canada-42170100 (archived at https://perma.cc/8YG2-BQAX).

14   Zara Stone, "Everything You Need to Know About Sophia, the
     World's First Robot Citizen," *Forbes*, November 7, 2017, https://
     www.forbes.com/sites/zarastone/2017/11/07/everything-you-need-to-
     know-about-sophia-the-worlds-first-robot-citizen/#40a3bbe846fa
     (archived at https://perma.cc/C93L-UFFJ).

15   Erico Guizzo, "How Aldebaran Robotics Built Its Friendly
     Humanoid Robot Pepper," *IEEE Spectrum*, December 24, 2014,
     https://spectrum.ieee.org/robotics/home-robots/how-aldebaran-
     robotics-built-its-friendly-humanoid-robot-pepper (archived at
     https://perma.cc/8U25-4SZP).

16   Chuck Martin, "Consumer Robots on the Rise," *Media Post*,
     February 1, 2019, https://www.mediapost.com/publications/
     article/331377/consumer-robots-on-the-rise.html?utm_source=
     newsletter&utm_medium=email&utm_content=readnow&utm_
     campaign=112693&hashid=syo_DgYFgZsS4BaDXDyumENKG94
     (archived at https://perma.cc/5GGS-XVTE).

17   Nicole Ault, "Beauty Brands Stand to Gain from Virtual Advisers,"
     Retail Dive, https://www.retaildive.com/news/beauty-brands-stand-
     to-gain-from-virtual-advisers/529046/ (archived at https://perma.cc/
     ZE5Q-L8UY).

18   Weiquan Wang and Izak Benbasat, "Recommendation Agents for
     Electronic Commerce: Effects of Explanation Facilities on Trusting
     Beliefs," *Journal of Management Information Systems* 23, no. 4
     (2007): 217–46, https://www.tandfonline.com/doi/abs/10.2753/
     MIS0742-1222230410 (archived at https://perma.cc/SEN6-ESND).

19   Bernard Marr, "5 Amazing Examples of Natural Language Processing
     (NLP) in Practice," *Forbes*, June 8, 2020, https://www.forbes.com/
     sites/bernardmarr/2019/06/03/5-amazing-examples-of-natural-
     language-processing-nlp-in-practice/#2dc2fec81b30 (archived at
     https://perma.cc/EF8Z-SCRZ).

20   Giuseppe Manuel Brescia, "You Are Invited to Take Advantage
     of the Chambermaid," *Smuggledwords.com*, April 18, 2010,
     https://smuggledwords.wordpress.com/2010/04/18/you-are-invited-

to-take-advantage-of-the-chambermaid/ (archived at https://perma.cc/ PP2J-WTUX).

21 Patrick Kulp, "Chatbots Can Make as Many Sales as Humans," *Adweek*, September 29, 2019, https://www.adweek.com/digital/ chatbots-can-make-as-many-sales-as-humans/ (archived at https://perma.cc/PXJ7-WBVT).

22 Sarah Halzack, "The Chatbots Are Coming—And They Want to Help You Buy Stuff," *The Washington Post*, April 13, 2016, https://www.washingtonpost.com/news/business/wp/2016/04/13/ the-chatbots-are-coming-and-they-want-to-help-you-buy-stuff/ (archived at https://perma.cc/EFH6-M6RN).

23 Carl I. Hovland and W. Weiss, "The Influence of Source Credibility on Communication Effectiveness," *Public Opinion Quarterly* 15 (1952): 635–50; for a recent treatment, cf. Yong-Soon Kang and Paul M. Herr, "Beauty and the Beholder: Toward an Integrative Model of Communication Source Effects," *Journal of Consumer Research* 33 (June 2006): 123–30.

24 Judith A. Garretson and Scot Burton, "The Role of Spokescharacters as Advertisement and Package Cues in Integrated Marketing Communications," *Journal of Marketing* 69 (October 2005): 118–32.

25 "America's Most Liked Spokescharacters," *e-Poll Market Research Blog*, April 5, 2017, https://blog.epollresearch.com/2017/04/05/ americas-most-liked-spokescharacters/ (archived at https://perma.cc/ DV8J-4ZDM).

26 Michael Corkery, "Should Robots Have a Face?," *New York Times*, February 26, 2020, https://www.nytimes.com/2020/02/26/business/ robots-retail-jobs.html (archived at https://perma.cc/5E8F-HP3X).

27 Martina Čaićet et al., "Robotic Versus Human Coaches for Active Aging: An Automated Social Presence Perspective," *International Journal of Social Robotics* 12 (July 2019): 867–82, https://link.springer.com/article/10.1007/s12369-018-0507-2 (archived at https://perma.cc/HDQ6-NW84).

28 Masahiro Mori, "The Uncanny Valley: The Original Essay by Masahiro Mori," *iEEE Spectrum*, June 12, 2012, https://spectrum.ieee.org/ automaton/robotics/humanoids/the-uncanny-valley (archived at https://perma.cc/3LUP-9FPU).

29 Alva Noë, "Storytelling and the 'Uncanny Valley,'" *NPR*, January 20, 2012, https://www.npr.org/sections/13.7/2012/01/20/145504032/ story-telling-and-the-uncanny-valley (archived at https://perma.cc/ ACR4-G5FF).

30 David Rowell, "The Spectacular, Stranger Rise of Music Holograms,"
    Washington Post Magazine, October 30, 2019,
    https://www.washingtonpost.com/magazine/2019/10/30/dead-
    musicians-are-taking-stage-again-hologram-form-is-this-kind-encore-
    we-really-want/?arc404=true (archived at https://perma.cc/
    BE74-CKLH).

31 "Hologram Sales Person at the Galleria Mall!" *YouTube*, October 18,
    2018, https://www.youtube.com/watch?v=C6BPBh2jt0k (archived at
    https://perma.cc/P9JV-294F); https://www.youtube.com/watch?v=-
    O7xaFbkj1I (archived at https://perma.cc/7JLS-72N5).

32 Jon Christian, "'Digisexuals, Are Falling in love with—and Lusting
    for—Robots," *Futurism.com*, January 20, 2019, https://futurism.com/
    the-byte/digisexuals-love-lust-robots (archived at https://perma.cc/
    7MRQ-Y3BZ); "World's First Brothel Staffed Entirely by Robot Sex
    Workers Now Looking for Investors to Go Global," *The Sun*, July 30
    2017, https://www.thesun.co.uk/news/4131258/worlds-first-brothel-
    staffed-entirely-by-robot-sex-workers-now-looking-for-investors-to-
    go-global/ (archived at https://perma.cc/Y2WX-T67V).

33 http://whatwillmatter.com/2013/07/quote-observation-no-one-ever-
    said-on-their-deathbed-i-wish-i-spent-more-time-at-the-office-harold-
    kushner-be-careful-that-you-are-not-giving-up-today-something-
    valuable-that-you-can-neve/#:~:text=QUOTE%20%26%20
    OBSERVATION%3A%20%E2%80%9CNo%20one%20ever%20
    said%20on%20their%20deathbed,you%20can%20never%20
    get%20again (archived at https://perma.cc/H94Y-ZVT8).

34 Rachel Lerman and Jay Greene, "Big Tech Was First to Send Workers
    Home. Now It's in No Rush to Bring Them Back, *Washington Post*,
    May 18, 2020 https://www.washingtonpost.com/technology/
    2020/05/18/facebook-google-work-from-home/ (archived at
    https://perma.cc/PQ8D-WYL9).

35 Matthew Dollinger, "Starbucks, 'the Third Place', and Creating the
    Ultimate Customer Experience," *Fast Company*, June 11, 2008,
    https://www.fastcompany.com/887990/starbucks-third-place-and-
    creating-ultimate-customer-experience (archived at https://perma.cc/
    MNJ9-JSKF).

36 Ryan Browne, "70% of People Globally Work Remotely at Least
    Once a Week, Study Says," *CNBC.com*, May 30, 2018,
    https://www.cnbc.com/2018/05/30/70-percent-of-people-globally-
    work-remotely-at-least-once-a-week-iwg-study.html (archived at
    https://perma.cc/R4T3-MAAR).

37   Christena Nippert-Eng, *Home and Work: Negotiating Boundaries in Everyday Life* (Chicago: University of Chicago Press, 1996).

38   Steve Calechman, "How to Prevent a Child from Constantly Interrupting Your Zoom Call," *Fatherly.com*, May 7, 2020, https://www.fatherly.com/love-money/how-to-stop-interrupting-child-advice/ (archived at https://perma.cc/TM28-JFQV).

39   Rich Haridy, "The Right to Disconnect: The New Laws Banning After-Hours Work Emails," *New Atlas*, August 14, 2018, https://newatlas.com/right-to-disconnect-after-hours-work-emails/55879/ (archived at https://perma.cc/R8ZN-Q9EF).

40   Ben Tarnoff, "The New Status Symbol: It's Not What You Spend— It's How Hard You Work," *The Guardian*, April 24, 2017, https://www.theguardian.com/technology/2017/apr/24/new-status-symbol-hard-work-spending-ceos (archived at https://perma.cc/RFX9-GUB9).

41   "Thirty-Five Percent of Americans Shop Online While at Work, Says FindLaw.com Survey," *Thomson Reuters*, November 26, 2014, https://www.thomsonreuters.com/en/press-releases/2014/thirty-five-percent-of-americans-shop-online-while-at-work-says-findlaw-com-survey.html (archived at https://perma.cc/R6PQ-LYQM).

42   Jamie Carson, "10 Suits to Wear Outside the Office," *Shortlist*, July 8, 2016, https://www.shortlist.com/style/fashion/10-suits-to-wear-outside-the-office/28329 (archived at https://perma.cc/SV44-QYZC).

43   Carmine Gallo, "70% of Your Employees Hate Their Jobs," *Forbes*, November 11, 2011, https://www.forbes.com/sites/carminegallo/2011/11/11/your-emotionally-disconnected-employees/#5df1eb9542d5 (archived at https://perma.cc/3VLU-L2LC).

44   Allan Scheweyer, "The Economics of Engagement," *Incentive Research Foundation*, January 5, 2010, http://theirf.org/research/the-economics-of-engagement/206/ (archived at https://perma.cc/G3JN-N9KA).

45   Jacquelyn Smith, "The Best Workplace Luxuries," *Forbes*, August 24, 2012, https://www.forbes.com/sites/jacquelynsmith/2012/08/24/the-best-workplace-luxuries/#6a08945c636c (archived at https://perma.cc/X85X-3U9B).

46   Quoted in Jennifer O'Donnell, "Are You a Free-Range or Helicopter Parent?," *verywell*, December 22, 2016, https://www.verywell.com/what-are-helicopter-parents-3288380 (archived at https://perma.cc/ESU2-YJP8); cf. also Sid Kirchheimer, "Overscheduled Child May

Lead to a Bored Teen," *WebMD*, https://www.webmd.com/parenting/features/overscheduled-child-may-lead-to-bored-teen#1 (archived at https://perma.cc/8SKK-3PTG).

47 Ben Tarnoff, "The New Status Symbol: It's Not What You Spend—It's How Hard You Work," *The Guardian*, April 24, 2017, https://www.theguardian.com/technology/2017/apr/24/new-status-symbol-hard-work-spending-ceos (archived at https://perma.cc/RFX9-GUB9).

48 http://static.gym-pact.com/ (archived at https://perma.cc/4MGZ-NEUL).

49 Harrison Weber, "Give This App Your Embarrassing Photos and It Blackmails You into Getting Things Done," *Thenextweb*, May 9, 2012, https://thenextweb.com/apps/2012/05/09/give-this-app-your-embarrassing-photos-and-it-blackmails-you-into-getting-things-done/ (archived at https://perma.cc/5B85-PM9X).

50 Melanie Swan, "The Quantified Self: Fundamental Disruption in Big Data Science and Biological Discovery," *Big Data* 1, no. 2 (2013): 85–99.

51 John D. Fair, "Physical Culture," *Encyclopedia Britannica*, August 2, 2016, https://www.britannica.com/topic/physical-culture (archived at https://perma.cc/ML6X-P4M9).

52 Cathal Gurrin, "A Privacy by Design Approach to Lifelogging," in *Digital Enlightenment: A Handbook*, ed. K. O'Hara et al. (IOS Press, 2014): 49–61.

53 Quoted in Anna Neifer, "Biohackers Are Implanting LED Lights Under Their Skin," *Motherboard*, November 9, 2015, http://motherboard.vice.com/read/biohackers-are-implanting-led-lights-under-their-skin (archived at https://perma.cc/LJ9H-2BUP).

INDEX

CPSIA information can be obtained
at www.ICGtesting.com
Printed in the USA
JSHW011956250121
11207JS00011B/152